POSITIVISM TODAY

Issues in Law and Society
General Editor: Michael Freeman

Titles in the Series:

Children's Rights: A Comparative Perspective
Edited by Michael Freeman

Divorce: Where Next?
Edited by Michael Freeman

Exploring the Boundaries of Contract
Edited by Roger Halson

Law as Communication
Edited by David Nelken

Iraqgate: The Constitutional Implications of the Matrix-Churchill Affairs
Edited by Rodney Austin

Positivism Today
Edited by Stephen Guest

Governing Childhood
Edited by Anne McGillivray

Legislation and the Courts
Edited by Michael Freeman

Positivism Today

Edited by
STEPHEN GUEST
University College London

Dartmouth

Aldershot • Brookfield USA • Singapore • Sydney

Published by
Dartmouth Publishing Company Limited
Gower House
Croft Road
Aldershot
Hants GU11 3HR
England

Dartmouth Publishing Company
Old Post Road
Brookfield
Vermont 05036
USA

British Library Cataloguing in Publication Data
Positivism today. - (Issues in law and society)
1.Legal positivism 2.Law - Philosophy
I.Guest, Stephen
340.1'12

Library of Congress Cataloging-in-Publication Data
Positivism today / edited by Stephen Guest.
p. cm.
ISBN 1-85521-689-2. – ISBN 1-85521-696-5 (pbk.)
1. Legal positivism. I. Guest, Stephen.
K332.P67 1996
340'112–dc20 96-16810
CIP

ISBN 1 85521 689 2 (Hbk)
ISBN 1 85521 696 5 (Pbk)

Printed and bound in Great Britain by
Biddles Ltd, Guildford and King's Lynn

CONTENTS

LIST OF CONTRIBUTORS

Ronald Dworkin is the Professor of Jurisprudence at Oxford and Professor of Law and Philosophy at New York University and Visiting Professor of Legal Philosophy at University College London

Michael Freeman is Professor of English Law at University College London and author of *Lloyd's Introduction to Jurisprudence*

Stephen Guest is Reader in Legal Theory at University College London and author of *Ronald Dworkin*

David Hutchinson is Lecturer in Laws at University College London and was formerly Legal Officer at the United Nations Secretariat

Andrew Lewis is Senior Lecturer in Laws at University College London and Editor of *The Journal of Legal History*

Philip Roberts was Lecturer in Laws at University College London and is at present with the solicitors Boodle Hatfield. He read for his doctorate in philosophy and linguistics at Edinburgh University and was formerly Head of Training at Slaughter and May

Philip Schofield is Reader in the History of Legal and Political Thought at University College London and Joint General Editor of the *Collected Works of Jeremy Bentham*

William Twining is Quain Professor of Jurisprudence at University College London and Chairman of the Bentham Project. He has recently published *Blackstone's Tower*

INTRODUCTION

STEPHEN GUEST

This is a set of essays produced by colleagues in the UCL Faculty of Laws who teach on the Jurisprudence and Legal Theory courses both for the LL.B. and the University of London LL.M. The topic is an appropriate one given that one of first two professors, John Austin, who was appointed in 1826 as a professor of jurisprudence in the University of London founded in that year, has had a famous and profound effect on both the development and understanding of English law. He was, of course, the pupil of Jeremy Bentham whose famous doctrines of utilitarianism and positivism were so overwhelmingly influential upon Austin's thought. Jeremy Bentham, too, was instrumental in the background to the founding of UCL (and after whom the UCL Laws Faculty building is named Bentham House).

Why bother to re-examine legal positivism? Many people say that the idea is now dead. No-one really believes that law and morality are as separate as the doctrine proclaims and so any attempt to draw sharp lines between the two kinds of judgment is doomed to failure. But much of the criticism is superficial. A common but misguided criticism of Hans Kelsen's theory of law, for example, goes no further than saying that since law is so vitally concerned with people and people's role in society 'purifying' the law to 'purge' it of its ideological content is not credible. That is an insufficient argument because no positivist has ever denied the importance of moral reasons as part of the content of law; indeed, the insistence on the distinction is intended to emphasise our constant need to criticise and appraise the law from the best possible standpoint. (It seems banal to point out that Bentham's life was devoted to law *reform*). And further, although the attack appears in its most virulent form against the pure theory, Kelsen only meant by 'pure' that his theory was a theory of positivism. So there is no special reason why this criticism should be confined to Kelsen since he was only saying what many other positivists have said. Legal positivism is by no means an easy doctrine to criticise and it is apparent, too, that the doctrine has great merits.

But what, first of all, is this animal called 'Legal Positivism'? It consists of several closely related strands of propositions each of which twines with another; the most prominent form is that, to quote the definition supplied by H.L.A. Hart, the expounder of the clearest and most coherent form of the doctrine, in his *The Concept of Law*:

> Here we shall take Legal Positivism to mean the simple contention that it is in no sense a necessary truth that laws reproduce or satisfy certain demands of morality, though in fact they have often done so.[1]

This, I think, is the central strand in associated doctrines and is affirmed in Austin's claim that the 'merit of law is one thing; its demerit another' and Bentham's distinction between expositorial jurisprudence (the propounding of law as it *is*) and censorial jurisprudence (the calculation of the moral worth - measured in utilitarian terms - of the law as it *ought* to be). In a short sentence, this main strand of positivism claims that moral judgments alone are irrelevant to identifying law. But the other strands are important. One is positivism as (in Joseph Raz's terms) the identification of law in its *source* (the 'sources' thesis). Here emphasis is laid not so much upon a distinction between morality and law but on the historical/empirical conditions of the identification of law. Nevertheless, given a reasonable assumption that the Humean 'is' - 'ought' is true, it follows that if the law is identified as an 'is' then moral 'oughts' are distinguishable. And, of course, there are historical and philosophical connotations arising from different uses of 'positivism' at different times, by different people, for different purposes. From the sources thesis it is easy to jump from legal positivism to logical positivism (the philosophical doctrine that the truth of all propositions rests ultimately on empirical truths). At one stage, 'positivism' was most commonly equated with 'the command theory' and there are still vestiges of that idea floating amongst international lawyers who will declare that that international is not positive law 'because' its major source lies in custom and not legislative or judicial 'commands'. Also fairly common is the equation of 'legal positivism' with a particular way of doing Jurisprudence, namely, by 'studying meanings', engaging in 'logical niceties' and 'existing entities' to no practical avail (although adherents to this sort of vague exercise are rare birds indeed).[2]

But there should be no difficulty in seeing what I mean by the 'central strand' of legal positivism. We are able (rightly or wrongly) to see at least this difference between moral and legal rules: that with legal rules more significance is attached to their status as law by facts about their creation and not their content. That is not to say that there are no moral rules which owe their status to such facts, since promises create moral obligations in a way that is independent of their status; rather, it is that more significance is attached in the case of law. We are less inclined to question, as we might a promise, the content of a legal rule when we ask ourselves the question, should we carry it out, or avail ourselves of the facility it offers, or obey it. It is a strange idea, for example, to ask whether we should do what is morally right; but not so strange (although strange to some) to ask whether we should do what is legally required of us or it is legally permitted that we do. This distinction arises from our attaching so much significance to the status of legal rules.

Because of these characteristic differences between legal and moral rules we can ask questions about legal positivism which search the *point* of thinking about the law in this way. This is where it becomes exciting. If we ask the question of point we move away from a descriptive account of law in terms (say) of empirical sources of legal authority to an account based on the practical human value in making some of actions dependent upon legal determination rather than upon moral determination. We should ask directly: What is served by perpetuating the idea that human determinations are higher in some senses than moral - perhaps, God-given - determinations? Taking a line like this easily ends up in a value-laden account, perhaps in the conclusion that positivism itself is a good, or bad, moral theory, a sub-theory of a general theory of political morality. Some philosophers reasonably say (Jerry Postema is one) that Bentham's theory of legal positivism itself was borne of his utilitarianism, meaning that Bentham thought that the greatest happiness of the greatest number would be served best by *our adopting* a distinction between law and morality. It appears paradoxical only if you forget that Bentham's aim was the improvement of law by constant criticism in the light of utilitarian principles. Ideally, for him, the law should have a fully utilitarian content but the only way to get to that state was through the intellectually clear position of seeing the law purely as a creature of man's own devising.

Other jurists (and I suspect Austin was one) simply take the line that law is 'out there' to be described, in much the same sense as we might suppose that Australia is 'out there' to be drawn in form of a map. The 'sources' thesis appears to be such a purely descriptive account. This mapping enterprise might take the form of describing the linguistic discourse of the law; the equivalent to Australia 'out there' is the legal language itself, for after all there is no 'reality' beneath the language which can be separated from the language itself for inspection. This kind of theory (and the earlier parts of *The Concept of Law* certainly lend themselves to an understanding such as this, as I later argue in my paper) might be termed a 'semantic theory', meaning not merely that it is a theory of 'law words' but a theory of the law 'out there' as understood through an analysis of legal discourse. Certainly, this is what Hart conceived of himself to be doing when he said in the Preface to *The Concept of Law* that 'the suggestion that inquiries into the meanings of words merely throws light on words is false.'

Different questions of methodology thus arise; certainly if there is anything in common to positivists it is not that they think that law can be described 'out there'. But there are other questions. Is it a characteristic of legal positivism that it commits us to a particular form of legal reasoning? Certainly it was a common view to Bentham, Austin, Hart and Kelsen that judges when deciding disputed points of law were 'making' new law and not 'applying' law (although the meaning of these terms is open to serious debate). Bentham, for example, thought that the business of law-creation was not at all something judges should engage in and he pursued the idea of a special legislative chamber to which *legislative* questions should be sent by judges faced with legally unresolvable problems such as whether rollerblading is forbidden in the park. Austin, on the other hand, thought that legal systems would not last for half an hour if judges could not make new laws and that one of the judicial roles was to be deputy legislator. Kelsen thought that the 'dynamism' of a legal system arose from the introduction of norms of fresh content by judges and Hart fairly consistently maintained that judges had limited powers as law-makers, like Austin, of the deputed sort. But a contemporary positivist like Neil MacCormick thinks that judicial creation is ultimately rooted in the social conventions (describable in 'is'-propositions) of the institutions of which judges are just a part.[3]

Another sort of question is that concerned with the scope of jurisprudence. If positivism is to be thought of as primarily a descriptive account of law as it is (and so Nazi law is law) does that mean that positivism has a claim to universality which other theories, say, natural law, lack? It is fairly common to assert (but I think wrongly) that Dworkin's theory of adjudication, which rests, ultimately, on the equality of respect due to all members of the community, is particular only to those societies, such as the United Kingdom and the United States, where the legal practices most closely fit the descriptive aspect of his theory. In other countries, there is insufficient by way of institutional 'fit' (to use his term) reflecting this basic principle to say with the requisite degree of 'force' that there is law in any but the most trivial semantic sense. But so much spins on the notion of 'a universal theory'. Dworkin's theory is universal in the sense that it *applies* to the Nazi system by *discounting* it as law; if it were particular only to the US and UK systems it would have nothing to say about Nazi law at all. We would otherwise have to say that the economists' idea of a perfect market is not applicable to the real world since there are no perfect markets in the real world. How, then, could we describe any markets as imperfect? And, taking Hart's own avowal in his recently published *Postscript* of the universal descriptivity of his theory, he himself would come to the same conclusions about, say, Islamic law, where there are no rules of recognition empirically determinable which 'cure defects' of 'uncertainty'.

Yet another set of questions arise as to the day to day *effects* of positivist thinking. One reason why a study of positivism is tackled by all jurists at some time or another is that in reading and teaching law, jurists come across a positivist 'mind-set'. In debates in so many law faculties over how students should be taught - over what they should be learning - two camps frequently emerge: the so-termed 'black letter' lawyers and the others. The 'black letter' lawyers exhibit one of the main traits of the positivist frame of mind, which is to demand exactitude, logic and rigorous attention to the *ipsissima verba*; it is regarded as waffly to be otherwise. The reason is that positivism has a claim to a scientific rigour: it is rooted in certainty (remember: Hart's rule of recognition was to 'cure' the 'defect' of uncertainty) and empirical verifiability; besides that, all that is left is logic according to severe deductive principles. You can see the virtue; you *must* get the law *right*; you *must* pay attention to logic. The sloppy student gets a good come-uppance at the hands of the confident black-letterite. But other ruinous qualities attach to this way of thinking about law. Nothing exists outside the four corners - the black-letters; notoriously, such lawyers flourish in the forests of deeds, documents and detail (ordinary Chancery practice is the paradigm). The other kind of lawyer quests rather than declaims and is to be found in the tortious kingdom and other such plushy areas; his type is keener on argument rather than combativeness. Everyone recognises these two caricatures - the chop-logician, knock-down arguer versus the waffler.

I'm of two minds as to the value of each; they reflect in their different emphases different good qualities, just like the natural division of emphasis between those centre left and centre right of the political spectrum. It is interesting that those positivistic in bent come to law faculties actually like that. When I taught the law of contract to first years it was always interesting to see students form divisions on something as simple as the postal rule. I would tell them what such cases as *Adams v. Lindsell* said and then ask them whether a contract has been completed when a letter of acceptance has not been fully pushed into a posting-box, balancing there, half-in, half-out. There are those who say defiantly that it is; there are those who say defiantly it hasn't; there are those voles who say 'may be it has; may be it hasn't'. I tend to favour the latter cast of mind (where the student understands that reasons have to be given) but I appreciate there is a danger of inculcating sloppiness; if I encourage this way of going about things am I in fact not producing the best kind of lawyer? The sit-on-the-fence cast of mind is not conducive to the decision-incisiveness that the practical edge (one of those things that makes the study of law attractive) that is required. On the other hand, the combative approach is too concerned with the psychological impact; worse, I think, it suggests that the answer comes before the reasons and is and I think on that account - that it is irrational - I disapprove of the positivist frame of mind.

Ronald Dworkin, our Visiting Professor of Legal Philosophy, writes on the problems posed by legal positivism over the truth of falsity of propositions of law which are indeterminate, that is to say, where all reasonable lawyers would agree that there no *demonstrable answer* to the disputed question. He concludes that to suppose that where there is no such answer a 'default' position is reached in which propositions of law are neither true nor false is wrong. Why? Because such positions only trivially describe the psychological state of uncertainty we feel when contemplating a controversial claim. Indeterminacy claims, as he calls them, exist elsewhere than in the law and are as much internal and substantive positions as any other; thus positivism which claims the lack of truth value to legal propositions in hard cases cannot do so by default and, in the absence of good reasons to support that claim by a substantive argument internal to positivism, fails as a successful theory of law. Michael Freeman, in an important essay which connects democracy with principles of statutory interpretation, argues that our approach to statutory construction today is heavily influenced by the over-formalistic approach of the classical positivists. He looks at theoretical ways of understanding legislation and the role of judges in interpreting it, emphasising ways in which judicial construction can be used to promote bureaucratic ideals. In my paper, I take issue with Hart's claims in his *Preface* that his work on positivism is not evaluative but 'neutral-descriptive'; I argue that, despite what he says, elements of his construction of 'secondary' rules from his 'primary' rules, his treatment of the Nazi grudge informer case, and the general liberal tenor of his desire, at times passionate, to drive a 'wedge' between the individual and the state, is achieved in accordance with moral motive. If I'm right, it follows that his work is not neutral and thus open to morally argumentative debate. David Hutchinson skilfully analyses the extent to which international law can be regarded as positivist in slant and says that there are good reasons for discarding positivist versions of the law-finding process in preference for naturalist accounts. Nevertheless, carefully testing international law against Dworkin's helpful idea of institutional 'fit' (devised, one assumes, for municipal systems) Hutchinson concludes that naturalist accounts of international law would need to explain and justify more satisfactorily limitations of this sort; 'fit', he says, represents as central feature of our conception of how to identify law. Andrew Lewis examines the lessons to be drawn about positivism from legal history. He says that the essential claim of legal positivism is its striving to find theoretical underpinnings for the 'autonomy' of law and he argues that legal history can provide 'good reasons' for accepting this claim. The classic exposition is that of Weber who identified the crucial step as the emergence of a professional class of lawyers - the *honoratiores* - for whom law has an intrinsic value. Recent work by Frier and Brand on Roman law and Common law respectively, ties the development of an autonomous legal order firmly to the rise of a distinct and educated legal profession. In contrast, a recent work on the jury by Constable casts some doubt upon the completeness of positivism's picture of the operation of law. In a complex and sophisticated paper, Philip Roberts considers a characterisation and evaluation of legal positivism which draws upon concepts arising from the development of linguistic theory. In so doing, he proposes that an account of 'judicial competence' is a principal aim of legal theory and argues that legal positivism can never provide a satisfactory account of this and must give way to a thorough-going normative theory of law. Philip Schofield, well-known for his work with the Bentham Project at UCL considers the major thinkers, Jeremy Bentham, William Paley and John Austin, in the early history of utilitarianism, and in early utilitarian legal theory. He argues that Austin acknowledged his intellectual debt both to Bentham and Paley, and indeed that Austin took his moral theory from Paley, despite the wide-spread assumption that Bentham was the dominant influence on Austin's legal thought. Schofield compares and contrasts the legal thought of these three writers and provides a fresh reassessment of the relationship between them. Finally (one should say alphabetically) and certainly not least, William Twining, our Quain Professor of Jurisprudence, claims that the distinction between general and particular jurisprudence has not been prominent in recent Anglo-American writings in the area and he argues that recent events suggest that legal theory should become more self-consciously cosmopolitan in response to the processes of globalisation. He explores three phases of the history of the distinction within English positivism: the distinction made by Bentham and modified by Austin; the long-running debate between Thomas Erskine Holland and his critics, notably W.W. Buckland; and the recent suggestion that H.L.A. Hart's main work fell within general jurisprudence, whereas that of Ronald Dworkin is largely confined to particular jurisprudence.

NOTES

1 *The Concept of Law 2nd ed.* (1994) Oxford pp. 185-86.
2 Hart neatly sums up a number of meanings of 'positivism' in *The Concept of Law* at p. 302.
3 See his *Legal Reasoning and Legal Theory* (1978).

1 INDETERMINACY AND LAW

RONALD DWORKIN

In *Law's Empire*[1], I suggested that legal positivism is best understood interpretively, as an affirmative normative theory claiming that we make most sense of legal practice, and see it in the best possible light, by supposing that convention plays the role in fixing what the law of a society is that positivism describes. In this essay (which is drawn from a larger work in progress) I consider the philosophical basis of another way of regarding positivism: as following from what I later describe as the idea of indeterminacy by default. On this view, propositions of law can only be determinatively true or false when they can be *demonstrated* as one or the other. Positivism supposedly supplies criteria of demonstration: for example, Professor Hart's Rule of Recognition, which is a test for law accepted by at least the bulk of the officials of a legal jurisdiction. Positivism then claims that nothing that cannot be demonstrated to be true in some such 'positive' way, so that all responsible and competent lawyers will agree on its truth when they are aware of the facts including the institutional history, can be true. I shall offer, here, a general argument against the idea of an indeterminacy default on which the argument just set out rests.

Indeterminacy and Default

I begin with a threshold question. Do we need any positive reason to think some evaluative proposition indeterminate? Do we need a positive reason, for example, for thinking that it is neither true nor false that Antigone did the right thing in burying her brother, or that abortion is wicked? Though this may surprise some readers, a great many philosophers think the answer is: no. They think that indeterminacy is the *default* position In morality, ethics, art and law. There are, in fact, two versions of this default thesis: a first-personal version, which assumes that a judgment of indeterminacy is the right one for someone to reach in the course of his own, personal, first-level moral experience when he is deeply troubled by some moral issue, and a third-personal version, which assumes that a judgment of indeterminacy is the right one for external observers to reach when they find that other people disagree in the personal, first-level moral judgments they make. I shall discuss mainly the internal version of the thesis, because once we see why the default thesis fails in that version, we see why it falls in the other as well.

Suppose I am bewildered whether abortion is wicked. I see arguments or analogies that make it seem so sometimes, when I am in some moods. But I also see other arguments or analogies that make it seem not so at other times. I confess that I lack any secure or stable sense of which of these arguments is better. Then, according to the first-personal version of the default thesis, I ought just to conclude that the question of abortion is indeterminate. There is no right answer to that question, I should say, but only different answers. This premise assumes that indeterminacy is a theoretically less ambitious claim than either a fully positive or a fully negative judgment: that something more must be known or shown or supposed by someone who asserts a moral judgment of any kind, or who denies one, than by someone else who says that the matter in hand is just a matter of opinion or that the answer is indeterminate or something of that sort. If so, then the failure to supply that 'more' is enough to establish indeterminacy, which is therefore true by default.

It is certainly true that what we might call C-propositions, which are claims that we are or should be uncertain about some issue, are theoretically less ambitious than more positive or negative claims: C propositions do hold by default in the way just described. If I see arguments on all sides of some issue, and do not find, even after reflection, one set of arguments stronger than the others, then I am entitled without more to declare that I am uncertain, that I have no view of the matter.[2] I do not need a further, more substantive, reason, beyond my failure to be persuaded of any other view, for claiming uncertainty. But in all these respects indeterminacy differs from uncertainty. 'I am uncertain whether the proposition in question is true or false' is plainly consistent with 'It is one or the other,' but 'The proposition in question is neither true nor false' is not. The difference is sometimes obscured by the way in which philosophers have defined indeterminacy. John Mackie defined it as what is left when we exclude various other possibilities.[3] If it is not true that Picasso was a greater artist than Beethoven, or that Beethoven was greater than Picasso, or that they were exactly equal in talent, then any comparison between the two artists is indeterminate.

This definition is not wrong, but it may tempt to error, because it takes no notice of uncertainty and offers no way to distinguish it from indeterminacy. Someone might infer from it that if he does not think that Picasso was greater than Beethoven, or that Beethoven was greater than Picasso, or that they were exactly equal to one another, then he should think it indeterminate which was greater. But that he does not follow, for he may instead think, consistently with all the beliefs just reported, that though one is indeed better than the other, he does not know which. It is more helpful to describe indeterminacy more subjectively. If someone does not think A is better than B, or B better than A, or that they are exactly equal, and if he is not uncertain whether A is better than B, he thinks the comparison indeterminate. Once uncertainty is taken into account, in some such way, then the default thesis collapses because if one of the alternatives - uncertainty - holds by default, indeterminacy, which is different, cannot.

A belief in indeterminacy is a positive claim, and it needs a positive reason or assumption to support it. There are three possible views I might take about the abortion issue, excluding uncertainty, but I am as much (or as little) in need of an argument for the third view - indeterminacy - as I am of an argument for either of the other two. So the default thesis falls in its firstpersonal version. It therefore fails in its third-personal version as well. If (as a matter of their ordinary, every-day moral convictions) one person holds that abortion is wicked, a second that it is not, and a third that the issue is indeterminate, there are three, not two, substantive positions in the field, and a fourth-party observer needs as much or as little argument for siding with any one of the three as with either of the others.

Reasons of a Third Kind

So we need a positive reason to choose indeterminacy over the other options, as the best available substantive view of some matter. What kind of a reason do we need? Our reason must be one not simply for denying that we can identify a reason for believing some proposition true or a reason for believing it false - that second-order reason would only justify uncertainty - but a reason for thinking that there are no reasons for thinking it true or for thinking it false. The difference is important. Though reticence is generally appropriate under uncertainty, it would be wholly out of place for anyone genuinely convinced that the issue is not uncertain but indeterminate. The Catholic Church has declared, for example, that even those who are uncertain whether a foetus is a person with a right to live should oppose abortion, because abortion would be so terrible if it turned out that a foetus was a person. No comparable argument could move someone who is convinced that there is no 'fact of the matter' about whether a foetus is a person. He might of course have others reasons for taking a position about abortion - he might say that abortion displeases (or, I suppose, pleases) him, or that since those who think the foetus is a person are very upset by abortion it should be banned for that reason, or that since it is unjust for the state to limit liberty by taking up one on an indeterminate issue, abortion should be permitted for that reason. But he cannot have the reasons for reticence or agony or commitment to further thought that someone who thinks the issue uncertain has.

Someone who believes there is no right answer to a particular moral question thinks, then, that no one could have a reason of a certain kind for acting or for praising or for condemning in a certain way. What kind of reason he thinks no one could have depends, of course, on what mode of acting or praising or condemning is in play. If the issue is an aesthetic one - if the question has arisen, for example, whether Picasso was greater than Braque and he thinks no one could have a reason for preferring either to the other - then he thinks there are no aesthetic grounds that could justify either preference. But since whether there is a justification for some aesthetic position is patently an aesthetic question, his position, that there is no justification for either position, is an aesthetic one as well, and it must be supported, if at all, on aesthetic grounds. If the issue is a moral one - if he thinks that it is neither true nor false that abortion is immoral - then he thinks there is no moral reason for a view either way and his own reason for that second-order view must therefore be a moral reason as well.

We might now look for examples of second-order aesthetic or moral or other evaluative reasons that might be thought to justify a judgment of indeterminacy. Some people think that the concept of nobility can sensibly be used of wine: they think it can be used to make a kind of aesthetic judgment. But are they right - is this a legitimate use of the idea of nobility? Critics of wine-snobbery believe that the concept is simply out of place in this context. Petrus may taste better than Beaujolais, and its taste may linger longer, but it is silly to say that it is *nobler*. If that is our view - rather than the bizarre view that it is always uncertain whether one wine is nobler than another - we must have some basis for it. We would probably not be able explicitly to describe that basis - taste evades elucidation - but we could nevertheless rely on a felt sense that there is a limit to the legitimate range of the aesthetic. Music may be noble, we might say, but not wine. My point is not that we can explain in any satisfactory way why we fix the limit of the aesthetic at one point rather than another, but rather that our view, however far we can or will go in describing it, is an aesthetic rather than logical or philosophical or semantic one. If the semantics of 'noble' permit it to be used of music, they permit it to be used of food and drink, too. We reject the nobility of wine, perhaps, as oenophiles would say, out of prejudice or ignorance or fastidiousness. But if so, it is aesthetic prejudice or ignorance or fastidiousness, not some other kind.

Now consider the claim someone might make that, all things considered, Picasso was a greater genius than Beethoven. I assume that you, like me, are willing and think yourself able to make at least some comparisons of artistic merit: we think Picasso a greater painter than Balthus and also, though the case is closer, a greater painter than Braque, great though Braque was, and we think Beethoven a greater musician than Lloyd-Webber and Mozart a greater musician than Beethoven. So we believe that comparisons about the merits of particular artists are in principle sensible. I believe, as I said, that though Braque was a very important artist, all things considered Picasso was a greater one. If you challenge me, I will try to sustain that opinion in various ways: by pointing to Picasso's greater originality, inventiveness, range of qualities from playfulness to profundity, etc, while nevertheless admitting certain advantages in Braque's work: a more lyrical approach to cubism, for example. Because artistic merit is a complex subject and my claim is an all-things-considered one, the issue can tolerate a complex discussion: the conversation would not soon turn silly, as it would if I were trying to defend a claim about the superior quality of Petrus over Lafitte. I might or might not convince you, after sustained discussion, that I am right; you might or might not convince me that I am wrong. But if neither convinces the other, I will still continue in my opinion. I will count it as telling against my view that I could not convince you of it, but (with apologies) I will not count this as a refutation.

But if I were asked whether Picasso was a greater genius than Beethoven, my answer would be very different: I would say (unless and until I am talked out of *this* view, as I conceivably might be) that neither was greater than the other, not because they had exactly the same degree of merit (that is preposterous) but because there are no pertinent standards against which this particular comparison can be made. Now of course I must defend that distinction: why do I think it sensible to compare Picasso and Braque but not Picasso and Beethoven? The difference is not that people agree about standards for comparing artists in the same period or in the same genre. They don't, and it would not count as showing that the agreed standards were the right ones even if they did. The difference can't be based on any cultural or social fact of that sort, but must be based, if it makes sense at all, on more general, perhaps even quite theoretical, assumptions about the character of artistic achievement or evaluation.

Obviously I couldn't claim that my view about Picasso and Beethoven is true by default: I couldn't claim that it follows just from the fact that there are no agreed or self-evident standards for making the comparison between them. If I did, it would be claimed against me that the comparison between Picasso and Braque is equally indeterminate on the same test.

I would try to defend my judgment about Picasso and Beethoven in a very different way: I believe that artistic achievement can only be measured as a response to artistic situation and tradition[4] and, since Beethoven and Picasso succeeded at obviously a superlative level, but in response to very different traditions and challenges, it seems to me wrong to think they can be compared. I am not very convinced by this, in part because I do think one can rank artists across genres, traditions and challenges in certain ways. Shakespeare was a greater creative artist than Jasper Johns, and Picasso a greater one than

Vivaldi. I believe, that is, that only order-of-magnitude comparisons can be made across traditions and genres, though much more subtle (Picasso and Braque) comparisons can be made within them. This is not an evidently stable view, though I find it is the view I hold, and since I hold it I also believe that the comparison between Picasso and Beethoven is indeterminate.

This confessional account of my views about artistic merit illustrates the most important features of indeterminacy in a complex area. First, claims of indeterminacy are not true by default: they need if not argument, which may not be available at any impressive length, at least a basis in more abstract instincts or convictions. Second, these must be convictions or instincts within the domain about which the judgment is made: in the case of aesthetics they must be (as the 'theory' I just reported illustrates) aesthetic instincts or convictions. Third, indeterminacy is a substantive view to be ranked alongside the other substantive views in the neighbourhood - that Picasso was greater than Beethoven or *vice versa,* for example. We cannot demand any greater character or level of demonstration for either of the two latter substantive views than we demand for the former. It would obviously be unfair of me to complain, against anyone who said that Picasso was greater than Beethoven, that he could not prove this to everyone's satisfaction, or that he could not set out an impressive theoretical position from which that view flowed in some deductive or even smooth way. For that is exactly my situation, too. I claim that the comparison is indeterminate, but the best I can do, in explaining why, is something that will not convince everyone else either.

It is common for philosophers to ridicule, as woolly or inconclusive or dogmatic, the arguments of people who believe that one position in some deep controversy has the better of the case. They say these partisans overlook the obvious truth that there is no 'fact of the matter, no 'single right answer' to the issue in play. They do not pause to consider whether they have any substantive arguments for that equally substantive position, and, if they do, whether these might not also be ridiculed as vague or unpersuasive or as resting on instincts or even bare assertions in the same way. Absolute clarity is the privilege of fools and fanatics. The rest of us must do the best we can: we must choose amongst the three substantive views on offer by asking which strikes us, after reflection and due thought, as more plausible than the others. And if none does, we must then settle for the true default view, which is not indeterminacy but merely uncertainty.

These various lessons are equally applicable to morals and ethics. Is there a right answer' to the question of what Antigone should have done? That depends, plainly, on complex, highly theoretical issues of substantive morality. If we are drawn to a utilitarian morality, we will think that there is a right answer, even if, so many centuries after the play was written, we are deeply uncertain about what it is. We will think that the right answer depends on which of the acts open to Antigone (or, in a different version of utilitarianism, which of the rules that might have guided her choice) would have produced the greatest net balance of pleasure over pain in the long run. So if we think there is no right answer to Antigone's problem - that whatever she did was the wrong thing to do, for example - we must have rejected utilitarianism. And we must also have rejected a great many other moral theories or approaches or attitudes that would also have insisted on the existence of a right answer.

Our conclusion (or instinct) of indeterminacy reflects, then, a special conception of morality, a conception that emphasises, perhaps, the brute, unreflective character of duties of different kinds. We may not be able to say very much to the utilitarian in defence of our moral attitude; perhaps we cannot say even as much to him as he can to us. That does not mean that we are wrong - or right. Here, too, conviction is inescapable. We remain as unconvinced by his appeals to the fundamental importance of human welfare as he does by our reminders about the deep and uncompromising character of duty; neither of us must bow to the other just in virtue of the raw, logical force of the arguments either can deploy. But our view has no epistemic or logical head start over his. It is just as much grounded in a moral attitude or conception as any other view in the field: it needs, to repeat, as much or as little positive argument in its defence as they do.

Philosophers have overlooked that point in ethics and morals to an even greater degree than they have in aesthetics. It is a popular view, for example, that, at least within a certain range of options, there is 'no right answer' to what choices people should make about how to lead their lives. Suppose a young woman must choose whether to pursue a promising career as a public interest lawyer in Los Angeles or to emigrate to a kibbutz in Israel. (Of course, she will have many other options as well. But suppose these are the only two now in question.) She might be puzzled about a great deal that is involved in that choice. Which life would she find more satisfying in retrospect? In which career would she be more successful? In which would she contribute more to the well-being of others? She may be uncertain about the right answers to any of these questions taken separately, and she will very likely be uncertain about the right answer to the question how to weigh them against one another. Now suppose someone says that she is wrong - silly - to worry about any of this, or, indeed to worry about making the best choice at all, because once certain bad lives have been ruled out, there is no right answer to the question - it is indeterminate - which of the lives that remain is all things considered the best. This surprising view cannot be true by default - it would not follow, if she remained uncertain which life was best, that neither was. Once the fallacious default claim is set aside, it is apparent that as much argument or positive instinct or conviction is needed to support the indeterminacy claim as the claim that the best life, all things considered, really lies in emigration, just as any argument or instinct or conviction that supports the latter must be an ethical one, so must any argument, instinct or conviction that supports the former. It is not apparent, however, what kind of argument or instinct or conviction could support the latter - particularly given that *some* choice must be made - which perhaps explains why life-choices are so often matters of agonised reflection rather than coin-tosses.

Determinacy and Law

It is a popular thesis, as I said, that in very hard cases at law, when the legal profession is split about the right answer, there actually is none, because the law is indeterminate on the issue. This 'no right answer' thesis cannot be true by default in law any more than in aesthetics or morals. It doesn't follow from the fact that no knock-down argument demonstrates that the case for the plaintiff is better or worse than the case for the defendant, all things considered, that it is not, in fact, actually better or worse. Since the no-right-answer claim about law is a legal claim - it insists that no legal reason makes the case for one side stronger than the case for the other - it must rest on some theory or conception of law. It is not hard to find theories of law that do purport to support that conclusion: when legal positivism is understood interpretively, as itself a controversial and non-demonstrative normative thesis, at least in its simpler and stricter versions, it does offer an internal, affirmative case for indeterminacy. There are more complex and plausible legal theories that might also be thought to generate indeterminacy in certain cases: a theory that makes moral conclusions sometimes dispositive of legal argument might be combined, for example, with a view of morality that made some moral issues indeterminate, as in Antigone's case.[5] Because such indeterminacy-generating legal theories actually exist, in articulated and elaborate form, law provides a good illustration of my claim that the assertion of indeterminacy is a substantive position and therefore counts as a case of internal rather than external scepticism about the more positive views it challenges. Most contemporary legal scholars who find it self-evident that there is no right answer to controversial legal questions do not subscribe to legal positivism or to any other theory that offers positive legal arguments for indeterminacy.[6] They fall into the fallacy of supposing that indeterminacy holds by default.

We can make sense of claims of indeterminacy, then, only by treating them as internal, substantive positions based, as firmly as any other, on affirmative theories or assumptions about the fundamental character of the domain to which they belong. I should now emphasise that last qualification. It would be a serious mistake to export a justification designed for one domain - for example, the tenuous justification I sketched for accepting some indeterminacy in matters of artistic comparison - to another without very great care. Though my own views about artistic merit are in some ways similar to my views about ethical merit - what makes one life more successful than another - I would not accept arguments that might seem to follow from a direct transplant of my opinions about art into the ethical domain. I would not accept, for example, that since the two lives we imagined a moment ago - public service law in Los Angeles and kibbutz life in Israel - are drawn from dramatically different ethical ideals or traditions, they cannot sensibly be compared. I would insist, rather, that though we measure the success or failure of a life in terms of its response to circumstances, the circumstances of modern life include choices among very different ethical traditions or conceptions, and that such choices are now part of the challenge of living well. Other people, it is true, would find the argument I just rejected much more appealing: Isaiah Berlin, for example, does believe that comparisons over very different kinds of lives are indeterminate. The disagreement reflects different views about the basic character of the particular domain in question, not the application to all domains of some standard and transcendent test of indeterminacy everywhere. Berlin might, for example, find less indeterminacy in comparisons of artistic merit over different forms of art and different centuries than I do.

Determinacy can be affected, moreover, by locating what might seem to be the same issue in a different domain. In law, for example, the functional need for a decision is itself a factor, because any argument that the law is indeterminate about some issue must recognise the consequences of that being true, and take these into account. Consider the difference between the aesthetic question raised by the pure form of the question about Picasso and Beethoven, and the different question that would be raised if Congress had instructed that a great statue be raised depicting one or the other, whichever was the greater artist. This kind of 'delegation' does not preserve the issue that is delegated unchanged; the delegation changes the question because it adds a context of purpose and a demand for action.

So the question becomes: given that Congress has instructed, at a particular time, that a statue be raised, and supplied that test for deciding whose statue it should be, which of the decisions the agency might make is the right one? A great deal beyond pure aesthetic judgment is then relevant. Which choice, if made by Congress itself, would have been the better, all things considered? Would one choice, for example, better match the public's opinion of the two artists? Would one choice be more likely to foster greater appreciation for the arts in general? Not responding at all - building no statue - is of course part of the set of options. But it wouldn't follow that that was the best option just from the failure of the pure aesthetic judgment to deliver a verdict.

For the agency must treat that fact as part of its challenge. Given the congressional instruction, and given the failure of the pure aesthetic judgment, what should be done? The range of factors pertinent to that new question is much larger than the range pertinent to the pure aesthetic Judgment, and the case for indeterminacy is correspondingly weaker.

One final point. Archimedean proponents of indeterminacy sometimes declare themselves to be against 'theory,' with the exception of their own. They say 'theory' is produced by philosophers who fail to understand that, from the philosophical or Archimedean perspective, there are no right answers to the questions these theories purportedly address. We can now see (as a coda to the argument as a whole) that the supposed alliance between indeterminacy and an anti-theory stance is as bogus as everything else in the Archimedean architecture. C-propositions, which concede uncertainty, might be said to be (at least relatively) untheoretical. But indeterminacy claims, as we have just seen, are different from uncertainty claims; the former require positive support, and there is no reason to think that the positive support they need draws any less on theory than other positive claims do. On the contrary, in the global form in which they are characteristically defended, they are likely to be much more ambitious because much more general.

Consider the legal claim just discussed: that when lawyers disagree, and there is no knock-down argument available to reconcile them, it follows that the case for neither side is better than the case for the other. There are an unlimited number of reasons why some but not all lawyers might think that one side had the better of a particular legal argument. Someone defending the view that no such reason can in fact tip the balance either way in any controversial case faces an enormously difficult task, much more difficult than that faced by someone who wants to argue for one decision rather than another in a particular case. How can he avoid appealing to some very general and abstract theory, like legal positivism? Someone defending a global claim of indeterminacy about morals or ethics or aesthetics - that there is never a right answer to any question about what we ought to do or how we ought to live or what is wonderful - has an even greater problem, and his need for a very abstract theory delivering these global conclusions seems even more evident. These are truly heroic claims, of vast theoretical pretension, and trying to dress them in the modest clothes of common sense or raw intuition is more comic than persuasive.

NOTES

1 Harvard University Press (1986).
2 Say 'all' sides of an issue so that this claim includes the possibility that I see no good reason for thinking the issue indeterminate either.
3 Mackie, John, 'The Third Theory of Law' *Phil & Pub Aff* vol.1 no.1 (1977) 3.
4 I describe and defend a similar (but, as I shall insist in a moment, different) view about ethics in 'Foundations of Liberal Equality', *XI Tanner Foundation Lecture Series*, 1.
5 John Mackie once argued that a legal theory that made moral argument relevant would characteristically produce indeterminacy. See his 'The Third Theory of Law' *op cit.*
6 See the discussion of Critical Legal Studies in *Law's Empire* (1986) Fontana ch.2.

2 POSITIVISM AND STATUTORY CONSTRUCTION: An Essay in the Retrieval of Democracy

MICHAEL FREEMAN

It is a striking fact that discussion of statutory interpretation (or construction as I prefer to call it[1]) in this country has been so lacking in theoretical underpinning or insight. In part this may be a consequence of pedagogy: the 'relegation' of the teaching of the so-called 'rules' of statutory construction to first year English Legal System courses. The 'rules' have had to be inculcated into an impressionable audience to socialise them into 'thinking like lawyers,' a craft[2] generations of law teachers have identified with rule-following.[3] Even when there have been major changes, as was signalled by the House of Lords in *Pepper* v. *Hart*,[4] it is the mechanics that command attention, not the wider theoretical (and in particular constitutional) ramifications of using non-statutory material to impose meaning on statutory language.[5]

Nearly half a century ago the Denning-Simonds confrontation threatened to ignite interest in the judicial role, but the debate was not sustained, nor, it has to be added, was it one nourished by much in the way of theoretical insight. Lord Denning's view was thought then to be radical, even heretical, and yet all he was calling for was a return to the contextualism of *Heydon*'s case.[6] Said Denning: 'A judge should ask himself the question: if the makers of the Act had themselves come across this ruck in the texture of it, how would they have straightened it out? He must then do as they would have done. A judge must not alter the material of which it is woven, but he can and should iron out the creases.'[7] To Lord Simonds this was 'a naked usurpation of the legislative function under the thin guise of interpretation' and it was 'the less justifiable when it is guesswork with what material the legislature would, if it had discovered the gap, have filled it in.' Gaps, Simonds opined, should be filled by amending legislation.[8] It is an interesting reflection on the state of thinking about the judicial role that the Denning recipe for repairing legislation should have been thought then, and I daresay by many still now, to be radical at all. Denning was in no sense deviating from the originalist imperative. His view was premised on positivism, observed fidelity to the legislature, accepted without qualification legislative supremacy. A better illustration of a 'tacit command'[9] it would be difficult to find! Let us, Denning is saying, assist the sovereign in its objective to wield power over the population by spelling out its will, which it itself has failed to do, perhaps because of the imperfections of language.[10]

The half-century since the Denning-Simonds conflict has seen the judiciary wield the weapon of judicial review increasingly and with ever more force.[11] Decisions taken by ministers and even by Parliament are undermined, even struck down by the judges. It was the judges who struck down the Foreign Secretary's decision to give aid to the Pergau Dam.[12] They threw out the Home Secretary's new Criminal Injuries Compensation scheme, although Parliament had passed the legislation.[13] Not long ago a judiciary, far more conservative than it is today, was loath to become embroiled in the political process.[14] Its greater willingness to do so now has led interest groups, particularly those representing minority lobbies ill-represented in Parliament, to use the courts as fora for political change. Greenpeace, Friends of the Earth, the World Development Movement, Stonewall and Amnesty International are amongst those bringing their campaigns to the courtroom.[15] When gay personnel dismissed from the armed forces used judicial review to challenge government policy they lost, but there was no doubt they attracted the sympathy of Simon Brown L.J., who described the government's policy as 'wrong' and 'damaging to human rights.'[16]

Because of this frenzied activity, questions have begun to be asked about judges and politics, about judges and the democratic process: there have been plaudits as well as brickbats. But this has remained very largely within the confines of the permissible limits of judicial review. There has been little or no spillover into the arena of statutory construction. Contemporary accounts of this are still firmly rooted within unproblematic positivism. Students[17] are still taught that 'what the Queen in Parliament enacts is law,' that legislative intention is to be located in plain language, that there are rules of statutory interpretation of which the most important is the literal rule. Are students supposed to assume that those who enact legislation do so in the knowledge of the existence of the canons of construction, let alone with these in mind? They are not, of course, supposed to assume that Parliament can dictate the absurd:[18] and so they are taught there is a 'golden rule,' a safety valve, but it is noteworthy that what they are then told is that a meaning leading to an absurd result should not be imputed to the legislature because the result could not have been the legislature's intent -a reiteration of the positivist argument. They could equally be instructed or at least asked to weigh up the different views, that the absurd result is not right, just or fair. But to many law teachers to open up this alternative perspective - the natural law argument - would be to invite at best scepticism, at worst unhealthy challenge to authority.[19]

To an American audience this account of attitudes towards statutory construction will conjure up images of a distant past when American theories largely tracked those in England.[20] When Lon Fuller came to publish his wonderful parable 'The Speluncean Explorers,'[21] ironically in the same year as Denning L.J. was writing his opinion in *Seaford Court Estates*, he put into the mouth of Justice Keen the positivist model still implicit in the 'English theory.' 'We now have,' said Keen, 'a clear-cut principle, which is the supremacy of the legislative branch of our government. From that principle flows the obligation of the judiciary to enforce faithfully the written law, and to interpret that law in accordance with its plain meaning without reference to our personal desires or our individual conceptions of justice. I am not concerned with the question whether the principle that forbids the judicial revision of statutes is right or wrong, desirable or undesirable: I observe merely that this principle has become a tacit premise underlying the whole of the legal and governmental order I am sworn to administer.'[22]

American approaches to statutory construction have long left behind the Keen model, itself a reconstruction of the ideas of Holmes.[23] For reasons too many to expound upon here - these include not only the written constitution[24] but also the critical and constitutional thought, particularly of the last fifteen years[25] - American legal scholarship has located thinking about statutory construction within theories of democratic politics and in doing so has asked questions not often heard on this side of the Atlantic. We are familiar with one variant of this approach, that exemplified by the writings of Ronald Dworkin, in particular in his *Law's Empire*.[26] Even this, however, has not had the impact it should. Whether this is because the chapter on statutory construction is late in the book, deemed peripheral[27] to the central thesis or just thought 'difficult' is not known. But certainly there is greater familiarity with his exegesis of the common law - few students of Dworkin are not familiar with his analysis of *McLoughlin* v. *O'Brian*[28] - than with his discussion of the role of courts in statutory construction. Dworkin's jurisprudence is distinctive but he is not alone in raising questions about the judicial role, in particular in siting this within a theory of democratic politics. Of course, implicit in every construction of a statute is a theory of democracy. We have seen that far too often this amounts to little more than a rhetorical concern for legislative supremacy. This orthodoxy has now been challenged.

The remainder of this paper examines these challenges and their implications. It starts with the familiar (or relatively so) and moves into less well-known terrain, including that of critical legal thinking. In doing so it will show that thinkers for whom Dworkin has no time[29] - he certainly has never tried to show them in their 'best light'[30] - have more in common with him than he or his defenders[31] may be prepared to concede. The primary aim of this paper, though, is to throw light on democracy, its meaning and its processes and to evacate or rediscover the judicial role. At the same time light will be thrown on what we understand by legislation: when does this end and when is its meaning fixed. Orthodox (positivist) opinion holds that the meaning of a statement is fixed at the end of the process of legislative enactment. But is this so? And what consequences flow from a finding that rejects statis for dynamism?

'The Best it Can Be'[32]

For Ronald Dworkin legislatures and courts are in partnership to make of each statute 'the best it can be.' The emphasis on partnership is key: within the positivist tradition the relationship is close to conceptualisation as one of principal and agent (and agents do their principal's bidding).[33] As part of his theory of 'law as integrity'[34] Dworkin argues that his Herculean judge can, through reflective interpretation, find the 'best justification' for each statute.[35] By thus doing he assists the political system to become a 'community of principle' rather than merely a 'rulebook community.'[36] For Dworkin interpretation is quintessential to the judicial vision of realising the ideals of 'political integrity and fairness and procedural due process as these apply specifically to legislation in a democracy.'[37] Judges must read statutes 'in whatever way follows from the best interpretation of the legislative process as a whole.'[38] They must refuse to treat statutes as mere 'negotiated compromises that carry no more or deeper meaning than the text of the statute declares.'[39] Employing the metaphor of the 'chain novel,'[40] Dworkin reconstructs the judge as partner with the legislature in the production of statutory meaning. Each is seen as co-author in the chain novel of the law-making process. Neither institutional participant has a monopoly in the creation of meaning: each in the chain must both interpret existing material and shape what will follow. Dworkin would not allow judges to succumb to crude consequentialism: judges are not given the freedom to choose the 'best substantive result.'[41] Rather, they must find 'the best justification ... of a past legislative event.'[42] That flows from 'the community's present commitment to a background scheme of political morality.'[43] The conventional, positivist account of statutes presuppose 'a fixed moment when the statute was spoken, when it acquired all the meaning it ever has'.[44] But, Dworkin insists

> 'Hercules' view requires no such structure. He understands the idea of a statute's purpose or intention, not as some combination of the purposes or intentions of particular legislators, but as the upshot of integrity, of taking the interpretive attitude toward the political events that include the statute's enactment ... . Nor does he suppose any canonical moment of speech toward which his historical research bends; the history he interprets begins before a statute is enacted and continues to the moment when he must decide what it now declares.'[45]

Hercules' method then 'rejects the assumption of a canonical moment at which a statute is born and has all and only the meaning it will ever have. Hercules interprets not just the statute's text but its life, the process that begins before it becomes law and extends far beyond that moment.'[46] The Herculean ideal is not to 'amend out-of-date statutes to suit new times,' but to recognise 'what the old statutes have since become.'[47]

Dworkin seems to assume that Hercules will encounter statutes in much the same way as he confronts the common law and he accordingly pays little attention to problems which may cause greater difficulties in interpreting statutes. And, just as he appears to see few difficulties, so neither do his sympathizers[48] or his critics. Dworkin on statutory construction has attracted little critical interest. The key concept for Dworkin's judge interpreting statutes is, what he calls, legislative convictions.[49] These are the values which legislators bring to the task of legislating.[50] The judge then develops these values in much the same mode that he elaborates principles in non-statutory contexts. He argues that these legislative convictions are a consequence of the legislature promoting a community of principle.[51] But care must be taken with what is meant by 'principle' in this context. It does not have any substantive meaning. Rather, it seems to be identified with coherence, sufficient to satisfy minimum rationality standards and avoid arbitrary statutes. Can Hercules then have a special role in working out legislative policy, if we accept Dworkin's distinction between principles and policies? Hercules' strength, as is made clear throughout *Law's Empire*,[52] lies in the application and elaboration of principles. This could lead us to one of two conclusions: either the model of the judge as a collaborator with the legislature cannot be sustained or Dworkin's distinction between principles and policies is defective. I think it is the latter, but this is not the place to expand upon this view. I turn instead to other anti-positivist models of statutory construction, initially to those which, like Dworkin, adopt a complementary or collaborative framework.

A Collaborative Exercise

The origins of seeing courts as collaborators with legislatures in producing statutory meaning can be traced to Willard Hurst[53] and to the influential 'law as process' writings of Henry Hart and Albert Sacks.[54] In *Dealing with Statutes*, Hurst urged that courts recognised that the statutory text 'derives its vitality'[55] from both the past and the future. For Hurst it is structural deficiencies within legislatures that limit their abilities to create effective statutes. It is for courts to compensate. This cognition of the 'realities'[56] of institutional structures demands, Hurst argues, an 'approach both more pragmatic and more deferential to the functions of courts under the separation of powers,' one which stresses 'custom-built determinations, fashioned out of materials immediate and special to the legislation at issue.' He contrasts this with, what he considers, the unhelpful formalism of 'broad, standardised formulas.'[57]

For Hart and Sacks interpretation is conceived as the 'creative elaboration' of meaning by judges.[58] They do not hide their belief that courts have to decide what meaning 'ought' to be given to the directions of the statute. Nevertheless, the primacy of the legislative role in policy-making is acknowledged, though at the same time the legislature's dependence on courts to use 'good faith and good sense' in construing ambiguous[59] language to ensure that the statutory 'purpose' is effectuated is also recognised.[60] The work of Hart and Sacks looks forward to seeing the courts as an instrument of democracy, but their feet are still rooted in earlier essentialist thinking. Thus, to them it is obvious that a court is forbidden from substituting 'its own ideas for what the legislature has duly enacted.'[61]

To positivists the temporal frame is clear: the statute is a single dateable event which ends upon enactment. But to Hurst and to Hart and Sacks it is equally clear that judges can take into account facts and considerations that the legislature could not foresee.[62] No legislature could have anticipated, for example, the computer revolution or the development of assisted reproduction if it were deliberating in 1930. Nor could it have envisaged greater tolerance of cohabitation or gay relationships.

Some contemporary legal scholarship goes even further. Thus, to Eskridge and Frickey 'evolving and current values'[63] can be worth as much, if not more, than historical legislative choices. They urge 'dynamic interpretation'[64] to keep legislation relevant, coherent and reflective of contemporary values. They would, it may be supposed, thus approve of the Court of Appeal's decision in 1975 to include a long-standing relationship of cohabitation within the concept of 'family,'[65] though this clearly was not intended by Parliament in 1920.[66] Guido Calabresi would invest courts with even greater powers. He has urged that a court be empowered to declare a law 'obsolete' if it finds it 'out of phase with the whole legal framework.'[67] Outdated statutes, he argues, have only a weak claim to majority support. The reason why judges can justifiably act in this way is that they have, so he argues, sufficient detachment.

Eskridge and Frickey belong to the new pragmatic movement in legal thinking.[68] They advocate, what they call, 'practical reasoning' in statutory interpretation.[69] The approach is based on Aristotle's practical reasoning (*phronesis*)[70] and 'starts with the proposition that one can determine what is right in specific cases, even without a universal theory of what is right.'[71] Eskridge and Frickey are influenced also by the hermeneutics of Gadamer.[72] According to Eskridge and Frickey, Gadamer believed that interpretation 'is the search for common ground between interpreter and text.'[73] The judge looks for a 'fusion' of the interpreter's 'horizon' and the historical 'horizon.' 'Hermeneutics suggests that the text lacks meaning *until* it is interpreted ... One does not "understand" a text in the abstract, without an "application" of the text to a specific problem.'[74] Practical reasoning has three basic principles. First, statutory construction is a creative process. Secondly, the judge has a choice among different answers. The range of choices is 'somewhat constrained by the text, the statute's history, and the circumstances of its application.'[75] Nevertheless, the 'actual choice will not be "objectively" determinable.[76] Third, in making choices, interpreters normally are driven by multiple values. These multiple values form the 'web of beliefs'[77] against which a judge will check his decision. They argue that a combination of pragmatism and hermeneutics can bring 'all the relevant factors and all of our problem-solving skills to bear on difficult questions of statutory meaning in concrete situations'[78], and in so doing can legitimate statutory interpretation through 'deliberation and candor.'[79] Even without 'apparent consensus in society or in the legal community, the interpreter can often create some kind of agreement in the context of the narrow case, and through the case enlighten attitudes in the larger community.'[80] They reject 'foundationalism,'[81] whether it focuses on intent, text purpose. Each of these theories may seek its legitimacy within democracy, but, Eskridge and Frickey argue, this is a 'chimera'[82] because none of the three can transcend the problem of indeterminacy.

The most unashamedly pragmatist of all is Judge Richard Posner.[83] For him conventional, positivist approaches to statutory interpretation place 'too much emphasis on authority, certitude, rhetoric and tradition, and 'too little on consequences and on social-scientific techniques for measuring consequences.'[84] Accordingly, it is his view that perhaps 'the best thing to do when a statute is invoked is to examine the consequences of giving the invoker what he wants and then estimate whether those consequences will on the whole be good ones.'[85] He confines judges, however, within the limits, such as they are, of 'reasonableness.'[86] This he defines to include 'sensitivity to the limits of judicial knowledge and to the desirability of stability in law.'[87]

Critical Discourses

The challenges depicted so far do not entirely negate the premises of positivism. They accept the legislative process as essentially democratic and enlist the courts as partners in a process of refinement. They recognise that courts have skills that legislatures lack, but legislatures, in the eyes of all the jurists discussed thus far, remain primary law makers. There are now also those who advocate exploiting statutory ambiguity as a vehicle for social transformation. The court is seen to have the potentiality to reconstruct society, to create a more genuine democracy than legislatures have succeeded in constructing. This vision of statutory construction emerges both out of civic republicanism[88] and from what may be generically classified as critical discourses,[89] feminism,[90] critical race theory[91] and postmodernist legal thinking.[92] There are strands of civic republicanism in Eskridge and Frickey, but it is in the writing of Cass Sunstein[93] that the true bridge to this transformative approach is found.

Like Eskridge and Frickey, he rejects the view that statutory meaning is fixed at the moment of statutory creation. He, too, argues for a dynamic theory of statutory meaning. Into this dynamic process of interpretation he feeds 'background norms'[94] and larger public values. Democracy, he argues, is about deliberation and dialogue. Part of the judicial role is the correction of 'malfunctions in the legislative process.'[95] He offers an extensive and rank-ordered catalogue of principles which he claims will enhance such values as 'the promotion of public deliberation, the protection of historically-disadvantaged groups, and the minimisation of naked interest group transfers.'[96] The view projected here is of interpretation as compensation. Interpretive principles assist, what has been called, 'as if' interpretation,[97] in which statutes are treated 'as if' they were the product of a democracy truly representative of all interests, rather than of a 'dominated dialogue'[98] which republicanism associates within pluralist politics.[99]

The critical discourses associated with feminist jurisprudence, critical race theory and postmodernism have not produced a lot of material on statutory construction.[100] Perhaps, as Schank admits, 'the very act of attempting to apply [postmodernism] to a practice is essentially an antipostmodern activity.'[101] But Schank's very useful survey article apart, there are now significant sources upon which to draw.

An excellent illustration of the problem and the approach is the article by Torres and Milun on the Mashpee Indian case.[102] The issue in the case was whether the Mashpees were a 'tribe' within the meaning of the Indian Non-Intercourse Act of 1790. The Act prohibits the transfer of Indian tribal land to non-Indians without approval of the federal government. The tribe claimed its land had been taken from it, between 1834 and 1870, without the required federal consent. According to the Mashpee, the Commonwealth of Massachusetts had permitted the land to be sold to non-Indians and had transferred common Indian lands to the Town of Mashpee. The Town of Mashpee in its defence denied that the Mashpee were a tribe. A forty day trial on the threshold issue led to a victory for the Town over the Tribe. The Mashpees lost the case because their history of 'assimilation' and 'integration' into the surrounding culture was found to destroy the element of 'community' that the court, following an earlier case[103] about a very different Indian grouping, interpreted the non-Intercourse Act to require to demonstrate tribal status. The testimony revealed the criteria of the earlier case as generalised ethnological categories that failed to capture the specifics of what it means to belong to the Mashpee people. As Torres and Milun note: 'Because of this disjunction between the between the ethno-legal categories and the Mashpee's lived experience, the Tribe's testimony and evidence never quite "signified" within the idiom established by the precedent.'[104] There were, in other words, 'culturally divergent versions of "the truth"'[105] and the court, because of its 'limited kind of cultural vision ... from the perspective of the dominant culture'[106] was unable to perceive a truly 'pluralistic conception of justice' which requires the incorporation of those conflicting views. The lived experience of the Mashpee was translated by the court into an 'objective, acontextual legal category.'[107] And 'once "Tribe" became exclusively a legal construct, it embodied all of the subsidiary or provisional social meanings that gave it life within a pseudo-objective legal form. By entering the universe of legal discourse, the term "Tribe", in the context of the Non-Intercourse Act, has no meaning for the internal perspective of people claiming that status.'[108] Although Torres and Milun are pessimistic - they see law as an 'ineffective form of politics,'[109] particularly for those who would change the dominant order -it is possible to envisage a court capable of hearing the silenced voice of the Mashpee. A court which did this would advance democracy by infusing into statutory meaning a perspective long marginalized. The Mashpee decision is a particularly good case study but the problem has arisen in other countries and contexts as well: in Israel in the controversy over who is a 'Jew'[110] and in Britain over whether Rastafarians constitute a race for the purposes of the Race Relations Acts.

A second example of the influence of critical discourses on statutory construction are several of the 'judgments' found in the recently - continued Speluncean Explorers' saga.[111] The hypothetical 'Newgarth' statute is re-interpreted in these 'contemporary proceedings' using very different perspectives from those which appear in Fuller's original.[112] Thus Naomi Cahn[113] is critical of the way Fuller's judges ignore context and fail to examine relationships and dependence. Of legislative intent she writes:

> 'I am not ... arguing that we jettison all attempts to understand why a particular statute was enacted; rather, I am suggesting that legislative intent is not gospel, that it is but one of multiple factors to be considered in interpreting the statute before us, and that we need to speak of legislative *intents*.'[114]

And drawing on the work of Carol Gilligan[115] she states the challenge as the need to acknowledge 'the different strands at play in our decisions. Instead of seeking to find our answers only in a hierarchy of rights, our decision should integrate care *and* justice.'[116] But, even then, she acknowledges, 'we will not reach the one "just" result' for there are only 'contingent judgments.'[117] Both Coombs[118] and Greene[119] emphasise the privileged position of the supposed defendants in the Speluncean case. 'Dare I suggest,' writes Mary Coombs in her opinion, 'that sympathy with these particular defendants, rather than the many others subject to [the statute prohibiting killing] might reflect an easy identification with the plight of other accomplished, privileged men who responded with logic, determination and manly courage to their dilemma?'[120] And Dwight Greene, after observing the parallel between the cave and many of today's ghettos, also 'removed morally from the force of a legal order'[121], comments: 'Surely, this Court would be unwilling to excuse a group of Melanoderms [his compendious term for ethnic minorities] from such a ghetto who formed their own social contract and imposed its outcomes on others within the community who dissented from that contract.'[122]

There are similarities between the civic republicanism of Cass Sunstein and these critical discourses - both challenge originalism, both seek to redress imbalances caused by defects in the legislative process - but the differences are of greater significance. For republicans what the courts need to do is of an adjustive nature: there is a uniquely correct result and the legislature would have reached it if only those whose interests are suppressed had been able to participate in the legislative process. Judges should interpret the statute 'as if'[123] there had been a full and fully informed democratic dialogue. Critical theorists reject the single correct answer and emphasise the social contingency of truth. Further, they do not justify using the courts to undermine oppression and correct exclusion by pretending that the political process could have achieved this. Rather the courts constitute an alternative space where different notions of the 'good' can be articulated. They create the opportunity to challenge what otherwise might seem inevitable and unproblematic, in Martha Minow's words 'natural, uncoerced and good.'[124]

The Democratic Process as Undemocratic

An inevitable response to the theme of this paper is that I have got it the wrong way round. Surely, the argument goes it is legislatures which are democratic whilst courts should be restrained from making law because they are not. On the contrary they are unelected, unrepresentative and unanswerable.[125] That there is a lot wrong with judiciaries and the judicial process is not denied - and ways of making courts more democratic clearly need to be addressed. This will be done, albeit briefly. But of greater significance to us here is the supposed contrast, and to unpick this it is necessary first to examine some of the premises and principles of democratic pluralism.

Orthodox constitutional theory views legislation as 'the vector of competing interests.'[126] As Sullivan neatly puts it:

> 'Factions differ in their agendas and in the importance they ascribe to various issues. Legislative outcomes reflect compromise, trading and tactical deals to exchange support; no law is likely to represent what any faction would prefer if left to its own devices.'[127]

The ultimate result is 'political equilibrium.'[128] The model has utilitarian underpinnings in that it strives to respect current preferences and to avoid the risks of tyranny associated with active and self-conscious preference-shaping by public officials.'[129] The case for pluralism weakened if some preferences can be shown to be objectionable or the product of unjust background institutions. Pluralism also tends to ignore the power of some groups to limit the number and nature of issues set for democratic resolution. It also overlooks the fact that preferences tend to be formed against a backdrop of disparities in power and limitations in both opportunities and information.

Further, it is unclear why, on pluralist assumptions, 'laws should not be bought and sold like commodities in a marketplace; such a process of sale might accurately aggregate preferences.' Civic republicanism, by contrast, requires laws to be supported by argument and reasons and 'private-regarding reasons are an insufficient basis for legislation.'[130] The deliberative model is, of course, the one we also expect our courts to adopt.

Utilitarian malfunctions must also be embraced. Public choice theory has shown that cycling problems, strategic and manipulative behaviour, sheer chance and other factors prevent majoritarianism from providing an accurate aggregation of preferences. There is also 'too much slippage between legislative outcomes and constituent desires.'[131]

Another problem is that pluralist approaches place no premium on political participation. The absence of participation may well reflect 'a collective action problem or an adaptation to practices that are believed intractable.'[132] Of greater significance still is the fact that, where participation is absent, so are many of the positive qualities that should accompany political life - 'self-development, feelings of empathy, social solidarity'[133] and other virtues that have come to be associated with citizenship.

Overarching all these concerns is the legislative structure. In Britain this is bi-cameral with a semi-hereditary House of Lords - a contemporary observer can still find 'some merit'[134] in this though she acknowledges it has 'no claim to democratic legitimacy'[135] - able to obstruct legislation, as it did attempts to inject considerations of fairness and justice into the 'poll-tax' legislation.[136] A two-party system ensures that minority interests, whether of ethnic minorities, the disabled[137] or the gay, count for very little. And, with the coming of 'elective dictatorship'[138], the power of elected representatives has waned. A democratic constitution is in the end undemocratic if it gives all power to its elected government. And when the executive clothes itself with the legitimacy of Parliament it pulls the wool over the eyes of a gullible public. Some of Parliament's responses, like the extension of the Select Committee system,[139] though far from an unqualified success,[140] are positive: other, like meeting less often,[141] thus reducing the opportunity for scrutiny of executive fiat, are not.

The responses of the judiciary are more interesting. To a considerable degree they have become guardians of our democratic values. The politically illiterate condemn this activity as a trespass into the political arena. The language used is often less temperate than Lord Simonds' ringing attack on Lord Justice Denning.[142] But it would have been timorous and unwise for the judges to have declined to act, on some supposedly 'political question' doctrine,[143] when litigants have challenged the propriety of actions of public bodies. In involving themselves they have played politics only in the wider and historically more accurate meaning of that concept by invoking ethical principles about how the state should be run. And so they have adjudicated on such questions of acute political controversy as the ban (since removed) on *viva voce* broadcasts by terrorist sympathizers,[144] the rights of persons claiming refugee status,[145] local government finance,[146] a local authority's ban on hunting across its land,[147] the armed services' ban on gay personnel,[148] grant-maintained schools,[149] the disposal of nuclear waste,[150] the government's decision to ratify the Maastricht Treaty[151]. They have held the High Court to be competent to give relief, whether by interim injunction[152] or final declaration,[153] where the effect has been to disapply United Kingdom legislation as incompatible with the law of the European Union.

They have even held the exercise of the Royal prerogative to be judicially reviewable,[154] and, in *Pepper* v. *Hart*,[155] treated the Bill of Rights as a statute like any other.[156]

That courts have these powers is not the result of legislation. As Mr Justice Laws has noted, in a remarkably frank and insightful article,[157]

> 'They are, categorically, judicial creations. They owe neither their existence nor their acceptance to the will of the legislature. They have nothing to do with the intention of Parliament, save as a fig-leaf to cover their true origins.'[158]

And he retorts: 'We do not need the fig-leaf any more.'[159] Even if the *ultra vires* prong could be justified in terms of the will of the legislature,[160] that which the courts label 'Wednesbury unreasonableness'[161] could only by full stretch of the imagination be similarly rationalised. To say it can be explained by imputing to Parliament an intention that statutory decision-makers should act reasonably and fairly is as rooted in fiction as is legislative intent itself.

The rules of statutory construction are, of course, also judicial creations. That there are three can only be explained historically.[162] The dominance, until very recently,[163] of the literal rule can be traced to the middle third of the nineteenth century.[164] It emerged with positivism,[165] the growth of parliamentary supremacy[166] and the articulation of a separation of powers doctrine.[167] But if judges can rethink the way they interpret statutes, such a process does not end with the formulation of new 'rules.' If new powers can be created to examine the propriety of statutory material, why should the role of the judiciary in statutory construction be so limited?

Judicial Supremacy?

One reading of this paper points to judicial, rather then legislative, supremacy. Although the legal source of the doctrine of sovereignty is in the judges[168] - again a fact not always recognised - this is not the true implication. Some, Bishop Hoadly perhaps[169] or some of the American Legal Realists,[170] may have subscribed to such a view, but it ignores the many constraints which confine the judiciary.[171] As Berger and Luckmann explain:

> 'to engage in judging is to represent the role of the judge. The judging individual is not acting 'on his own,' but *qua* judge ... The role represents an entire institutional nexus of conduct. The role of judge stands in relation to other roles, the totality of which comprises the institutions of law.'[172]

The judicial role is circumscribed in a number of ways. A judge cannot act on his or her own initiative. S/he must wait for a case or controversy to be submitted for adjudication. Judges are reactive, not proactive. And they must react: once seised of a *lis* a decision must be reached. Further, judges are under a duty to articulate a reasoned basis for their decisions. Unlike the legislature, they must justify their decisions. A statute by contrast 'normally contains no argumentative or justificatory statement; it simply asserts: this is forbidden, this is required, this is authorized.'[173] To find the reasons for legislative enactment *Hansard* must be consulted, and possibly the reports of committees and commissions. The practice of a preamble, more common when judges in pre-positivist days sought out the 'mischief' of the statute, is moribund.

Judges are further confronted by, what Fuller called, a 'problem of system.'[174] In language almost prescient of Dworkin's 'chain novel' metaphor[175] Fuller explained: 'The rules applied to the decision of individual controversies cannot simply be isolated exercises of judicial wisdom. They must be brought into, and maintained in, some systematic interrelationship; they must display some coherent internal structure.'[176] A legislature, by contrast, can take 'leaps in the dark': there is no logical necessity for any statute to be related to any other. It may be that the root of this difference lies in the fact that judges are able to act in this way because they are confronted with real human problems. Justice demands that these be treated equally, and equality of treatment demands system. Legislatures, on the other hand, see issues in an abstract, generalised fashion. Because of pressure on time, legislators know that they will not be able to reconsider the question at hand for some considerable time. But judges can take minor steps which elicit new information and allow them to pull back 'without excessive loss if the new information indicates unexpected trouble.'[177] They can do this because they know that in due course new problems similar to the first will arise, and they will be able to test the rule against the new facts. The rule, as initially formulated and subsequently restated or modified, enables the judge to focus attention on unresolved problems.

Recognition of the role judges can play in furthering democratic ideals requires us to rethink both the judicial process and the judiciary. Ironically, it may cause us to re-examine one of the most radical of recent changes in the judicial process as far as it affects the construction of statutes. The move to allow judges to consult *travaux préparatoires*[178] was generally welcomed but how much consideration was given to one of its more regressive consequences? A consultation of background materials, and in particular *Hansard*, can lead to construing statutes in terms of outdated understandings. If in *Dyson Holdings* v. *Fox* in 1975[179] *Hansard* had been consulted on how Parliament in 1920 (when the relevant statute was passed) had understood who was included within the concept of a tenant's 'family,' the court would not have been able to take into account the interests of a woman who had cohabited with a tenant for 21 years. It would, of course, also have reached the conclusion it did, eleven years later, that a lesbian relationship was not a family relationship for the purposes of Rent Act protection.[180] That such a conclusion was wrong - and would not have been reached by any of the theorists discussed in this paper - is a matter to which I must return. What must be recognised here is that the decision in *Pepper* v. *Hart* adopts essentially a positivist model of statutory construction, without investigating its theoretical, institutional or political difficulties.[181] I am not advocating that judges should not be able to consult preliminary materials: only that they should understand them for what they are.

There are ways of improving the judicial process. If statutes are to be interpreted more democratically, access to the judicial system has to be opened up, rather than, as at present, foreclosed by the curtailment of legal aid. When barriers are placed before those who wish to litigate, what can be aired before courts becomes a variable of wealth and status. The 'have nots'[182] get no more of a 'look in' than they do in legislative politics. What statutes are construed, and how, thus becomes to a considerable degree dependent upon how legal services are delivered. Nor is it only the means test that needs to be re-examined: the 'merit' test which limits litigation to that which reasonable persons of reasonable means would undertake and which perceive poverty in absolute rather than relative terms obstructs not only access but the ability to participate in a democratic process. The 'test case' is one of the few opportunities that ordinary people get (or would get if there were not also differential access to justice) to participate in the law-making process.[183]

Greater acceptance and use of the *amicus curiae* brief is also important if the range of parties interested in litigation is to be broadened. Greater tolerance of group actions would also facilitate the participation in the judicial process of many individuals whose ability to use the courts is currently frustrated.

There must be changes too in the policies relating to judicial selection and training. The Lord Chief Justice is right to resist those who advocate something close to affirmative action: whether he is right to draw a comparison with who gets to be a brain surgeon is more dubious.[184] The pool of those from whom the judiciary is currently selected excludes many who have the ability and the skills to adjudicate conflict. Opening up appointment policies beyond the cosy 'old boys network' will also broaden the base from which appointments are sought. It is indefensible, if nevertheless understandable, that so few women sit as judges of our higher courts and that most of those who do have been confined to the ghetto of the Family Division. This millennium is likely to end before this country's highest court receives its first female appointment.[185] As I write this, an English law professor is being appointed to the International Court of Justice in The Hague.[186] The chances of any of her colleagues being appointed to the bench in England is slim in the extreme. But appointments of academic lawyers and of solicitors - only one solicitor as yet has reached the High Court bench - would widen the social composition of the judiciary. This might not have any significance beyond the symbolic, but the importance even of this should not be underestimated.

More emphasis needs to be placed also on training the judiciary: advocacy skills and legal knowledge and craft can be guaranteed, but more than this is required of our judges. The establishment of a judicial training college, to which new appointments would be sent and where sabbaticals could be taken, would encourage judges to think about their role and give them greater insights into the society they are judging.

These are important matters - and they need a fuller consideration than can be given in this paper. They are especially important if the profile of the judiciary in the reconstruction of democracy is to be taken seriously.

Conclusion

The model of construing statutes adopted in this paper is an attempt to get beyond fictions - that there is a legislative will, that it can be found, that interpretation can be neutral. These fictions are deeply embedded within positivist thought which continues to cast a deep shadow over legal thinking. It also embraces an image of pluralist politics so that the will of the sovereign is deemed to form a vector of democracy. Those, by contrast, who emphasise judicial activism have not, at least until the jurists discussed in this paper, addressed the implications of such activism for democratic politics. I argue that the judges can be a power for good, that they can redress imbalances caused by the failures of the political process, that they can rescue legislation from the deadhand of history. This requires to see legislation as a living organism rather than an historical product. It was judges who created our constitution, judges who invented the so-called rules of statutory construction. It was judges who first decided that recourse to *travaux préparatoires* was impermissible and then that it could be consulted. It is judges who have created and expanded the powers of judicial review. This is particularly germane to the theme of this paper, for it is in the context of judicial review that we have seen minority interest groups able to challenge the power of the state in a way short of demonstrations or civil disobedience otherwise denied to them. With the distinct possibility that we will soon incorporate the European Convention on Human Rights into United Kingdom law, the questions raised in this paper take on a new significance for one concern of opponents of such a move is that entrenchment of rights can be backward-looking. It is the legacy of positivism which induces this fear. This now needs to be transcended. That it can be done is shown by the approaches to statutory construction which have been described in this paper. And they privilege the contemporary over the historical.

NOTES

1 See M.D.A. Freeman, *Lloyd's Introduction To Jurisprudence* (6th edition, 1994) (London: Sweet and Maxwell), 1289.

2 Using Karl Llewellyn's expression: see *The Common Law Tradition: Deciding Appeals* (Boston: Little, Brown, 1960).

3 See W. Twining and D. Miers, *How to do Things with Rules* (London: Weidenfeld and Nicolson, 3rd ed., 1991, ch. 10.

4 [1993] 1 All E.R. 42.

5 *Cf* William N. Eskridge, 'Legislative History Values' 66 *Chicago-Kent Law Review* 365 (1992).

6 1584 3 Co. Rep 7 b.

7 *Seaford Court Estates Ltd v Asher* [1949] 2 K.B. 481,499

8 *Magor and St Mellons R.D.C.* v *Newport Corporation* [1952] AC 189, 191. Lord Simonds was responding directly to opinions expressed by Denning L.J. in the Court of Appeal in the *Magor* case (see [1950] 2 All E.R. 1226, 1236), but these reiterated his sentiments in *Seaford Court Estates*. Of course in *Shaw* v *D.P.P* [1962] A.C. 220, 268, he had no difficulty filling in gaps in legislation to uphold public morality.

9 This can be traced to Hobbes's *Leviathan*, ch. xxvi (and see H.L.A. Hart, *The Concept of Law* (Oxford: Clarendon Press, 2nd ed, 1994, 63-64).

10 Denning L.J. refers in *Seaford Court Estates* to the absence of 'mathematical precision' in the English language (*op cit*, at 498).

11 See David Pannick, 'Who is Subject to Judicial Review and in Respect of What?,' (1992) *Public Law* 1.

12 *R* v *Secretary of State for Foreign Affairs ex parte World Development Movement Ltd* [1995] 1 All E.R. 611.

13 *R* v *Criminal Injuries Compensation Board ex parte P* [1995] 1 WLR 845.

14 Though it did in more insidious ways, as J.A.G. Griffith, *The Politics of the Judiciary* (London: Fontana Press, 1977) demonstrates.

15 See Polly Toynbee, 'Judicial Review is a mere Elastoplast,' *The Independent*, 2 August 1995

16 *R v. Minister of Defence ex parte Smith, The Times,* 13 June 1995

17 See for example Nicola Lacey's experience as quoted in 'Feminist Legal Theory Beyond Neutrality,' (1995) 48 *Current Legal Problems* 1, 2.

18 See Baron Parke in *Perry* v *Skinner* [1837] 2 M & W 471, 476.

19 See Duncan Kennedy, 'Legal Education as Training for Hierarchy' in David Kairys (ed.), *The Politics of Law* New York: Pantheon Books, 1982).

20 See William S Blatt, 'The History of Statutory Interpretation: A Study in Form and Substance' (1985) 6 *Cardozo Law Review* 799.

21 'The Case of the Spelucean Explorers,' (1945) 62 *Harvard L.R.* 417

22 *Ibid*, 633.

23 'The Theory of Legal Interpretation' (1899) 12 *Harvard Law Review* 417.

24 Hence the controversy over the appointment of Robert Bock (who failed) and Clarence Thomas (who was appointed).

25 A good example of which is Cass R. Sunstein, *The Partial Constitution* (Cambridge, Mass.: Harvard

University Press, 1993)

26 But see also *Taking Rights Seriously* (London: Duckworth, 1977) and *A Matter of Principle* (Cambridge, Mass: Harvard University Press, 1986).

27 Most commentators write as if Dworkin addressed only common law problems.

28 [1983] 1 AC 410, discussed by Dworkin in *Law's Empire* (London: Fontana, 1986), 23-29, 238-250.

29 I think particularly here of critical thinkers, but surprisingly he has not taken much interest in others considered in this article, Posner excepted.

30 See J.M. Balkin, 'Understanding Legal Understanding: The Legal Subject and the Problem of Legal Coherence' (1993) 103 *Yale Law Journal* 105, 134-135 (note 50).

31 Most obviously Stephen Guest.

32 Ronald Dworkin, *Law's Empire* (London: Fontana, 1986), 348.

33 See Cass Sunstein, 'Interpreting Statutes in the Regulatory State,' (1989) 103 *Harvard Law Review*, 407.

34 *Op cit*, note 32, 95-96 and ch. 7, *passim*.

35 *Ibid*, 335

36 *Ibid,* 338, 345

37 *Ibid,* 338

38 *Ibid,* 337

39 *Ibid,* 345

40 *Ibid,* 228-238

41 *Ibid,* 338

42 *Idem*

43 *Ibid,* 346

44 *Ibid,* 316

45 *Idem*

46 *Ibid,* 348

47 *Ibid,* 350

48 Stephen Guest, *Ronald Dworkin* (Edinburgh: Edinburgh University Press, 1992) pays little attention to Dworkin on statutory construction.

49 *Op cit*, note 32, 328-330.

50 *Ibid*, 327.

51 *Ibid*, 328-330.

52 *Ibid*, 240-150. See also *Taking Rights Seriously*, *op cit*, note 26.

53 J. Willard Hurst, *Dealing with Statutes* (Princeton NJ: Princeton University Press, 1982)

54 Henry M. Hart and Albert M. Sacks, *The Legal Process: Basic Problems in the Making and Application of Law* (eds. William N. Eskridge and Philip Frickey (Brooklyn, NY: Foundation Press, 1994).

55 *Op cit*, note 51, 41, 45-46.

56 *Ibid*, 52

57 *Idem*

58 *Op cit*, note 52, 1380.

59 Dworkin argues that the approach to be adopted is no different when the language of the statute is clear (*op cit*, note 32, 351.

60 *Op cit*, note 52, 1374

61 *Ibid,* 1194

62 Thus Hurst argues that the statutory text 'derives its vitality' from both the past and the future (*op cit*, note 51, 41). There are similar sentiments in Hart and Sacks.

63 William N. Eskridge and Philip Frickey, *Cases and Materials on Legislation: Statutes and the Creation of Public Policy* (1988), 87.

64 See W. Eskridge, 'Dynamic Statutory Interpretation,' (1987) 135 *University of Pennsylanvia Law Review* 1479, 1481

65 *Dyson Holdings v Fox* [1976] Q.B. 503

66 When the Rent Act was first passed.

67 *A Common Law for the Age of Statutes* (Cambridge, Mass: Harvard University Press, 1982) 164

68 See the Symposium on the Renaissance of Pragmatism in American Legal Thought, 63 *Southern California Law Review* 1 (1990).
69 William N. Eskridge and Philip Frickey, 'Statutory Interpretation As Practical Reasoning,' 42 *Stanford Law Review* 321 (1990).
70 See Aristotle, *Nicomachean Ethics* chs. 5-11.
71 *Op.cit, note* 68, 323.
72 See H-G Gadamer, *Truth and Method* (J. Weinsheimer and D. Marshall trans, 1989). See W. Eskridge, 'Gadamer/Statutory Interpretation,' 90 *Columbia Law Review* 609 (1990). See also F. Mootz, 'The Ontological Basis of Legal Hermeneutics: A Proposed Model of Inquiry Based on the Work of Gadamer, Habermas and Ricoeur,' 68 *Boston University Law Review* 523 (1988) and Hoy, 'Interpreting the Law: Hermeneutical and Poststructuralist Perspectives,' 58 *Southern California Law Review* 135 (1985).
73 *Op.cit, note* 68, 323 citing Hans-Georg Gadamer, *Philosophical Hermeneutics* (David E. Linge trans. 1976).
74 *Ibid,* 346, citing Gadamer's *Truth and Method.*
75 *Ibid,* 347.
76 *Idem*.
77 *Idem*, And see W.V. Quine and J.S. Ullian, *The Web of Belief* (New York: Random House, 1970).
78 *Ibid*, 383.
79 *Ibid,* 384.
80 *Idem.*
81 Defined by Eskridge and Frickey as theory that 'seeks an objective ground ('foundation') that will reliably guide the interpretation of all statutes in all situations.' See *op cit,* note 62, 325.
82 *Ibid*, 383.
83 *Problems of Jurisprudence* (1990).
84 *Ibid,* 456.
85 *Idem*.
86 *Ibid*, 131.
87 *Idem*.
88 There is a good account of this in Craig, *Public Law and Democracy in the United Kingdom and the United States of America* (Clarendon Press: Oxford, 1990), ch. 10.
89 See Gary Minda 'The Jurisprudential Movements of the 1980s,' (1989) 50 *Ohio State Law Journal* 599.
90 Katherine T. Bartlett, 'Feminist Legal Methods' (1990) 163 *Harvard Law Review* 829 (particularly 877-880). See also Anne Phillips, *Engendering Democracy* (Cambridge: Polity Press, 1991) and Kathleen B. Jones, *Compassionate Authority* (New York: Routledge, 1993).
91 See Patricia J. Williams, *The Alchemy of Race and Rights* (Cambridge, Mass: Harvard University Press, 1991); Gerald Torres, 'Critical Race Theory: The Decline of the Universalist Ideal and the Hope of Plural Justice (1991) 75 *Minnesota Law Review* 993.
92 See J.M. Balkin, 'What is a Postmodern Constitutionalism?' (1992) 90 *Michigan Law Review* 1966.
93 See, in particular, 'Interpreting Statutes in the Regulatory State,' 103 *Harvard Law Review* 407 (1989).
94 *Ibid*, 469. See also William Eskridge, 'Public Values in Statutory Interpretation,' 137 *Univ of Pennsylvania Law Review* 1007 (1989).
95 *Op cit*, note 63, 383.
96 *Ibid*, 449.
97 On 'as if' interpretation see Jerry Mashaw, 'As if Republican Interpretation,' 97 *Yale Law Journal* 1685, 1688 (1988).
98 *Cf* Kathleen M. Sullivan, 'Rainbow Republicanism,' 97 *Yale Law Journal* 1713, 1718 (1988).
99 See David Held, *Models of Democracy* (Oxford: Oxford University Press, 1987): see particularly 186-220.
100 Including the work (not discussed in this article) of Stanley Fish: for example the collection *There's No Such Thing As Free Speech* (New York: Oxford University Press, 1994).
101 'Understanding Postmodern Thought and its Implications for Statutory Interpretation,' 65 *Southern California Law Review* 2505, 2574 (1992).

102 'Translating Yonnodio by Precedent and Evidence: the Mashpee Indian Case,' (1990) *Duke Law Journal* 625.
103 *Montoya* v *United States* 180 U.S. 261 (1901).
104 *Op cit*, note 100, 634-635.
105 *Ibid*, 639.
106 *Ibid*, 632.
107 *Ibid*, 646.
108 *Ibid*, 655.
109 *Ibid*, 657.
110 'Who is a Jew?: Some Semiotic Observations on a Judgment of the Israel Supreme Court,' (1993) 6 *International Journal for the Semiotics of Law* 115.
111 On which see William N. Eskridge, Jr, 'The Case of the Speluncean Explorers: Twentieth Century Statutory Interpretation in a Nutshell,' 61 *George Washington Law Review* 1731 (1993). See also note 112.
112 Lon L. Fuller, 'The Case of the Speluncean Explorers,' 62 *Harvard Law Review* 616 (1949).
113 'The Case of the Speluncean Explorers: Contemporary Proceedings,' 61 *George Washington Law Review* 1754, 1755 (1993).
114 *Ibid*, at 1758.
115 In particular in a *Different Voice: Psychological Theory and Women's Development* (Cambridge, Mass: Harvard University Press, 1982).
116 *Op cit*, note 112, 1763.
117 *Idem*.
118 *Op cit*, note 112, 1785.
119 *Ibid*, 1790.
120 *Ibid*, 1787.
121 *Ibid*, 1794.
122 *Idem*.
123 See Jerry Mashaw, 'As if Republican Interpretation' 97 *Yale Law Journal* 1685 (1988).
124 *Making all the Difference: Inclusion, Exclusion and American Law* (Ithaca, NY, Cornell University Press, 1990), 53.
125 This is, of course, one of Ronald Dworkin's central objections to judicial lawmaking. See *Taking Rights Seriously* (London: Duckworth, 1977), Ch. 4. But Dworkin is simultaneously an opponent of both judicial activism and judicial restraint (as acknowledged in Lloyd's *Introduction to Jurisprudence*, *op cit*, 5th ed. 1985, omitted from 6th ed., London: Stevens, 1985, note 1, 1126).
126 See Kathleen Sullivan, 'Unconstitutional Conditions,' 102 *Harvard Law Review* 1413, 1469. (1989).
127 *Idem*.
128 See Cass R. Sunstein, 'Beyond the Republican Revival,' 97 *Yale Law Journal* 1539 (1988).
129 *Ibid*, 1543.
130 *Ibid*, 1544.
131 *Ibid*, 1546.
132 *Ibid*, 1547.
133 *Idem*. And see Carole Pateman, *Participation and Democratic Theory* (Cambridge: CUP, 1970) and Jon Elster, *Sour Grapes: Studies in the Subversion of Rationality* (Cambridge: CUP, 1983).
134 Dawn Oliver, *Government in the United Kingdom* (Milton Keynes: Open University 1991) 55.
135 *Ibid*, 49.
136 'Backwoodsmen' were responsible for defeating an amendment that would have related liability to ability to pay. The amendment was defeated by 317 votes to 183 and, of the 317, 233 were hereditary peers.
137 This led to a dramatic (and dramatically suppressed) demonstration outside Parliament by the disabled in 1994 when legislation to improve their rights was being blocked.
138 Lord Hailsham's term in his 1978 Dimbleby lecture. He used it to describe the Labour government, but was strangely muted when Lord Chancellor in the Thatcher administration. See also John Keane, *Democracy and Civil Society* (London: Verso, 1988) ch. 5.

139 House of Commons Select Committee on *Procedure*, HC 588 (1977-1978).
140 See K. Ewing and C. Gearty, *Freedom Under Thatcher* (Oxford: Clarendon Press, 1990).
141 Parliament has since 1994 worked for little more than three days a week.
142 See, *op cit*, note 8.
143 See for example *Tito* v *Waddell (No. 2)* [1977] 3 All E.R. 129, 216-223. In the U.S. see the attitude of the Supreme Court to the Vietnam War in *Mora* v *McNamara* 398 U.S. 934 [1967].
144 *R* v *Secretary of State for the Home Department ex parte Brind* [1991] 1 AC 696.
145 *R* v *Secretary off State for the Home Department ex parte Bugdaycay* [1987] AC 514.
146 *R* v *Secretary of State for the Environment ex parte Hammersmith and Fulham LBC* [1991] 1 AC 521.
147 *R* v *Somerset C.C., ex parte Fewings* [1995] 3 All E.R. 20.
148 *R* v *Minister of Defence ex parte Smith The times*, 13 June 1995.
149 *R* v *Secretary of State for Education and Science ex parte Avon C.C.* [1991] 1 AC 558.
150 *R* v *Inspectorate of Pollution ex parte Greenpeace Ltd (No. 2)* [1994] 1 WLR 570.
151 *R* v *Secretary of State for Foreign and Commonwealth Affairs ex parte Rees-Mogg* [1994] QB 552.
152 *Factortame Ltd* v *Secretary of State for Transport (No. 2)* [1991] 1 AC 603.
153 *Equal Opportunities Commission* v *Secretary of State for Employment* [1994] 2 WLR 509.
154 *R* v *Secretary of State for Home Department ex parte Bentley* [1994] 2 WLR 101. This question had been left open in the *GCHQ* case ([1985] AC 374).
155 [1992] AC 593, 638-639.
156 How far this goes is in part, assessed by G. Marshall, 'Impugning Parliamentary Immunity,' (1994) *Public Law* 509.
157 'Law and Democracy,' (1995) *Public Law* 72. See also Sir John Laws, 'Is the High Court the Guardian of Fundamental Constitutional Rights?' (1993) *Public Law* 59.
158 *Ibid*, 79.
159 *Idem*.
160 See, for agreement, *ibid*, 78-79.
161 *Associated Provincial Picture Houses* v *Wednesbury Corporation* [1948] 1 KB 223.
162 See, *op cit*, note 1, 1291-1292. See also William S. Blatt, 'The History of Statutory Interpretation: A Study in Form and Substance,' [1985] 6 *Cardozo Law Review* 794. Robert S. Summers and Geoffrey Marshall, 'The Argument from Ordinary Meaning in Statutory Interpretation,' [1992] 43 *Northern Ireland Law Quarterly* 213, describe statutory construction as 'as old as written law.'
163 Initially under the influence of interpreting European legislation but latterly more generally, the courts have come to construe statutes more purposefully.
164 Thus Blackstone in his *Commentaries* vol. 1, 91-92 still spoke in language reminiscent of *Heydon's* case. See Robert J. Martineau, 'Craft and Technique, not Canons and Grand Theories: A Neo-Realist View of Statutory Construction,' [1993] 62 *George Washington Law Review* 1, 6.
165 The literal rule is virtually contemporaneous with the lectures of John Austin.
166 Hence the emphasis on legislative intent. In contract, property and tort a similar emphasis emerges at this time.
167 See Rebecca L. Brown, 'Separated Powers and Ordered Liberty,' [1991] 139 *University of Pennsylvania Law Review* 1513.
168 As interpreted, for example, by Hart, *op cit*, note 9, with his rule of recognition (see 94-110).
169 'Whoever hath an absolute authority to interpret ... laws it is he who is the lawgiver to all intents and purposes and not the person who first wrote or spake them,' as quoted in Hart, *op cit*, note 9, 141.
170 'the Constitution is what the judges say it is 'is attributed to Chief Justice Hughes of the U.S. Supreme Court.
171 I wrote on these many years ago. See M.D.A. Freeman, 'Standards of Adjudication, Judicial Law-Making and Prospective Overruling' [1973] 26 *Current Legal Problems* 166, 174-186.
172 *The Social Construction of Reality*, Berger and Luckmann - (Harmondsworth: Penguin), 92.
173 See Lon L. Fuller, *Anatomy of Law* (Harmondsworth: Penguin Books, 1971), 127. On Max Weber's views see Laurence Friedman (1966) *Wisconsin Law Review* 148, 158 *et seq*.
174 *Ibid*, 134.

175 See *op cit*.
176 *Op cit*, note 171, 134.
177 *Per* Martin Shapiro (1965) 2 *Law in Transition Quarterly* 134, 140. See also Vilhelm Aubert in *Legal Essays to Castberg*, Oslo: Universitetsforlaget (1963): 'The safest strategy for the judge is to hide some of his footprints, so as not to commit himself and other judges beyond the minimum necessary' (p. 41, 45).
178 Taken in *Pepper* v *Hart* (*op cit*, note 4).
179 [1976] Q.B. 503.
180 *Harrogate Borough Council* v *Simpson* [1986] 2 FLR 91.
181 On these difficulties, though not directly in relation to *Pepper* v *Hart* see William Eskridge, *op cit*, note 5.
182 See Marc Galanter, 'Why the "Haves" Come Out Ahead: Speculations on the Limits of Social Change,' (1974) 9 *Law and Society Review* 95.
183 See Tony Prosser, *Test Cases for the Poor: Legal Techniques in the Politics of Social Welfare* (London: CPAG, 1983.
184 As he did, in widely-reported remarks, in 1995.
185 One, Butler-Sloss L.J., has reached the Court of Appeal, provoking all manner of problem over how to address her!
186 Professor Rosalyn Higgins of the London School of Economics.

3 TWO STRANDS IN HART'S THEORY OF LAW: A Comment on the *Postscript* to Hart's *The Concept of Law*

STEPHEN GUEST

Hart's theory of legal positivism has a long and distinguished history. It is not merely that it has withstood serious and sustained attacks from different quarters but it appears to have been accepted by large numbers of lawyers, judges included, in the United Kingdom, and the various jurisdictions of the new and old commonwealth. Its main tenet asserts '... it is in no sense a necessary truth that laws reproduce or satisfy certain demands of morality, though they have in fact done so.'[1] If you talk to a group of first year students in the first week of their course, you discover that they, too, accept a positivist view of law. They can, for example, see clearly the difference between their own personal moral judgments about, say, abortion, and the legal question whether abortions are permitted under the Abortion Act 1967, the Infant Life (Preservation) Act 1934 and the common law (e.g. *R. v. Bourne*).[2] It is not just that students can see this without further study of law, but that they can see the *sense* of it. They say that if the law were otherwise, and merged with our 'personal and subjective' views of morality, the law would be different for each according to their personal moral perspective: abortion would be illegal for some but not for others. Early on in discussion, students will tell you that the law must be 'objective' and 'certain' and something to which all people can refer.

Two points emerge, both crucial to understanding Hart's theory of legal positivism: these students understand that they think of law, as an unanalysed matter of fact, in the way Hart describes. He says that we naturally draw a distinction between our judgments of law and our judgments of morality, this natural fact being discerned by a close examination of our linguistic practices (for example, how can you 'peel off' the language from the reality of the law?). His 'essay in descriptive sociology' (so famously referred to in the Preface to his *The Concept of Law*) *describes* the way we talk about law and, therefore, the way we both think and engage in the practices of law. But these students also understand that, independently of the fact they think that law and morality are different in the way legal positivism supposes, it is *a good thing* to think in this way. That is what they mean when they say that 'you couldn't have the law otherwise because that would mean that law would be one thing for some and another thing for others!' They mean, in other words, that there is a (moral) virtue in the theory since the law is 'seen as' - but 'constructed' is probably a better term - something of a *publicly ascertainable* nature.

These two aspects to Hart's theory are insufficiently understood. One reason is that people find it enormously difficult in general to distinguish between descriptive and normative claims. They find it particularly so in the case of law since there is the additional complication there that the language of the law (the 'law-related discourse' which Hart describes by use of his - to many, mystifyingly called - 'linguistic philosophy') is itself normative. Another reason is more profound and it is that people find it difficult to suppose *a theory itself* could be normative. After all, a theory of law is about 'law' and any theory should be an explanation at a sufficiently high level (employing breadth plus an economy of concepts) of *what the law is*. There are people who find that they can make the first leap - understand law descriptively as a normative enterprise - but not understand theorising as a normative enterprise.

But it is not difficult except for the way theorists sometimes present their theories. We are put off-guard by Hart's claim that his work *The Concept of Law* is an 'essay in descriptive sociology' and by his subsequent clearly descriptive use of terms (notoriously) such as 'being obliged' and 'being under an obligation'. But we should be careful. If we leap to his Chapter 9 we find him saying such things as that the choice between two conceptions of law (a 'narrower' natural law theory and a 'wider' positivist theory - the latter being his one) saying that the choice should *not* be determined as a matter of linguistic propriety. He says 'Plainly we cannot grapple adequately with this issue if we see it as one concerning the proprieties of linguistic usage.'[3]

Hart clearly offers more than a descriptive account of the law. He has not just analysed how we who engage in the law happen to think now about law (and therefore reflect, use and endorse the linguistic practices of law) but also goes on to say that he proposes that way of thinking about law as a *good*, meaning a *moral*, thing. If this is right then the light he throws on law is more strongly value-laden - judgmental - than he says it is in his now well-known *Postscript*. For what he must be offering are moral views which *justify* his according moral priority over other possible conceptions of law *and these justifications must be moral ones*. I am in no doubt that this is what he does. He achieves it first, by openly investing his central set of elements constituting law in terms with characteristics showing the moral superiority of a society which has adopted a set of rules which allow for progress (rules conferring public and private powers), for efficient handling of disputes (rules conferring powers of adjudication) and rules that create the possibility of publicly ascertainable - *certain* - criteria of what is to count as law.

If I am right, then Hart's theory can be attacked on moral grounds, and that means that he has joined a debate about what is appropriate, right, good, valuable and so on, about the conceptions of law which are on imaginative offer to us and it would follow that his approach is controversial in a way which ordinary language cannot tackle. What, then, is disappointing about his *Postscript* is that he appears to have lost the insight which he gave us, in 1982, in the Preface to his *Essays in Jurisprudence and Legal Philosophy*. In particular he admitted that the 'methods of linguistic philosophy ... are neutral between moral and political principles ...' and thus 'not suitable for resolving or clarifying those controversies which arise .. from the divergence between partly overlapping concepts reflecting a divergence of basic point of view ...'[4] And shortly before this passage he admits that this was a 'general defect' of his early invocation, for jurisprudence, of linguistic philosophy.

To cut a long story short: if Hart is talking morals, we can join the argument from morals. This means that it is an evaluative and not a descriptive wedge he badly wishes to insert between the individual and the state ('What surely is most needed in order to make men clear-sighted in confronting the official abuse of power, is that they should preserve the sense that the certification of something as legally valid is not conclusive of the question of obedience.')[5] It also means, I think, that he has conceded that theories of law are, in Dworkin's extremely wide sense, *interpretive*. Hart's best sense of law is one that values - sees and endorses the point of - certainty, public ascertainability and the host of virtues surrounding these important principles (such as the right not to have one's reasonable expectations frustrated). Indeed, once we see that Hart's project of this kind, we can see a familiar ring to the virtues extolled. They are the virtues of (dare one say?) the Chancery bar.[6]

The nature of legal theory

In the *Postscript* Hart affirms that he intended his theory of law to be both descriptive and general, in the sense that it was not to be thought of as tied to any one particular legal system. By 'descriptive' theory he says that he intended it to be 'morally neutral' and with no 'justificatory aims', adding further that this is 'a radically different enterprise' from that envisaged by Dworkin which, he says, is 'in part evaluative and justificatory and addressed to a particular legal culture''. He then says that because of these differences, he and Dworkin are not in conflict (something which, for example, Finnis has maintained in *Natural Law and Natural Rights*[7]), but rather that they are each writing with different aims in mind.

Early on, Hart takes issue with Dworkin's claim that positivist legal theory can be restated as an interpretive theory.[8] He thinks that Dworkin's view is 'mistaken' but the reasons Hart gives are disappointingly brief. He simply says that we *can* understand legal systems from the moderate external point of view, namely, the point of view of someone who understands that some people accept certain rules (i.e. adopt the internal point of view) when not himself accepting those rules. Hart concedes that such a person must understand what the internal point of view is:

> 'It is true that for this purpose the descriptive theorist must understand what it is to adopt the internal point of view and in that limited sense he must be able to put himself in the place of an insider; but that is not to endorse the insider's internal point of view or in any other way to surrender his descriptive stance'.

Later on, Hart says: 'Description may still be description, even when what is described is an evaluation.' I think much of this is just unargued for assertion. Here is the problem: to what extent can you make sense of a human practice without being a person who is (as it were) part of that practice? Let us take mathematics. Could you produce a descriptive account of mathematics (what mathematics is; what it can achieve; what sorts of problems it deals with; etc, etc) without yourself being a mathematician of some sort? It is easy to imagine that the more versed in mathematics a person is, the better account that person will give. Why? Because what is interesting about mathematics is what it is that people who are engaged it are doing - who better to give an account, then, than someone engaged in mathematics?

There is a quicker way to this point: could a person who was entirely innumerate tell us anything at all about mathematics? Could a person who was stone-deaf give us an adequate description of what music is? In the case of law, the more detached a person is (in Hart's terms, the more 'external') the less rich the explanation will become. It seems to me that this defence of Dworkin becomes all that much more stronger when we turn to law because there we have description of practice which is difficult to separate from commitment and evaluation, if not moral judgment. Could someone who has no idea at all of what 'commitment to general social rules for human life in society' provide an adequate explanation of what law is about?

Some will feel that this argument is too quick a way with Hart. They might wish to make the following reply: 'True, one could not be entirely ignorant of mathematics to be able to produce a theory of mathematics for one purpose of theorising is to explain to people who want to know how to understand - to do - the subject of the theory. Nevertheless, to suppose that knowledge of all sorts of things that are not actually *doing* mathematics but contribute to understanding mathematics was only peripheral to a theory of mathematics, or not part of a theory of mathematics at all is going too far. You don't need to be able to do algebra, or calculus, to be able to make general remarks of the sort 'mathematics discovers relationships between things in the real world' or that mathematics is one of the 'finer forms of intellectual enquiry,' or that mathematical developments 'aided the production of the atomic bomb.' And the argument is much stronger for law. If only lawyers could produce appropriate accounts of law, we would have no room for the person who can sit back and watch what is going on: the moderate external view point allows us to see the Nazi, committed to his ideologically loaded law, from the point of view of someone who is not so committed. That gap in understanding provides a richer account of law than the account given by the philosopher Nazi judge. The Nazi judge, or the pure mathematician, is in the important sense *too involved* for a decent theory to be forthcoming. The best theory will be the one that can maintain an intellectual *distance*.'

Certainly these are views that are taken by many sociologists (for example, Roger Cotterrell[9]). The insider's point of view is either too narrowly focused and therefore inappropriate emphasis distorts the insider's theory. Worse, the theorist is too caught up in the heat of things, too involved, to produce a clear picture. Those in the CLS movement, too, are bothered by the inward, self-gestating ('autopoietic') quality of legal theory which 'privileges' the point of view of the (theoretical) committed judge.

The general sentiments expressed are important since they arise from a fear of disguised partiality on the part of a theorist who has various reasons for promoting particular views. The arguments of the committed supporter of apartheid take a different hue when we discover that he is a white South African; so, too, does the discovery that the supporter of racial discrimination is a neo-Nazi. It is not just vested interest (the South African owns a large amount of property; he has an interest in his own political security) but also the intellectual entanglement which makes the truth distorted (the Nazi is passionate; the passion blinds him). But these arguments are insufficient and do not sideline the insider viewpoint. The key to it what follows lies in what 'inappropriate' emphasis, or what a 'clear' picture is, since the idea of a 'privileged' viewpoint is no less 'privileged' than an 'unprivileged' one. What counts as a criterion of 'appropriateness' or 'clear' or 'unprivileged' but connection to a central account of these concepts?

Imagine what a theory of mathematics would be like which did not refer to mathematical calculations at all, or to a theory of law which did not refer to laws at all. It is not merely difficult but *impossible*. Let's try it for mathematics: mathematics is 'what goes on inside Departments of Mathematics'; 'mathematics doctorates are rarely more than 30 pages long'; mathematicians 'say little at College committees'. This is banal stuff but note: the identification of mathematicians here requires some knowledge of what counts as a mathematician. To do the exercise fully requires that the word 'mathematics' or 'mathematician' be placed in quotations, since the non-mathematical theorist of mathematics does not know sufficient about mathematics to identify mathematicians except by relying on what others say to him. Now can a theory of mathematics be produced in this way? No.

Let's try the exercise for law. It is not that a knowledge of intricate details within Chancery is required; the insider's viewpoint need not as narrow as that; but in producing a theory of law, the first stage must be that of the identification of the subject-matter and that requires acquaintance with legal argument at least to the point of being able to operate the basic ideas of adjudication, rule-identification, rule-application and rule-following.

So identification of subject-matter is required as a necessary part of theory production. But the objection might be returned to that this is only a minor matter and that this much can be conceded without the insider's viewpoint becoming 'privileged.' Does this work, though? Let us go back to the Mathematics Department. We discover that there are doubts about the identification of the subject-matter. We established that elimination of the insider point of view meant that we could only rely on what others told us constituted correct use of terms such as 'mathematics.' What do we do if we discover that these reporters differ amongst themselves as to what constitutes 'mathematics'? We find, for example, that some mathematicians say of a colleague 'he doesn't do mathematics - he just tinkers' or (rudely) 'he twiddles his thumbs as far as *mathematics* is concerned'. The proposed outsider view of all this is just sidelined by hypothesis since it can't resolve the question of what constitutes mathematics. And the same is true for law: to have no idea about what centrally a lawyer does is a no-start position and if that conclusion sounds startling to you, you should wonder why you are surprised.

The stronger argument for privileging the outsider view lies in the problem of partiality. But these problems can be tackled directly; what is wrong is the partiality. Someone who claimed commitment to apartheid but who is then discovered to have had business interests in the continuance of apartheid can have his views attacked: 'you only say that because ...' amounts in these sorts of circumstance to saying 'you are not *really* committed to ...' And that is quite a different argument altogether from the claim that the insider viewpoint distorts.[10] Take the medical profession; the insider view is that of healer. To give an account of what healing it is not necessary to adopt a psychological point of view of a particular healer; nor a representative group. Or, rather, to choose a particular healer, or to choose what counted as a representative group is to make a choice on grounds which reveal what it is to do that think that counts as healing - to give an account of *what healing is about*.

These considerations can be enlightened by consideration of cases such as the Nazi cases, in which stark but nevertheless real distinctions are so horribly etched. Consider the position of the medical profession in Nazi Germany as described in Robert Jay Lifton's brilliant psychological study: 'In the beginning it was almost impossible. Afterward it became almost routine. That's the only way to put it.' The account he gives is of initial inner turmoil then corruption but the important point is that it is corruption which takes place, and not a transformation of what 'healing' means. Speaking of the position of ordinary practising psychiatrists who became involved in the thirties Nazi eugenics programme, he reports:

> Dr. E. went on to explain that he and other psychiatrists came to distinguish between 'dishonest' opinions from those experts who acted out of 'sheer political motivation,' on the one hand; and, on the other, other, 'honest' judgments from those experts, much fewer in number, who based their opinions on general medical considerations. As he talked, it became clear to me that a focus on this distinction had enabled him and his colleagues to avoid moral truths concerning the 'euthanasia' project: to avoid recognising that what they viewed as 'honest medical opinions' about schizophrenic or mentally deficient patients became the basis for mass murder of these patients. Yet his visible pain as he discussed these matters suggested that he could not avoid that recognition, and probably had not even then.[11]

Now in this extreme sort of situation, a description of 'what is going on' is inadequate to describe the special kind of wrongness. There is no form of healing at all. And so with the Nazi legal system; we cannot just *describe* the legal system (the Nuremberg laws; the laws institutionalising the camps; and so) without making similar sorts of judgment to the one Lifton makes in the quoted passage showing the specific adoption of a point of view.

This argument does not, of course, dispose of the question whether Nazi law is law or not; my point is the different one that questions of what counts as law are arguable questions of the sort 'what is mathematics? and 'what is healing?' and are not of the 'universal descriptive; evaluatively neutral' sort. A principle of selection must be at work, despite Hart's claims. We do not 'just describe'; we describe something which we have already carved out as an object of interest; that interest is as much the subject of inter-personal debate as the choice between, to take Hart's example, 'wider' and 'narrower' conceptions of law.

The nature of legal positivism

As a semantic theory. Hart takes exception to Dworkin's having labelled him as one of those linguistic theorists guilty of the 'semantic sting'. That criticism, to be found in Chapter one of *Law's Empire*, is that no adequate account of law can be based on a description solely of how people speak (the truth conditions of law = linguistic practices). Hart denies that he ever had such a theory and says that the charge 'confuses the meaning of a concept with the criteria for its application'. He clearly means by this the distinction that Dworkin makes great use of between the elaboration of a 'concept' and a 'conception', with the clear implication that he (Hart) thinks that his theory allows for the elaboration of a conception of law. This is interesting in the light of the way the first four chapters of *The Concept of Law* develop for there one would certainly be led to believe that Hart's aim was in fact to capture 'linguistic practices' that are a 'plain fact' about the world.

Take his famous distinction between 'being obliged to do something' and 'being under an obligation to do something'. Certainly it is presented in the book as of great importance and it is true to say that the distinction, once pointed out, is very effective in drawing our attention to the difference we *in fact* draw between two very different kinds of situation. Hart's approach is via the three 'crucial questions' which he says need to be addressed by a theory of law: What is the relationship between mere coercion and law? what is the relation between 'legal' and 'moral' obligation? and what is a social rule? The famous distinction addresses the first question and much of the ensuing argument, extending well into the middle of *The Concept of Law*, depends upon it. Further, the question itself is one that has been viewed as a central one by other significant jurists. In Kelsen's terms: how do we distinguish between the bank robber and the tax inspector? In the real world (for Kelsen: the world of 'causality' as opposed to the world of 'imputation') there is nothing to distinguish them; we need, instead, to transcend the real world to an assumption that the tax inspector's demand is an 'ought' of 'objective validity'. Hart's answer is that we do *in fact* draw a significant distinction between the social situations; he 'proves' this fact by showing us the language that we *in fact* use (and we agree that we use language correctly in this way). Now what more argument does he use to draw the distinction? Our attention is arrested by our recognising in ourselves what we in fact do. (Much of the power of linguistic philosophy derives from this feature; both the power to convince and to reveal). Hart then proceeds to an elaboration of the basic distinction between the bank robber and the tax inspector. The tax inspector acts in accordance with standards; these standards can only be understood as different from habits or mere regularity; we use rules; what is more these rules confer powers; powers are distinct from duties; (and signs are different from signals; predictions different from justifications; and so on and so forth ...) A reduction, as by Dworkin, of these arguments to the form of:

> <<the truth conditions of law = the truth conditions of the 'language we use in legal discourse'>>

is sweeping but correct.

But as I have pointed out, by the end of the book, especially in the very important Chapter 9, it becomes clearer that Hart is choosing between conceptions of law on grounds other than our linguistic use.[12] A possible way of understanding his famous step from the 'pre-legal' to the 'legal' society makes sense in terms of something other than a recording of linguistic use. He imagines a simple society in which there are primary rules of obligation alone and finds certain problems within that society. These problems turn out to be social problems and Hart then posits the existence of a type of rule which will lead towards the solving of these problems. The idea is that of the power-conferring rule. He is then able to draw a distinction between duty and power-conferring rules which neatly accounts for the less malign way we *in fact* think about law than is supposed by the Austinian account in which laws are primarily to be seen as imposing duties.[13] How does he achieve this? The social 'defects', as he calls them, are those of lack of social progress through legislation ('cured' by power-conferring rules of 'change', inefficiency of law enforcement ('cured' by power-conferring rules of 'adjudication') and uncertainty ('cured' by power-conferring rules of 'recognition'). Our attention is drawn to the obvious practical merits of the power-conferring rules. Society is better off with a legislature, courts and police, and with publicly ascertainable criteria of identification of law. But to what extent is the power of the argument dependent upon that of: this is *in fact* the way we view the law (as including power-conferring rules)?

The answer, I think, is that Hart was basically straddling two stools in *The Concept of Law*. He possessed too much insight into the nature of law and philosophy in general, ever to affirm that all questions could be answered by the correct characterisation of linguistic practices. Nevertheless, he was heavily involved in the influential school at Oxford in the late forties and during the fifties, which was the heyday of the movement in linguistic philosophy, and I think that he is simply unclear, quite understandably, throughout his book on the point of what precisely was the methodology he was employing.

As an interpretive theory. The issue Hart takes up here is that he disagrees with Dworkin that the point or purpose of law or legal practice is to justify state power: '... it certainly is not and never has been my view that law has this as its point or purpose.' He refers, for example, to his invocation of the 'pre-legal' world and says that the proposed introduction of the secondary rules, of adjudication, of recognition and of change, was not intended to answer any question about the justification of the application of the coercive powers of the state. This is an important assertion for it raises the question of the whole point of Chapter 9 since, in it, Hart justified his legal positivism on the grounds that it made clear that the certification of legal validity should not finish the question of obedience.

The point of the rule of recognition is to clear the air here: to make certain (in Hart's language, 'cure the defect' of uncertainty) what is law and what is a matter for personal conscience. Why? To halt the abuse of state coercive power. The use of retrospective lawmaking was, for example, the 'evil' that had to be balanced against the 'evil' of letting the Nazi grudge informer go free of punishment. Hart's concern cannot therefore here be unconnected with the justification of the application of state power. Indeed, he is at pains in the construction of his theory that laws can be identified independently of personal moral judgment to justify this on the ground that it shows - for good moral reasons - why we should think of legal justifications having no moral content.

Without much more by way of elaboration I think that there is a good case for saying that, despite what Hart says, his concerns *are* parasitic on concerns about the way we should view the justifications that are advanced for applying law. Put it in this way. Why is Hart bothered about drawing the sharp distinction between the state and the individual? In his discussion of how best the law (or legal theory) should solve the Nazi grudge informer case, Hart becomes the most morally involved of all of his writings. At the beginning of the fourth section of his paper in which he initiated the famous Hart-Fuller debate he recounts the passion with which natural lawyers attacked the positivist distinction:

> '[This] criticism of the separation of law and morals is of a very different character; it certainly is less an intellectual argument against the utilitarian distinction than a passionate appeal supported not by detailed reasoning but by reminders of a terrible experience. For it consists of the testimony of those who have descended into Hell, and, like Ulysses or Dante, brought back a message for human beings. Only in this case the Hell was not beneath or beyond earth, but on it; it was a Hell created on earth by men for other men.'[14]

It was in the context of this account that Hart defended the 'utilitarian distinction'; clearly, 'we speak differently' has little appeal; much stronger is the moral value with which we attach to the distinction.[15] And so Hart answered the objection by saying that legal positivism settles the moral issue of what a legal system should do with a grudge informer better than natural law. His short criticism, to be found in *The Concept of Law*, was that the natural law way (proposed by Radbruch) that laws should be declared invalid if contrary to (at least to common and deeply held conventional) morality is 'too crude a way with delicate and complex moral issues.'[16] The better way, he says, to deal with the problem of punishing the Nazi informers under the law would have been to do this by retrospective law declaring the Nazi statute to invalid. This approach to legally justifying punishing the informer supposedly brings to view the full nature (the 'delicacy') of the moral issues involved. His suggested solution introduces another element into the equation of justification. This is that, although we think it was wrong to do what the woman did, we also think it wrong to punish a person when what they did was permitted by the state, that is, was lawful. The moral principle here, and one endorsed by many legal systems, is that of *nulla poena sine lege*. The rationale of this principle - which, as he says, is enshrined in most legal systems - is that if you are acting within the law at any one time then it should not be later declared that what you were doing was against the law.

Hart is not, of course, saying that this principle can *never* be sacrificed to some other moral principle, but rather that a transgression of that principle is part of the equation, and must be taken into account in determining whether the woman should be punished. So he says: 'Odious as retrospective criminal legislation and punishment may be, to have pursued it openly in this case would at least have had the merits of candour. It would have made plain that in punishing the woman a choice had to be made between two evils ...' The two 'evils' he refers to are first, letting the woman go unpunished and secondly, introducing retrospective legislation. The Radbruchean, natural law approach, just simply says: 'what the woman did was wrong and she should be punished, and it is irrelevant that she thought that she was doing what she was permitted to do, or that when she did it, it was permitted by the enacted law.'

So it does not follow, as it is commonly supposed that it does, that Radbruch and Hart have different views about the outcome of the case. It is just that they would have approached it in different ways. Why, then, does it matter if the outcome is the same? Well, the argument is that the outcome *could have been different*. Hart's justification for punishing the woman by a retrospective law is a result of a better mixture of justification: it involves a weighing up between the rightness of punishing a Nazi informer and the wrongness of retroactively enforced decisions. Radbruch's approach cannot allow the wrongness of retroactively enforced decisions as relevant for, by definition, if the law is morally bad, then it is not a law at all and so cannot be extinguished by retroactive decision. It would be possible, therefore, by Hart's and Radbruch's methods to come to different decisions simply because the judgment Hart recommends is a more complex one than Radbruch's, having an extra ingredient in the argument, and merely having the extra ingredient in the argument *could* turn the decision in another way.

But Hart goes further than just saying that we should be candid about our approach to the problem of how to deal with the Nazi informer. He says also that to adopt Radbruch's approach would be to obscure a very powerful form of moral criticism, that of being able to criticise legislation. He says that to say plainly that something can be a law but too evil to be obeyed then we rivet people's attention. That is, such a statement makes, as he says, 'an immediate and obvious claim to our moral attention' for it raises the general question of our obligation to obey law. On the other hand, it is obscure to say that immoral laws are *not* laws at all. In fact, many people would simply disbelieve that as a dubious proposition.

Note again the pull for Hart of the way *we actually think* about law. To repeat his point: we understand his viewpoint because we accept, in our thinking and the way we speak, that one can criticise laws in this sort of way. Here Hart is a unfair to Radbruch because he appeals to the way we currently think. Radbruch can just answer it by saying we do *but should not*. So it is Hart's *prescriptive* point that Radbruch's proposal blurs over the various moral issues involved that is the better one. It meets the *morality* of Radbruch's point head on, and so is an open admission by Hart that the choice between Radbruch's natural law approach and his own approach is to be settled by choosing morally between them.

Hart says that we could choose between two rival conceptions of law: First, the wide, positivist, conception of law that considers as law all rules which are valid by the *formal* tests of a legal system, even although some of them might offend against society's morality or our own morality, and second, the narrow, Radbruchean, conception of law that considers as law only those rules, passed as formally valid, that are not morally offensive. Hart prefers the first conception. The first reason he gives is that it is, as he says, *descriptively* better to think of law in this way. It is fairly clear that he means by this again that it more accords with the way *we actually think* about law, saying that '... nothing is to be gained in the theoretical or scientific study of law as a social phenomenon by adopting the narrower concept: it would lead us to exclude certain rules even though they exhibit all the other complex characteristics of law.'[17] The second reason is that the first conception 'grossly oversimplifies' the variety of moral issues.

Hart is right, I think, at least in pointing to three kinds of confusion could be created by adopting the narrower conception. If we teach ourselves to think of laws as essentially moral then, since we have different views about morality, some laws will be valid for some people but not for others. For example, some people would consider, morally, that they have no obligation to pay taxes. If the narrower conception of law were adopted how would the courts decide whether people had legal obligations, say, to pay income tax? The narrower conception of law could only operate successfully if there were not only one set of true moral standards, which is at least a debatable proposition (although not as strange as it might appear since we all talk that way!), but a set of true moral standards that was *objectively ascertainable*. (Or, second best, it could be achieved morality were defined in a way that departed from our usual critical sense to mean: what people agree on makes for moral truth).

If we trained ourselves to view law in this narrow way, then we might become indifferent to the fact that Parliament passed legislation affecting us. That is, the narrower conception of law trains us to concentrate only on the particular action that we judge to be morally right and this side-steps the major issue of whether we have some sort of obligation to obey (even if only *prima facie*) just on the ground that a legislature had produced it. Surely, in any matter of civil disobedience, that something was said in a *statute* must be an *ingredient* in any judgment whether to obey it. But it would follow from Radbruch's narrow conception of the law that you could not commit civil disobedience against an immoral law because such a law does not exist, in fact, it cannot. And a third sort of confusion would be that thrown up by the Nazi informer case. We might, in short, ride rough-shod over the important principle of *nulla poena sine lege*.

Hart's arguments can be summed up in his own words. What follows are his *moral* reasons for preferring the wider conception of law that separates law from morality by declaring all rules formally identifiable by reference to the factual test of the rule of recognition *ipso facto*:

> 'What surely is most needed in order to make men clear sighted in confronting the official abuse of power, is that they should preserve the sense that the certification of something as legally valid is not conclusive of the question of obedience. ... A concept of law which allows the invalidity of law to be distinguished from its immorality enables us to see the complexity and variety of these separate issues; whereas a narrow concept of law which denies legal validity to such rules may blind us to them.'[18]

All these arguments support the view that Hart has a moral theory of law. The connection between law and morality is sophisticated one, true, but it is there. It is not a relationship between the meaning of 'law' and 'morality' but between the meaning of 'theory of law' and 'morality'. Although Hart's conception of law is one that separates 'law' and 'morality', it is clear that he thinks that this conception - the wider conception - is *morally* better than the narrower one. We could argue, therefore, that he connects law and morality in the necessary sense that a *theory* of law must serve a moral purpose and that we must view as law only those rules that are law according to the morally best conception of law. Further, if Hart wants to get 'inside' the law and make judgments about what counts as a good justification (retrospective legislation if necessary, in the Nazi informer case) then it becomes very difficult to see how he can view legal theory as concerned with descriptive accounts of the law and this corroborates my view that, for Hart, it is impossible to look at a practice from the outside (see above, particularly in relation to the innumerate person producing a description of mathematics).

Soft positivism. 'Soft' positivism is the view that there are controversial - uncertain - rules of law; so, for example, soft conventionalism allows for the following two rules to be captured by a rule of recognition which recognises the rule 'Vehicles are prohibited in the park': 'skateboards are prohibited' and its contradictory 'skateboards are permitted'. This is the area of the penumbra. Dworkin's view is that a. since a decision has to be made between these rules, and b. because in legal practice there clearly is use made of non-rule standards (he calls them 'principles'), there is much more sophistication to legal argument than even soft positivism could allow.

It has never been quite clear (until the *Postscript*) what Hart's view was since in Chapter 7 of *The Concept of Law* he endorses a much more sophisticated account of legal reasoning in hard cases than appears to be implied by his rigid criteria of what counts as law. In fact, Chapter 7 is a much more accurate account of legal reasoning (akin to Neil MacCormick's account in his *Legal Reasoning and Legal Theory*[19]) than is implied by the remainder of *The Concept of Law*. The reason is to be found in Hart's account of the famous rule or rules of recognition. We must not forget that it was to cure the defect of uncertainty. What, indeed, does the defect consist of? It is not in itself a psychological feeling (there will always be people who feel uncertain about things); rather, it lies in an inherent incapacity to find out what the law is - the remedy lies in clear, publicly ascertainable criteria. What is so wrong with uncertainty? One lies in the idea of the principle of *nulla poena sine lege* but that is only one of a number of moral virtues connected with certainty. Another is that of security; for how can we plan our lives if what the state permits or prohibits is not a publicly ascertainable matter? Further connected with these two ideas but also different is the virtue in having one's (reasonable) expectations fulfilled; if the state constantly chops and changes its legislation, the law lacks a virtue. (In fact, many of Lon Fuller's principles of law-making are tied up with this idea of the state's demands being made 'certain' by the rule of recognition, leading to a consistency of dealing - fairness - in the relations between the state and citizen.)

It follows, therefore, that the rule of recognition *makes the law certain*. In the court cases in which there is adjudication on a point of law *just because* there is no certainty (because why else would the case come to court on a point of law?) if follows further that there is no law. If the law is made certain by the rule of recognition, for the various virtues listed above, then how can uncertain law be law at all? Thus soft positivism is not an option for Hart; he must stick to his guns and deny that there are any controversial points of law, and that means that there is no law which binds judges or parties in hard cases.

Morality and the nature of rules

The practice theory of rules. Hart thinks that Dworkin's arguments that not all legal rules can be identified by referring to a social practice[20] shows a serious misunderstanding of what the rule of recognition was intended to be about. Hart claims that Dworkin assumes that the rule is supposed to determine completely the legal result in every case. Not so, he says: '... the function of the rule is to determine only the general conditions which correct legal decisions must satisfy in modern systems of law.'[21] This is simply the argument that the rule of recognition is designed to cure the defect of uncertainty. Hart's argument amounts to saying that the uncertainty is cured by seeing that the law identified can be incurably ambiguous. In the end, under his theory the law is 'vehicles are prohibited, etc ...' and it is asking too much to expect that there should be determination of the ambiguity inherent in the word 'vehicle'.

To understand this point fully it is necessary to go into Dworkin's criticism in *Taking Rights Seriously* of the idea of the existence of social rules being necessary to identify judicial duties.[22] He argues that they are not necessary since it is possible for us to assert the existence of duties, in general, without it being necessary to point to a social rule to that effect. A good example is that of vegetarians who assert that we all have duties not to eat meat, even although there is no social rule saying that we ought not to eat meat (and, in fact, a clear social rule saying that we may eat meat). This seems a good argument to me. Dworkin then moves to saying that there is therefore nothing wrong with asserting that, in hard cases, judges are bound by duties which cannot be identified by reference to social rules (viz. the social rule of recognition). He considers one possible objection to this which is the simple contention that the social rule theory of duty only applies to law for, In the end, the vegetarian only invokes a moral duty in us all not to eat meat. But he is right to dismiss that argument (which is very common) by saying that it amounts to the following: 'In general, duties can exist either as the result of a social rule, or as existing in some other way independently of social rules; but in the case of law a social rule is required; that social rule is a rule of recognition which declares affirmatively whether a rule is a valid rule of law imposing a legal duty'. Dworkin says that is just an assertion of positivism and that theory cannot refer to itself in support.

Hart's response to this is interesting and important for it shows a possible shift in Hart's position. First, Hart concedes that Dworkin is correct in maintaining a distinction between rules accepted socially as a matter of convention and rules which have the appearance of being conventionally accepted but, instead, only represent a consensus of convention. I can illustrate this distinction in the following way. In England, everyone accepts a moral rule prohibiting murder; there is a coincidence of our views. Each view, however, is supported by independent reasons each of us has for our conviction that murder is morally wrong. So, if asked, I would say 'finishes a life; invades physical integrity; causes pain; etc, etc'. They are my independent reasons for saying why murder is wrong. Compare murder with the rule that men must take their hats off in church. There we say that the rule exists just because everyone accepts that rule ('it is the accepted convention'). The difference is striking when we consider what a conventional justification would sound like for murder. It sounds wrong to give as the reason for thinking murder wrong that 'it is the convention' or 'everybody thinks it's wrong' because these sorts of justification aren't strong enough. The fact that other people think that something is wrong, at the very least for murder, is insufficient justification for why you should think it wrong. You have to make up your own mind. (This distinction, incidentally, is identical to the distinction that both Bentham and Austin draw between 'positive' and 'critical' morality).

But having conceded this difference, which amounts to Hart's conceding that there could be reasons of the legal sort which give rise to non social-rule identified legal duties, Hart then says that Dworkin's account of social rules is too strong for:

> '... it seems to require not only that the participants who appeal to rules as establishing duties or providing reasons for action must believe that there are good moral grounds or justification for conforming to the rules, but that there must actually be such good grounds.'[23]

The reply for Dworkin would be to say that this cannot be a criticism of his view that there can be legal duties in the hard cases. Sometimes a. judges give the wrong grounds and b. it is reasonable to suppose that there are good grounds that could have been advanced: certainly saying both of these things is compatible with the way judges and lawyers reason. Hart is really saying that legal positivism does not require that there be good moral grounds for justifying decisions in hard cases and Dworkin can answer that by simply saying that it amounts to positivism citing itself in its own support. If judges and lawyers argue as if there were good legal grounds that are at the same time good moral grounds then that fact must be one in support of a legal theory that accounts for it (as Dworkin's theory purports to account for how judges and lawyers argues then it must be a better theory). Nevertheless, Hart maintains that, despite the controversial nature of law in hard cases, it is a misconception to suppose that the rule of recognition can dispose completely of any question of law, declaring '... the function of the rule is to determine only the general conditions which correct legal decisions must satisfy in modern systems of law.'[24]

Rules and principles. Hart also thinks that Dworkin is wrong to suppose that there is such a sharp distinction between rules and principles. There is undeniably a difference (he is willing to concede) since principles are less specific and principles perhaps embody reasons, while 'non-conclusive' in the way rules are, which are of a particularly weighty kind. But he thinks Dworkin exaggerates the differences and refers to the *Riggs v. Palmer* decision which Dworkin famously uses to show how principles decide cases.[25] Hart thinks this decision shows clearly not a clash between two principles but a clash between a rule and a principle. Hart just asserts that there was a clear rule of succession that a murderer could inherit from the estate of the person he murdered; Dworkin denies that there was any such rule but that there was a general principle, outweighed by another in that case ('no man should profit from his own wrong'), that the clear words of a valid will should be closely adhered to. Certainly many lawyers would not have thought that there was such a rule; it appeared to many (in England, too) that this was a controversial point and was sufficiently controversial to warrant appeal in *Riggs*.

Pedigree and interpretation. Hart thinks that while 'large theoretical differences' exist between Dworkin and himself on the question of the identification of valid law, nevertheless they both share the view that there are certain basic facts of legislative history which each of them thinks limit the application of law by judges: '... his explanation of the judicial identification of the sources of law is substantially the same as mine.'[26] But the main difference, he says, lies in the fact that there are few legal systems outside the US and the UK in which legal reasoning takes the form of the all-embracing kind ('holistic') that Dworkin says is involved in the idea of constructive interpretation. Hart therefore rejects any kind of view which says that moral judgments about what people's rights are part of the identification of their legal rights, since legal rights and duties are the point at which the law protects or restricts individual freedom by allowing individuals the power 'to avail themselves of the law's coercive machinery'. They are thus independent of the 'moral merits' of the law; presumably because they are only expressive of your 'right to take the matter to court'.

Hart still maintains the view that the Nazi-type legal system, while undeniably of moral wickedness, was nevertheless law since the various features it shares with other modern municipal legal systems are too great for a 'universal-descriptive' legal theory to ignore. He points to Dworkin's suggestion that such a legal system might be a described as such in his 'pre-interpretive sense' and then says that Dworkin's concession there about the flexibility of legal language strengthens rather than weakens the positivist's case:

> '... it does little more than convey the message that while he insists that in a descriptive jurisprudence the law may be identified without reference to morality, things are otherwise for a justificatory interpretive jurisprudence according to which the identification of the law always involves a moral judgment as to what best justifies the settled law.'[27]

Consequently, in line with what Hart argues at first in his Postscript, that he is concerned with universal description and Dworkin is concerned with justification of state coercive powers, Hart rather reasonably concludes that, in characterising the Nazi legal system, he and Dworkin are really talking at cross purposes.

Hard cases. Hart addresses the question of the difference between himself and Dworkin as one of how best the 'unregulated cases' (as Hart appears to call hard cases) should be resolved. His answer is straightforwardly but disappointingly assertive: he thinks that there just are cases where judges exercise their judicial discretion by acting as 'judicial law-makers' and he does not think that this poses a great threat to democracy. This at least is in line with *The Concept of Law* bar Chapter 7 and is echoed in the *Preface* to his *Essays in Jurisprudence and Philosophy*:

> 'For though the search for and use of principles underlying the law defers the moment, it cannot eliminate the need for judicial law-making, since in any hard case different principles supporting competing analogies may present themselves and the judge will have to choose between them, relying like a conscientious legislator on his sense of what is best and not on any already established order of priorities among principles already prescribed for him by the law.'[28]

And he acknowledges the problems that this idea can get him into. But it is difficult to agree with him on the following statement: '... the delegation of limited legislative powers to the executive is a familiar feature of modern democracies and such delegation to the judiciary seems a no greater menace to democracy.' It is disappointing because it draws insufficient attention to the great differences of role and function between the legislature and the judiciary. The legislature must make laws for the community as a whole and we not only *in fact* don't think that judges are like that at all but we strongly think that they *ought not* to be thought of in that way. We think that they should concern themselves with the merits of the dispute relating to the respective rights and duties of the parties before them.

Hart also takes Dworkin to task for saying that it is a defect of legal positivism that it supposes that judicial discretion in unregulated cases is retrospective in effect (which Hart must concede happens if he allows for judicial law-making). He simply says that if there were law there, in the cases, or the arguments, or whatever, as Dworkin supposes, it wouldn't be retrospective, true, but it would be as equally surprising to the defendant what decision the judge came to as in the positivist position whereby the law is 'made' by the judge. In defence of Dworkin, surely if we are to choose between two theories of adjudication, we must choose the one that says that, characteristically, the judge is punishing (or awarding compensation or whatever) for acts which at the time that they were done were against or within the law. The defendant who is surprised by a decision that is the result of retrospective legislation is worse off in this sense than the defendant who is surprised at a decision about the law existing at the time he did the act. It is a matter of whether we accept a principle of the rule of law: no one should be punished, or whatever, unless there is a law which prohibited (or whatever) the act at the time that it was done. In one guise this is the *nulla poena sine lege* principle and we could remember in this connection that it was this principle which Hart so effectively invoked in the important Chapter 9 of *The Concept of Law*.

NOTES

1 *The Concept of Law 2nd ed.* (1994) pp.185-86.

2 [1939] 1 KB 687.

3 See *The Concept of Law* p.209.

4 See the preface to his *Essays in Jurisprudence and Philosophy* (1983) Oxford.

5 *The Concept of Law* p.210.

6 I have my tongue in my cheek; Hart was at the Chancery bar for twelve years. But I'm reminded of a passage in Balzac's *Old Goriot*:

> 'There are no such things as principles, there are only events; there are no laws, there are only circumstances ... If there were fixed principles and laws nations would not change them as easily as we change our shirts. I shall hold an unalterable opinion when I find three minds agreed on the application of a principle, and I shall wait a long time! There are not three judges in the law-courts with the same opinion about a point of law.' (Penguin Classics, trans. Crawford, p. 134)

7 (1980) Oxford. See generally Chapter one and, in particular, the footnotes.

8 See, for example, the chapter entitled 'Conventionalism' in Dworkin's *Law's Empire* and, in particular, the lengthy and very useful footnote 3 on page 429 of that book.

9 See his *Law's Community: Legal Theory in Sociological Perspective* (1995) Oxford.

10 I make similar sorts of arguments in my 'Meaning and Statutory Interpretation' in *Statutory Interpretation* ed. Michael Freeman (1996) Aldershot: Dartmouth.

11 See *The Nazi Doctors: a Study in the Psychology of Evil* Robert Jay Lifton (1987) London: MacMillan. Martin Amis's unfairly criticised *Time's Arrow* confronts the problem head on. There such contradiction, such madness in the idea of a doctor intentionally killing healthy people (not even patients), that it reduces to the absurdity that Time goes backward: only then does killing become healing.

12 Note the very telling sentence on p.209 when discussing the Nazi grudge informer case: 'Plainly, we cannot grapple adequately with this issue if we see it as one concerning the proprieties of linguistic usage.'

13 But Austin can easily be defended; he obviously, like Bentham, thought that the 'key' was the sanction. But he did not think that there were no power-conferring rules; rather, he thought that law was fundamentally about power, and his theory of law is constructed carefully to bring this fact out. Hart skates along the surface of law, in other words, not bringing out the underlying truths. True, we can marry, make contracts, and so on, according to Austin, but these sorts of activities only make sense on the understanding that ultimately marriages will be backed up, contracts will be enforced, wills will be carried out and so on. In the end, legal right means legal might. How is all this possible, though? Austin has a reflexive view of legal powers; a person has a power to do something by virtue of the sovereign's 'tacit command' that other people obey that person in the area of competence tacitly allocated to that person. Austin explained judge-made law in this way: the judge had the power - the jurisdiction - to apply law by virtue of the sovereign's command for people to obey him. So, if an executor did not carry out the terms of a valid will, which had been granted probate, the judge had the power to make the appropriate order, invested with the power of the sovereign. There is a lot of sense in this; clearly, what are legal powers unless there is a 'sting' to them? Also, given the reference to the sovereign's power here, much sense is given to the idea that the judge should not usurp the function of the legislature (see Diplock, L.J. in the famous flick-knife case of *Fisher v. Bell* [1961] 1 QB 394), because the judge will only have the power where the sovereign has 'tacitly commanded', and that means that the judge has to put himself in the position, in the case of interpreting statutes, whereby he imagines what is that the sovereign would have commanded had he been aware of the circumstances. And even the criticism, made by a number of people, including Hart, that the idea of 'tacit' command is flawed, is not wholly convincing. To use Hart's own example, we can imagine a sergeant telling one of his men to take over, adding 'do what I'd do in any situation that arises'. This is a simple idea; it just means that if the delegated man has to make a judgment in special circumstances, he is empowered only to do 'what his sergeant would have done'. In fact, 'do what I'd have done' makes perfectly good sense, and so why not with the idea of tacit command?

14 See *Essays in Jurisprudence and Philosophy* p. 73.

15 See p. 78: 'I have endeavoured to show that, in spite of all that has been learned and experienced since the Utilitarians wrote, and in spite of the defects of other parts of their doctrine, their protest against the confusion of what is and what ought to be law has a moral as well as an intellectual value.'

16 See p. 207.

17 See p. 205.

18 See pp. 207 and 208.

19 (1978) Oxford.

20 See *Taking Rights Seriously* Chapter 3.

21 *Postscript* 258.

22 See *Taking Rights Seriously* Chapter 2.

23 *Preface* p. 257.

24 *Preface* p. 258.

25 *Riggs v. Palmer* 115 NY 506, 22 NE 188 (1889); see *Taking Rights Seriously* p.23.

26 *Preface* p. 267.

28 At p. 7.

4 POSITIVISM AND INTERNATIONAL LAW

DAVID HUTCHINSON

'The doctrine of sovereign immunity is based on international law. It is one of the rules of international law that a sovereign state should not be impleaded in the courts of another sovereign state against its will. Like all rules of international law, this rule is said to arise out of the consensus of the civilised nations of the world. All nations agree on it. So it is part of the law of nations.'

'To my mind this notion of consensus is a fiction. The nations are not in the least agreed on the doctrine of sovereign immunity. The courts of every country differ in their application of it. Some grant absolute immunity. Others grant limited immunity, with each defining the limits differently. There is no consensus whatever. Yet this does not mean that there is no rule of international law on the subject. It only means that we differ as to what that rule is.'

Lord Denning M.R. in the case of *Trendtex Trading Corporation Ltd.* v. *Central Bank of Nigeria*.[1]

International law serves legal philosophers well. It acts as a testing-ground for the various 'definitions' and accounts of 'law' which they propose. Its institutions and practices provide valuable material for consideration when pondering such matters as the nature and significance of Hart's 'steps' from a 'pre-legal' to a 'legal world'[2] or assessing Raz's analysis of the roles and importance of 'primary organs'.[3] The technique which is used to identify its rules can also afford plenty of useful food for thought when considering the theories which have been propounded regarding the nature of the process of legal reasoning. This paper represents an international lawyer's attempt to make a small contribution in the last of these three domains.

The process of international law-finding may be described, in the broadest outline, as follows. In order to determine what provision is made by customary international law on a particular point, international lawyers will typically examine whether the generality of States evinces attitudes which are concordant regarding just what it is that customary international law provides. In the language of international law, they will look for an *opinio juris* which is shared among States in general regarding what the law is on the matter in hand[4] - an *opinio generalis juris generalis*, in Professor Cheng's terminology.[5] If they find one, they will then typically go on to see whether States, in their day-to-day conduct, have conformed with the rule which is favoured by that *opinio*.[6] If their conduct on the whole accords with that rule, then they will conclude that that rule exists. If it does not, then the conclusion will usually be drawn that that rule is not part of the law which is currently in force.[7] If there simply is no conduct to examine - perhaps because States have not yet been faced with facts which would call for application of the rule -, the responses of international lawyers will differ: some will decline to assert the existence of the rule which the *opinio juris* supports,[8] while others will be prepared to take that step.[9]

Of course, matters are more complicated than this simple thumb-nail sketch may suggest. In particular, there is disagreement among international lawyers about particular features of this law-finding process. How many States need to be identified as supporting the proposition that a particular rule is a rule of general international law for it in fact to be so? Do certain specific States need to support that proposition and, if so, which? What level of discordance between the conduct of States and a hypothesised rule is consistent with the existence of that rule as law? Precisely which States are bound by a rule which has the support of States in general? And so on. These questions, large though they may be, are essentially matters of detail and can be put to one side; for it is the basic elements of the process by which the provisions of customary international law are identified which are of concern here.

Superficially, at least, this process is readily amenable to a positivist understanding. Rules are created by human action and by human action alone.[10] The talk may be of the actions of States - that is, of incorporeal juridical persons -; but those actions are in fact the actions of humans, albeit ones which are identified by means of a series of highly refined rules which themselves form part of the international legal process. More significantly, the identification of the rules which those human actions create does not depend upon the application of precepts of morality. It turns simply upon the answer to a question of fact - facts about human actions -: do States in general maintain in common the attitude that a given proposition of law is a valid proposition of existing law? The propositions so supported may be morally good or they may be morally evil. That, however, is a question for so-called 'critical jurisprudence' and does not affect the existence of those propositions as law, nor their content - if it were possible to separate the existence of something from the identity of the thing which exists. Again, why it should be that States consider as law and, therefore, as binding upon them whatever legal proposition is supported by the generality of States may be an interesting question; but it is not one which needs to be answered in order to identify that law.

The problems which beset such an analysis are many. One, though, is of especial interest; for the question which it raises admits of no easy answer, whether on a positivist analysis or by the application of any other methodology.

The passage quoted above from Lord Denning's judgment in the celebrated *Trendtex* case describes a situation which is by no means rare in international law. Certain States evince the attitude that the rule of international law on a particular issue is one thing, while certain other States evince the attitude that it is another. Still other States may even evince yet another, different attitude on the matter. (The position in the 1960s and 1970s regarding the law relating to the expropriation of foreign-owned property was just this.[11]) Furthermore, the composition of each of these groups, whether quantitatively or qualitatively, may be such that it cannot be maintained that either of them - or any - constitutes the generality of international society and the other - or others - a recalcitrant minority. That being so, there will be no proposition of law which can be said to have the support of States in general.

In such a situation, the conclusion might seem unavoidable, on a positivist analysis, that there simply is no rule of general international law on the matter in hand. Attempts to avoid this result by maintaining that one view of the law will necessarily have support of a quantity and quality that can be said to be 'general' are unconvincing;[12] while assertions that this will soon be the case and that things are just passing through a stage in which it is 'unclear' what the law is would seem to avoid such an awkward conclusion by ignoring it or else to assume some other means of identifying that law. Admittedly, the inconveniences of such a conclusion are alleviated, to some extent, by the admission in international law of 'regional' or 'special' rules of customary law, which are identified by a process akin to that already described.[13] Thus, as between those States which share the attitude that the law is so-and-so, the law is indeed so-and-so; while, as between those States which share the attitude that it is such-and-such, such-and-such is the law.[14] Nevertheless, it remains the case that, as between a State which evinces the first attitude and a State whose attitude is of the second type, there would seem to be no rule of general international law which might regulate their mutual relations.

The inconvenience of such a situation is patent. To affirm a *non liquet* - that is, to say, in effect, that the law simply makes no regulation of the matter in hand, whether to prohibit some activity or to permit it - would be problematic for the States concerned, if not for States in general.[15] It would also run contrary to one of the essential characteristics of every legal system: namely, that it purports to be 'comprehensive', regulating, or providing for the regulation of, every aspect of the life or conduct of its subjects, even if only to confer on them the freedom to do as they wish.[16] Indeed, legal systems are often said to include a 'closure rule', the role of which is precisely to regulate those matters which are not regulated by specific rules which have been created by means of positive human action.[17] Just such a rule, familiar to U.K. constitutional lawyers, is the rule that that which is not prohibited is permitted.[18] A 'closure rule' of similar purport has been said to exist within the international legal system.[19] In fact, it has been maintained that a rule to this effect necessarily forms part of any legal system.[20] However, to apply that rule to a situation such as that which is under discussion would hardly be acceptable. So, for example, to have said to those States which maintained that compensation, assessed on the basis of market value, had to be paid to the previous owner of property which had been expropriated and also to those States which maintained that some lesser measure of compensation need be paid that, as between them, the law simply conferred a freedom on an expropriating State to compensate or not, as it wished, and, if it did decide to compensate, to utilise whatever measure it thought best would not have respected the views or met the interests of either of those groups of States. Indeed, it would have been to have given effect to the position which was favoured by yet another group of States, which very position was opposed by the first group and was at least not supported by the second. Moreover, were it the case, whenever support among States for some particular proposition disintegrates and becomes less than general, that such a 'closure rule' were to apply, legal development would be characterised by periodic returns to a kind of *tabula rasa*, which would not only be destabilising, but would also effectively discourage any purposeful attempt by States to develop or improve the law through the medium of their practices. Perhaps because of its potential to yield such results, as well as its ability to lead to conclusions which are morally repugnant,[21] such a 'closure rule', while it may often be supposed in the day-to-day practice of international affairs, has not consistently and in all contexts attracted the general support of States.[22] There are, therefore, some problems in asserting that it constitutes a positive rule of law, established by human action.[23] Perhaps it must, nevertheless, be accepted that it is analytically necessary or something of the sort[24] - even if the conceivability of a *non liquet* might be thought to indicate otherwise. Whatever the case, though, these difficulties indicate that, even if a 'closure rule' might ultimately have to be applied, *faute de mieux*, in order to resolve the problem which is here under consideration, some better alternative should be sought before resort is had to such a potentially unsatisfactory device.[25]

International lawyers have, accordingly, advanced various proposals as to how such a situation might be avoided, while respecting the tenets and retaining the supposed benefits of positivist methodology.

One such solution is to apply between States of conflicting camps the rule of general international law which last had the support of both, or all, those camps.[26] Indeed, one school of positivist thought - once flourishing, but now in decline, if not altogether extinct - would identify this rule as in fact being the existing rule of general international law on the matter in hand.[27] However, there is no evidence that such a conflict-resolving rule enjoys the general support of States - not surprisingly in view of the fact that it would tend to work to the benefit of the older, predominantly Northern States, at the expense of the more recently independent, predominantly Southern countries. As such, it cannot itself be said to be a positive rule of law. Nor can it be said to have any rational necessity to it, such that it inevitably forms part of a legal system of the type to which the international legal system belongs, without any need for its being positively created by and through human action.

Another solution which is sometimes mooted is to identify some rule which, while it is not the rule which is supported by either or any of the conflicting camps, might, nevertheless, accommodate and give effect, to some extent at least, to the views and, more importantly, the interests of each. International tribunals may be thought to have done just this on a number of occasions: in respect of the law relating to the delimitation of the base-line of coastal maritime zones, for example,[28] or with regard to the law which regulates the delimitation of maritime boundaries.[29] However, it is difficult to see how the existence of such a rule can be reconciled with positivist tenets. *Ex hypothesi*, no State has evinced the attitude that such a rule exists. Its identification cannot, therefore, be said to consist simply in a report of the views of States on what the law is. Indeed, it is partly for this reason that the judgments of international tribunals which have affirmed the existence of rules of this type have been criticised by some as representing instances of 'judicial legislation'.[30]

The suggestion might be advanced that the existence of a rule of this type does not in fact depend, in whole or in part, upon the application of moral precepts. First, the rule exists only if and in so far as it may be said to be evidenced by the practice of States. It is only if what States do can be said to represent instances of the application of the rule in question that that rule can be said to exist. Existence of the rule is, therefore, dependent upon human action. Secondly, the content of the rule depends upon the identification of a matter of fact: what each of the conflicting groups' interests are and what normative disposition may reconcile them. Such a contention is, however, difficult to maintain. Assume, for the moment, that the interests of those States which maintain a particular view of the law may be identified by conducting a factual investigation into what those States consider their interests to be. To reconcile those interests with the interests of another camp of States would, nevertheless, unavoidably involve the application of moral notions. To reconcile points of view requires a qualitative appraisal of what is significant in each and of what might be sacrificed without depriving it of its essence; and this, in turn, necessitates determination of what considerations justify the existence or possession of an interest, so that an evaluation can then be made of what matters more and what less in the position which is advanced with a view to securing it. Again, to assess what would be a fair bargain as between the interests involved would inescapably require application of notions of distributive justice. Moreover, it is doubtful that the interests of States are capable of identification without resort to moral precepts. It is rare for States explicitly to articulate their interests. That being so, some process of interpretation would almost inevitably be involved in determining what they were, interests being ascribed to States according to whatever were best capable of justifying the view of the law which they advanced.

These criticisms might conceivably be accommodated, while still retaining the tenets of positivism, by maintaining that, even if considerations of value, morality or justice fall to be applied in applying the solution under discussion, their involvement stems solely from the fact that they form part of a law-finding technique which exists and is applied because, and only because, the generality of States evinces the attitude that it exists as part of the *corpus juris*. Things could conceivably have been otherwise, it might be said, and they would have been, had States chosen to evince a common attitude which favoured some other way of dealing with the problem in hand. However, this manoeuvre is not very convincing, either. Were such a technique to depend for its existence on being posited by the conduct of States, it would be natural to expect States to recognise the legitimacy of its application to cases of the type in hand. Yet, not only do they frequently fail to apply it themselves, but many of them also censure those actors which do apply it. Thus, as has already been remarked,[31] the decisions of tribunals which have identified the law in the way under discussion have been criticised by some as finding little or no foundation in the practice of States. Application of the technique in question depends upon its rightness, then, and not upon its being recognised as right.

A solution which is sometimes advanced in the domestic sphere by thinkers of a positivist persuasion where the legal materials are under-determinative of the answer to a legal problem is to admit that there is no law - or that there is no single, correct answer to the question what it is that the law provides -,[32] but to maintain that new law will be made to regulate it - or an answer created and given - by any court to which a dispute on the matter is taken.[33] The difficulties with this version of events are well known.[34] They are magnified, though, at the international level, making it even more unsuited as a solution to the problem which is under consideration. Putting to one side the compatibility of any notion of judicial law-making with the traditions of the international legal system,[35] it is still rare that international disputes are taken to any form of adjudication and it is not often the case that one State party to a dispute can, against the wishes of the other, secure the binding decision of an international tribunal on the merits of the differences between them.[36] The problems which beset the claim that there is no law until it is made *de novo* by a judge are, accordingly, even more readily apparent at the international level than they are on the domestic plane. Law, which is not there to be applied by the actors to whom it is subsequently and retroactively addressed, fails in its most essential functions;[37] and that failure is obviously the greater the smaller are the prospects that the difficulties caused for those actors by the absence of any law to regulate their affairs will be resolved at some time in the future by the decision of some court or tribunal.[38] Concomitantly, the smaller the prospects of *lacunae* in the law being filled by acts of adjudicatory creativity, the harder still it becomes to characterise the legal propositions which States might advance in a situation of the type in hand as predictions of what an adjudicator might, at some later date, possibly decide the law to be, dressed up, for rhetoric's sake, as if what is predicted had already taken place.[39] In short, States consistently identify propositions of law as representing law which exists and is in force in cases in which, on this analysis, there is no law to identify. The error in this version of events, then, stems from a tendency to see the identification of the law as essentially a matter for officials, whereas primary responsibility for this task must lie with those who are expected to apply and govern themselves by the law.[40] It is not surprising, therefore, that Lord Denning recognised the bankruptcy of positivism in affording any plausible solution to the problem in hand. Instead, he advocated an approach which consisted 'above all [in] defining the rule [of general international law concerned] in terms which are consonant with justice', while 'seeking guidance' from the various practices of States.[41] At first sight, this approach might seem more promising. However, it, too, is not free from difficulties.

Although particular rules of law may occasionally direct that what should be done is simply that which is just, identifying the law is, on the whole, not a matter of determining, in any given case, what normative disposition can best be justified in the circumstances, all things considered.[42] If the law is about the doing of justice, it is, not justice *simpliciter* that is to be done, but, in the words of the old adage, 'justice according to law'.[43] In identifying the law, limits are imposed on the arguments from justice that may be made. It has been contended that the types of moral considerations that may be employed are limited, some forms of moral proposition or argument being excluded as inapposite or inappropriate.[44] However, the most important, and fundamental, limitation is that the normative propositions which may be advanced as justified by moral considerations must be ones which also 'fit' or 'explain' the legal materials of the particular legal system concerned. Most basically of all, it must be possible to identify elements of that material - precedent judicial decisions, for example - which may be understood as instances of the application of the normative proposition which is being advanced, even if, as a matter of historical fact, those who engaged in or were responsible for creating those materials actually thought that they were applying some different normative proposition or propositions. Without such supporting material, a normative proposition simply cannot be entertained as representing the law in force: in the words of Lord Justice Kerr, 'we cannot make forensic bricks without jurisprudential straw'.[45] More than this, though: it must also be possible to say that the materials of that system may, on the whole, be understood as instances of application of the normative proposition advanced. Some elements which cannot be 'explained' as instances of the application of the proposition may be dismissed as 'mistakes';[46] but, barring some astonishingly morally appealing argument to the contrary, the predominant part of the material, considered quantitatively or qualitatively, must be able to be seen to 'fit'.[47]

Following this approach, it may sometimes be possible, in a case of the type under consideration, to formulate a legal proposition which is morally attractive and which 'fits' with most, or even all, of the apparently conflicting practice on the matter in hand. It may be that none of the States belonging to either, or any, of the opposing camps has actually advanced the suggestion or supported the view that such a proposition represents the law which is in force; but, as long as the conduct of those groups of States may be understood as instances of the invocation or application of that proposition, that need not matter. The proposition in question may then properly be said to represent law in force. As has already been remarked,[48] international tribunals have done just this on a number of occasions.

Alternatively, it might sometimes be the case that one body of the practice of States on the matter in question may effectively be dismissed as 'mistaken', it being possible to identify a normative proposition which is morally attractive and which 'fits' with the remainder of State practice in the field.[49] However, that possibility may well not exist, either. The moral appeal of any normative proposition which may be said to 'explain' any significant part of the practice in question may not be especially strong. More importantly, though, the body of practice which resists 'explanation' may be too sizeable and too qualitatively significant to be dismissed as 'incorrect'. For example, it may be the practice of a significant body of States, perhaps including all or most of the States of a particular ideology or geographical region, with the consequence that the rule which one is tempted to advance could not be said to have support which is 'representative' of all the sections of international legal society. Any supposed rule of general international law which might be asserted contrary to their position and inconsistent with their practices would, therefore, be one which there would be little chance of being effective. Certainly, it would be wrong to deny the utility of asserting novel normative propositions with a view to bringing about changes in the practices of the community to which those propositions are said to apply. However, in practice-based systems, such as the international legal system, the validity of such propositions as statements of the law in force is limited to cases in which there is a realistic prospect that the practices of those to whom those propositions are said to apply will generally comport with them.[50] In other words, the fact that a rule is - or, perhaps more accurately, has the immediate prospect of being[51] - generally effective is a necessary precondition to its existence as a rule of customary international law in force.

In certain cases, this last factor is likely to pose a serious obstacle to finding any satisfactory solution to a problem of the type under consideration. Perhaps the only way in which this obstacle can be overcome is to look beyond the practice which poses the problem - that which is specific to the question in hand - and consider, too, the practices of States pertaining to other matters or issues. Having determined the moral considerations which can be understood to justify the practices of States in those other domains, one might then proceed to identify what normative proposition it is that those considerations justify as most appropriate for disposing justly of a case of the type in hand. As the quantum of practice which is taken into account is thus increased, it might be thought to become correspondingly easier to discount as 'mistaken' that section of practice pertaining to the problem in hand which does not 'fit' with the normative proposition which practice, examined more widely, can be understood to exemplify. At the same time, even if the specific proposition which one is contemplating applying to the case in hand does not benefit from support which is widespread enough to be described as general, the general support which exists for related propositions can be called in aid in order to sustain the conclusion that the considerations which underpin that proposition are indeed 'effective'.[52]

While resort to other propositions of law or to the practices which sustain them widens the range of interpretative material, making it possible, perhaps, to circumvent the difficulty which might be posed by the apparently limited effectiveness of any proposition which one is minded to advance, it might, at the same time, be thought to run up against yet another obstacle. Thus, not only must any proposition which one is minded to apply to the case in hand 'fit' in some way with at least a fair proportion of the mutually inconsistent practice pertaining to cases of that type; it must 'fit' with the practices of States on still other matters, too. Just such an extended notion of 'fit' constitutes a fundamental, if not defining, element of our legal practice. Any novel proposition which is advanced in a difficult case such as the type under consideration must satisfy it.[53] Yet it is not immediately apparent why this should be so; and, in the absence of any explanation, it is impossible to understand just what cogency there is in an argument which relies upon the fact that the proposition which it advances 'fits' the legal materials in such a manner.[54]

A number of explanations has been put forward as to why it is that only those normative propositions may be advanced as representing the law in force which 'fit' the existing legal materials in the way described. All, though, suffer from major weaknesses - weaknesses which, in the case of certain of them, are only magnified or added to when they are translated from the national level to the plane of international law.[55]

The first consists in justifying this limitation on the grounds of the certainty or predictability which it supposedly provides. It is of undoubted value, it is said, that persons should be able to plan their actions and conduct their affairs with knowledge of what it is that they may safely do without running the risk of incurring the unpleasant consequences which the law attaches to certain behaviour. Such considerations, of course, lie at the heart of the liberal ideal of the 'rule of law'.[56] Admittedly, the principal justification of that notion is rooted in the protection which it is supposed to afford to the freedom of the individual[57] - something which can hardly apply in respect of a legal system in which none of the legal persons are human beings. Nevertheless, it remains the case that there are obvious benefits if those who manage the legal affairs of an incorporeal legal person such as a State are afforded a stable and predictable framework in accordance with which they may plan its activities and order its affairs. Moreover, in the case of States, just as much as in the case of individuals, benefits will flow, it may be said, if one person is able to co-ordinate her actions and expectations with the actions and expectations of another, such that they may both be confident that for one to do such-and-such and the other to do so-and-so will have the consequence that, say, new legal relations stipulated in some identifiable text will arise between them.[58]

Assuming, then, that certainty and predictability of such a type are of value, the element of 'fit' may be said to be justified as preserving or promoting certainty as to what the law is and predictability as to what others will consider it to be. Admittedly, the law-finding technique of which that limitation forms part does not promote those ends in a thorough-going fashion. They would be much better secured were the law to be identified by some other technique, such as a test along the lines of that which was rejected which was by Lord Denning: namely, if States are in accord that such-and-such is the law (assuming, for present purposes, that it is not unduly difficult or controversial a thing to verify the existence of such a state of affairs), then it is the law, but, if there is no accord, then a 'closure rule' applies.[59] However, that would be to exclude the possibility that more beneficial, specific normative solutions might be applied to situations which, on this model, would fall to be regulated unswervingly by the blunt and indiscriminate instrument of the 'gap-closing' rule. It is no doubt for this reason, amongst others, that such a law-finding technique is not applied in international law - or to the practice-based parts of any other legal or normative system, for that matter. In contrast, the technique of law-finding of which the limitation of 'fit' forms part makes it possible, in situations in which States are not precisely in accord with regard to what provision it is that the law makes, for rules to be identified, advanced and applied which, if they are not optimally just, are, nonetheless, more beneficial than the simple application of any 'closing-rule' would be. Certainty is thereby lost, to be sure; but, at the same time, a significant and worthwhile measure of predictability might be thought to be preserved by the limitation of 'fit'. It serves as a restraint on the propositions which may be advanced regarding the current state of the law, excluding many as simply unsustainable, however just or beneficial they might be. It also might be said to make it possible to identify at least the range of propositions which may plausibly be advanced and acknowledged as well-founded.

This may be so. However, it is difficult to understand how an element which plays such a fundamental and important role in the process of law-finding as does the limitation of 'fit' can be said to find its justification in its ability to provide predictability in such an attenuated form.

This is all the more so in view of the fact that the law-finding technique of which that limitation forms part licenses, if it does not encourage, the advancement of innovative legal propositions. Surprises, if not welcomed, are by no means discouraged. There can be no certainty that propositions which may be advanced will be accepted by others as legitimate, nor can it predicted with confidence what propositions others may advance in response.[60] Any element of predictability which there may be about the technique is derivative or incidental, stemming from the fact that anyone, suitably trained, can apply it and so form some view of the range of propositions which may be advanced in any given context and make an estimation of what particular State is likely to advance which.[61]

The main problem, then, with this first, explanation of the limitation of 'fit' is that the justification which it advances for that aspect of the law-finding technique is at odds with the practical effects of that technique's other aspect. In contrast, the following explanations of that element involve no such tension. Indeed, in the case of the second of them, it is explained in a way which makes it inseparable from, if not inherent in, the other aspect of the law-finding process.

An explanation of the limitation of 'fit' which has sometimes been proffered in the national sphere is to justify it by reference to the doctrine of 'separation of powers'. It is recognised to be highly desirable that, in situations in which no previously established rule is clearly applicable, courts may, nevertheless, create and apply rules in order to bring about both the legal regulation of those situations and the regulation of similar situations which may arise in the future. It is also recognised that the rules so created and applied should be the best and most beneficial rules possible. However, were such a power of law-making to be untrammelled, the judiciary would enjoy the power to create new rules which might wreak wide-ranging changes upon and within the society concerned. The power to make such dramatic changes, it is said, ought to be confined to the legislature: only it has any popular mandate for the performance of such tasks; only it has the apparatus of the civil service at its disposal to provide it with the in-depth, expert advice which is needed when carrying out any large-scale regulatory reform; and so on. The limitation of 'fit' is said to serve the purpose of ensuring that judges do not enjoy any such power, limiting their law-making power in such a way as to ensure that any new rules which they might create do not effect large or dramatic changes in the economic, social or cultural organisation of society.[62]

This explanation is superficially attractive. Certainly, it would appear to be corroborated by the frequent refusal of judges to identify certain rules as law, in spite of their acknowledged desirability, on the ground that, since they do not 'fit' the existing legal material, power to create them lies solely with the legislature. However, such statements could just as well describe a consequence of the element of 'fit' as point to its justification; and the difficulties which beset justifying it in such terms indicate that the former, rather than the latter, is what they most probably do.

Chief among these difficulties is the fact that, if the requirement of 'fit' is warranted by the necessity of limiting the reach and repercussions of judicial legislation, it performs that task poorly indeed. One need look no further than the celebrated case of *Donoghue* v. *Stevenson*[63] - containing, in Lord Atkin's judgment, perhaps the paradigm of legal reasoning as far as English and Scottish lawyers are concerned - to appreciate that the need to 'fit' precedent legal materials does not preclude judges from identifying novel legal propositions which may have the most far-reaching economic and social consequences. Instances of such decisions could be multiplied, both in respect of the United Kingdom's legal system and the systems of other countries, the constitutional jurisprudence of the United States affording a particularly rich fund of examples.[64] Moreover, even if the limitation of 'fit' were better suited to its supposed task, doubts might be felt as to whether its existence might plausibly be justified by the need to limit judicial creativity. The factors which are said to give rise to that need could all be changed: judges could be elected or appointed by means of some democratic process; they could stand for election on some particular legislative or policy manifesto; they could receive the assistance of civil servants and other policy-researchers; and so on. Yet there is no reason to think that, were such reforms to be made, the character of the judicial task and, with it, the nature of law-finding technique would suddenly change. Experience in those jurisdictions whose judicial systems and legal processes contain elements of such 'reforms' tends to substantiate this conclusion.[65] In short, the limitation of 'fit' would seem to be rooted more in the nature of law than in the character of the institutions which administer it.

Were these difficulties not enough, they are only increased when this explanation of the limitation of 'fit' is applied to the international legal system. The proposition that there is no law until it is made by a court, which forms an essential part of this explanation, is still more evidently one which it is difficult to accept when it is applied to a system in which the prospects of adjudication are often remote or non-existent, as has already been remarked.[66] It is also not immediately obvious that the notion of 'separation of powers' has any sense in an international context. A division of function may be postulated between adjudicators and States, analogous to that suggested between courts and the legislature (with States, as the makers of international law, occupying the place of the legislature); yet the notion that international tribunals may engage in legislative activity of any sort is quite antagonistic to the most basic traditions of the international legal system.[67] Alternatively, the division of function which the limitation of 'fit' is supposed to ensure might possibly be adapted from one between institutions to one between the situations in which the subjects of international law might find themselves. Thus, in so far as States might find themselves in a situation which falls to be regulated by rules whose existence is not dependent upon a treaty, they may advance as constituting those rules not only those normative propositions which are clearly and unequivocally established by virtue of the explicit support of the generality of States, but also those propositions which would be most beneficial in the circumstances. However, if those rules would involve major changes in the organisation of international society, a treaty must be resorted to in order to create them. The limitation of 'fit' would then serve as a device to single out those propositions which would not involve such major changes. However, it is difficult to understand the legal discourse of States as being appropriate to such a version of events. States do not couch propositions of customary law in the manner of legislative proposals, nor do they conduct their arguments concerning the validity of those propositions predominantly in terms of their substantive merits; and, if we are asked to suppose that the fact that they do otherwise is because they are merely engaging in rhetoric, we must wonder who it is that is supposed to be 'taken in'. Moreover, it is not easy to see what reason there might be for drawing in such a manner the frontier between the propositions which States might and the propositions which States might not advance as customary law. Since States have expert policy-advice available to them in the same measure whether they are involved in applying customary law or negotiating a treaty, an explanation might conceivably be sought for the existence of a frontier of the type supposed in the legitimacy, or otherwise, of the law-creating process which is involved. Novel legal propositions involving far-reaching changes in the relations of States should need the specific consent of the State *vis-à-vis* which they are advanced before they become binding on it, it may be said, and the device for obtaining such consent is a treaty; whereas propositions involving less drastic changes do not need any acceptance of that sort to be binding upon other States. However, putting to one side the question whether 'consent' (whatever that may mean) has any role at all to play in explaining why international law is binding, it is by no means obvious why, if 'large scale' legislation should require the acceptance of other States before it becomes binding upon them, the same should not be so in the case of the supposedly 'small scale' law-making which is involved in the advancing of novel propositions of customary law.

Any supposed justification which may be sought for the limitation of 'fit' in the doctrine of 'separation of powers' simply cannot apply, then, in the sphere of international law, even were it to be free from problems at the national level.

A third explanation which has been advanced for the existence of the limitation of 'fit' is that it helps to ensure that there is a moral justification for the law allowing us to do what it allows us to do, requiring of us what it requires of us and threatening us with the unpleasant consequences which it does if we do not comply with its requirements. The argument by which this explanation is sustained is long and tortuous and it cannot be reproduced here.[68] However, in essence, it consists in an attempt to answer the question of how it may be that we consider there to be at least some justification for the fact that officials threaten us with coercion if we do not comply with the normative standards which they proclaim, in spite of the fact that those standards may not be the most just standards which may be conceived.[69] This assumption may be correct, it is said, if and in so far as those standards can be understood to constitute the expression of, or to be justified by, moral precepts which together form a single, coherent moral scheme.[70] This scheme, in turn, must have a certain type of content: it must consist in precepts which derive their moral force from the fact that they ensure that respect is given to individuals by virtue of their capacity to be self-governing or autonomous.[71] Most important, though, is that those precepts must be consistent with each other, springing from a single conception of what it is that respect for the autonomy of the human person requires. If and in so far as they do not, individuals who are treated by officials in accordance with one precept and individuals who are treated in accordance with another are not shown the same respect: the members of the one group are treated as possessing a humanity which members of the other group are treated as not enjoying. That is itself an immoral act, independently of whatever moral wrong may be done by virtue of the actual content of one or both of those precepts.[72] Conversely, to treat those persons in accordance with the same conception of what it is that their humanity and capacity for self-government require is to do something of value - to advance a moral end -, even if it is the case that that conception of what humanity and autonomy require is mistaken.[73] To that extent, then, if it is possible to understand the laws of a community as being based upon one such single conception, justification exists for the existence of those laws and the coercion which their enforcement involves.[74] The limitation of 'fit' helps to promote the advancement of this moral value, it is said[75] - a value which is distinct from the values of substantive and procedural justice and which may be termed 'integrity'.[76] Thus, it requires of a judge that she justify the decision which she proposes to give in the case before her by reference to moral considerations which would also serve to justify the decisions which were reached by her fellow judges in previous cases of the type in hand.[77] More widely than this, though, it also requires of her that those considerations derive their moral force from precepts which would, at the same time, justify decisions in domains other than that with which the instant case deals.[78] By this means, the limitation of 'fit' helps to promote the bringing-about of a state of affairs in which the laws of the community concerned may be understood to give expression to a single moral system.

This explanation is by no means free from difficulties. Foremost of these is that it is not immediately apparent what of moral value there is in the supposed virtue of 'integrity' on which it is founded. Suppose that some official were to treat your brother in a way other than that in which she ought to have done, if she were seeking to identify the best way to protect or to promote his capacity for self-government - perhaps because she entertained a faulty understanding of what that capacity consists in or of what should and should not be done in order best to ensure its preservation or advancement. Then, put to one side any possible consequentialist arguments, which may or may not apply as a matter of contingent fact.[79] It is difficult to see what moral good would be done, or what evil avoided, by some official - perhaps the same one, perhaps another - subsequently treating you in accordance with that same faulty conception. Better that you - and others after you - be treated correctly.[80] Perhaps it might be thought that this judgment simply reflects what is best 'on balance' and that there might be something which is lost in your being treated differently from your brother, even if it is preferable, all things considered, that you be treated as your humanity demands.[81] Of course, were that so, it would be to admit that the demands of justice always, or nearly always, override the demands of 'integrity'. That latter consideration could hardly then serve as a convincing explanation of the limitation of 'fit'; for that limitation is frequently invoked in legal practice as necessitating rejection of even the strongest demands of justice.[82] However, even at such a trivial level as that, it is impossible to see what argument can be made that some quality of the human person is honoured by visiting on you, for the reason that he received it, the less than ideal treatment which was meted out to your brother. *Ex hypothesi*, there is nothing in your capacity for self-government which calls for such sub-standard treatment. Moreover, nothing about that capacity is altered by the fact that your brother has been treated less than well, such that what respect for that capacity would entail is concomitantly changed. Again, your brother's capacity for self-government is in no way protected or enhanced by your receiving less than that which (considered independently of how he was treated) is your due.[83]

If this seems excessively 'rationalist', consideration of the matter at the level of intuition would not seem to yield any different conclusion. Any uneasiness which you might feel about receiving better treatment than did your brother would seem to amount to no more than regret that your brother was not treated as he should have been. The legitimacy of that sentiment depends upon how it was that your brother was treated: not how you may be treated. Indeed, that it does not depend upon any disparity in the treatment between the two of you is clear from the fact that such regret, if it is warranted, ought to exist prior to the meting out to you of whatever treatment it is that you are to receive. Perhaps, once you have been treated as you should be (considered independently of how it was that your brother was treated), you might experience some feelings of guilt before your brother about your good fortune; but that would seem to be as misplaced as the guilt which might be felt by someone who has had the good luck to have been born more talented than her sibling. Nothing changes, except that regret is replaced by indignation, if perspectives are altered and the situation is considered from the point of view of your brother. The natural corollary of his anger at the less than ideal treatment which he has received is a wish that the shortcomings in that treatment be made good, if that is possible,[84] rather than a desire that that same treatment be visited on others. Anything else would smack of vindictiveness or of jealousy at the anticipated good fortune of others - what has pithily been termed the 'politics of envy'.[85] Again, from the perspective of a bystander, things are no different. Any uneasiness regarding the disparity in treatment between you and your brother stems from pondering, perhaps vicariously, the bad luck of the brother who was treated less than well and who was not fortunate enough to be accorded the right and proper treatment which you received. If, and in so far as our intuitions may be other than these, and if and in so far as they may suggest that there is indeed something which is wrong in the very meting out of such differential treatment,[86] Rawls's advice might be recalled: that some of our intuitive judgments may have to be rejected if they cannot be justified by reference to the scheme of principles which the predominant part of our intuitions presuppose.[87]

This difficulty with such an explanation of the limitation of 'fit' is only added to if that explanation is translated to the level of international law. The persons of the international legal system are all incorporeal in nature, the principal such persons being, of course, States. Attempts have sometimes been made to maintain that individual human beings also constitute subjects of international law; but these, for good or ill, remain thoroughly unconvincing.[88] That being so, the virtue of 'integrity', since it allegedly finds its foundation in the respect which it supposedly ensures is paid to the human person,[89] simply cannot have any application.[90] An attempt might be made to argue otherwise by contending that what are represented by international lawyers as the individual legal rights of a State should be conceived of, in substance, as group rights which are vested in the society of individual citizens who compose that State. However, putting to one side the question of whether such disregard of legal form is legitimate,[91] such a contention is beset by so many problems that it would simply amount to heaping Pelion upon Ossa.[92]

The fourth, and last, explanation of the limitation of 'fit' which will be considered here seeks to justify that element of law-finding technique in a manner which bears a certain superficial similarity to the foregoing. It is acknowledged that the fact that a legal proposition can be seen to 'fit' with the existing materials or practices of a legal system hardly serves to show that that proposition is just. That calls, rather, for consideration of whether the consequences of the application of that proposition are ones which are morally worthwhile. To prove that it satisfies the limitation of 'fit' would, therefore, seem to be beside the point.[93] Nonetheless, it is said, while such proof may not help in any way to establish that that proposition is in itself just, it does show that it can be implemented without causing any practical problems and, to that extent, is one which can, as well as should, be applied; for to demonstrate that a proposition 'fits' the legal materials in the way which has been explained above is to verify that the values which it promotes or the ends which it advances are not inconsistent with the values or ends which are promoted or advanced by other propositions which form part of the legal system concerned. In short, the limitation of 'fit' is directed at minimising 'pragmatic conflict' within the law.[94]

This explanation does not involve any of the questionable ethical assumptions of the foregoing. Nevertheless, it remains subject to what is essentially the same central weakness and, moreover, is possessed of even less explanatory power. Thus, it is by no means clear why the fact that the application of a proposition would bring about a 'pragmatic conflict' in the law should constitute an impediment to its adoption. It might well be that existing rules of law can only be understood to promote the achievement of happiness, say, and not virtue, so that to espouse a proposition which advances virtue, and not happiness, would be to create a situation in which different propositions of law promoted different values which cannot form part of a single moral system. However, if virtue is to be valued rather than happiness, then it should be promoted, if at all possible, even if other domains of law are of such a nature that virtue will not be promoted as efficiently or effectively as it could otherwise have been. It might only be otherwise if the very existence of such 'discord' were apt to be productive of deleterious consequences; but it is difficult to see how it would be, in normal circumstances at least.[95]

Even assuming that the creation of such 'discord' were, for whatever reason, likely to be a source of practical problems, it is, nevertheless, the case that the limitation of 'fit' which the existence of that likelihood would justify would be very different in its nature and content from that which forms part of existing legal practice. First and foremost, that limitation would be *prima facie* in nature only. Thus, although the application of innovative and 'discordant' legal propositions might be calculated to create problems, those negative effects might well be outweighed by the good which application of those propositions would do. In such a case, there would be every reason to put the limitation of 'fit' to one side.[96] Yet the limitation of 'fit', as it is understood and applied in practice, simply is not dispensed with so easily, even in those cases in which the person who is called upon to identify the law enjoys power to overrule existing law and create new. Moreover, were judges concerned to avoid 'pragmatic conflicts' between the propositions which they are minded to espouse and other propositions which form part of the legal system concerned, they would be less concerned with whether the propositions which they are minded to adopt 'fit' the legal materials and more about whether they 'fit' with whatever propositions their fellow judges consider, or would be likely to consider, those materials to support. After all, if such conflicts are to be avoided, it is because of the supposed negative consequences of the law pursuing or promoting different and inconsistent ends: not of it advancing goals which differ from those which were pursued in the past. Yet the concern which judges show is with what the law is best understood to be, not with how other judges presently understand it or how it may be that they are likely to understand it in the near future; and, if it is thought that, though not couched in the form of a prediction, the law-finding technique of which the limitation of 'fit' forms part in fact operates in such a way that the propositions of law which it enables one to identify are ones which others, employing that same technique, will also identify, it may be recalled that the room which that technique allows to innovation and surprise makes it a quite unreliable predictor of the propositions which others will espouse.[97]

Therefore, none of the justifications which have been advanced for the limitation of 'fit' can be said to be convincing. Indeed, the shortcomings of most of those explanations are greater still, or at least more patent, when they are applied to the case of international law. Nonetheless, and notwithstanding their failure to provide any thoroughly satisfactory explanation of why it should be that the propositions which it yields should enjoy the status of law, naturalist accounts of the process of law-identification remain more convincing than their positivist counter-parts. The description of that process which they provide corresponds much more closely with how that process operates in practice, both at the national and at the international levels. More particularly - and evidence perhaps of their greater cogency -, they provide a more satisfactory way of coping with problems of the type which Lord Denning described in the *Trendtex* case. It is not that a solution cannot be found to such problems on any positivist analysis. However, that solution can hardly be described as satisfactory, consisting, as it does, in the simple application, *faute de mieux*, of the application of the blunt and undiscriminating instrument of a 'closure rule'. It is remarkable that international tribunals have avoided resort to such a solution, except in one famous case,[98] and the reception which was accorded to that decision might be thought only to go to prove the rule.[99] Doctrine, too, consistently fails to employ it.

There is, then, probably every reason to discard positivist versions of the law-finding process in preference for naturalist accounts. Yet, if it is to command complete confidence, any naturalist account of our law and legal practice must explain and justify more satisfactorily than has been done to date the limitation of 'fit', which represents such a central feature of our conception of how to identify law. Perhaps some other justification for that limitation may be found, more plausible than those which have been outlined above: one, even, which is particular to international law. There is, after all, no *a priori* reason why that limitation, as it is employed in the practice of international law - or in practice-based systems generally -, should not be justified by considerations which are different, in part or even in entirety, from those (if such there be) which support its existence as an institution of national law. The quest for such a justification, though, is one which must be left to some other occasion.

NOTES

1 [1977] QB 529 at 552F-H; [1977] 1 All ER 881 at 888*c-d*; [1977] 2 WLR 356 at 363H-364B.

2 Hart, H.L.A., *The Concept of Law* (1961), at pp. 89-96.

3 Raz, J., *Practical Reason and Norms* (1975), at pp. 132-148.

4 See, for example, *North Sea Continental Shelf, (Federal Republic of Germany / Denmark; Federal Republic of Germany / Netherlands), I.C.J. Reports*, 1969, p. 4 at para. 77.

5 Cheng, in Macdonald, R.St.J., and Johnston, D.M., eds., *The Structure and Process of International Law: essays in Legal Philosophy, Doctrine and Theory* (1983), p. 513 at p. 532.

6 See, for example, *Military and Paramilitary Activities in and against Nicaragua (Merits), I.C.J. Reports*, 1986, p. 14 at para. 184.

7 Cf. *Asylum Case (Columbia* v. *Peru), I.C.J. Reports*, 1950, p. 266 at p. 2**.

8 See, for example, Macgibbon, in Cheng, B., ed., *International Law: Teaching and Practice* (1982), p. 10 at pp. 19-22.

9 See, for example, Cheng, *Indian Journal of International Law*, 5 (1965), p. 23 at pp. 35-37 and 45.

10 Though see text at nn. 17-20, below, and n. 20.

11 See, for example, Fatouros, *Virginia Law Review*, 50 (1964), p. 783 at pp. 807-811.

12 While this assertion is not made by Cheng, he appears at times to entertain such an assumption: *loc. cit.* above (n. 5), at pp. 540-541.

13 For the possibility that such rules may exist, see *Asylum Case*, *loc. cit.* above (n. 7).

14 Cf. Cheng, *loc. cit.* above (n. 9), at p. 37.

15 For whether international law or legal practice knows of such an institution, see Lauterpacht, H., in Lauterpacht, E., ed., *International Law, Being the Collected Papers of Hersch Lauterpacht*, vol. 2, p. 213. The possibility of some type of *non liquet* is suggested by Raz's analysis of those situations which are imperfectly regulated by positively established rules of law. In such a situation, a legal proposition is neither true nor false. The contrary of that proposition is also neither true nor false. That being so, the law affords no answer to what may or may not be done. See Raz, J., *The Authority of Law* (1979), at pp. 70-75. The resulting indeterminacy is resolved within national legal systems by the existence of courts which have the power to provide an authoritative answer to the question of what may and what may not be done: *ibid.*, at pp. 58-59 and 172-175. However, in the absence of any court - or of any court with power to make such regulation - the indeterminacy would remain legally unresolved and unresolvable: *ibid.*, at p. 173. The fact that there is frequently no chance that a dispute between States may be resolved through adjudication (see text at n. 36, below) would, therefore, entail that often not only is there no answer, but also no answer can be given, to the question of what may and what may not be done under international law. Moreover, since no sharp line can be drawn between situations which are regulated and those which are regulated imperfectly (*ibid.*, at pp. 73-74, 173 n. 8 and 208), one might be tempted

to conclude that, as a practical matter, it is the case in respect of very many situations that there is no law to regulate them which is worth the name. Cf. Cheng, *loc. cit.* above (n. 5), at pp. 521-523 and 537.

16 For this characteristic, see Raz, *op. cit.* above (n. 3), at pp. 150-151. Raz explains this characteristic in terms of a claim of authority to regulate all activities, rather than in their actual regulation. This qualification should be understood in the light of his contentions that legal systems contain 'closure rules' in order to regulate matters which are not regulated by any specific rule which has been created by human action (see the text following this note and accompanying notes) and that judges enjoy a power - which they will exercise - to create rules in order to provide specific regulation for matters which are imperfectly regulated by those rules which have been created by human action - either because of the indeterminacy of the facts on which the content of those legal rules is dependent or because two or more such rules conflict, there being no further rule which clearly specifies which is to prevail (*op. cit.* above (preceding note), at pp. 172-175).

17 Raz, *op. cit.* above (n. 15), at pp. 75-77 and 192-193. Raz maintains that 'closure rules' apply in the absence of any 'positive' rule - that is, a rule which has been created by human action -, rather than where there is a positive rule, but there is uncertainty as to what it is that it provides: *ibid.*, at p. 77. That being so, it might possibly be thought that any 'closure rule' which there might be would not apply in a situation such as that which is under discussion, since positive legal materials do exist - the practices of various States - and what there is is uncertainty as to what rule those materials 'stand for'. However, on the positivist version of legal sources which is here assumed, no human action of the sort which would qualify as creating any rule has taken place. Consequently, no positive rule exists.

18 See, most famously, Dicey, A.V., *Introduction to the Study of the Law of the Constitution* (1885), Chapter V, *passim*.

19 *S.S. Lotus*, P.C.I.J., Series A No. 10, p. 4 at p. 18.

20 Raz maintains that 'closure rules' are analytic truths, rather than 'positive' human responses to the problems which would exist in the absence of such rules: *op. cit.* above (n. 15), at p. 77 n. 19. The content of such truths is necessarily along the lines of that described in the text: *ibid.*, at pp. 75-77.

21 Most infamously, prior to the late-1940s and the occurrence of any human action which might be capable of sustaining the existence of a positive rule of law to the contrary, the application of such a 'closure rule' would have legitimised the practice by a State of genocide against a racial or ethnic group of its own nationals.

22 See, for example, n. 99, below. Indeed, the approach which many States have adopted with regard to the law which regulates jurisdiction to prescribe rejects the assumption that the starting-point for analysis must be any freedom for States to extend the reach of their laws to whomsoever, whatsoever and wheresoever they might choose. According to Raz, the analogous problems which would arise within national legal systems are largely avoided by the existence of a judicial power to create new, positive rules in order to regulate in a more satisfactory fashion those situations or activities whose regulation by the 'closure rule' would be inappropriate or unjust: *op. cit.* above (n. 15), at pp. 192-193. The general absence of any prospect of non-consensual recourse to adjudication in the international legal system (see text at n. 36, below) entails, though, that that solution is often just not available at the international level. The reluctance of States sometimes to accept or to acknowledge application of the 'closure rule' might, consequently, be understood as reflecting the institutional deficiencies of the international legal system. However, it could just as well be thought to raise questions about analyses which depend upon the existence of institutions and the attribution to them of law-making powers in order to render workable or palatable the propositions which they involve.

23 While Raz maintains that there is necessarily a 'closure rule' in any legal system, even though it may not have been created by any human action (see n. 15, above), that does not exclude the possibility that human action might create a positive 'closure rule' and, moreover, that the rule so created may possess a different content from that which a non-posited 'closure rule' would bear. Article 38 (1) (*c*) of the Statute of the International Court of Justice has sometimes been talked of as if it were just such a rule, at least as far as disputes coming before the 'World Court' are concerned. See, for example, Lauterpacht, *op. cit.* above (n. 15), at pp. 221-222.

24 See n. 20, above.

25 Thus, Lauterpacht observes that, in international litigation, States seldom found their case upon the application of any 'closure rule', preferring to contend that, despite any appearances to the contrary, the legal materials support the proposition that a positive rule of international law has been created which is in their favour: *op. cit.* above (n. 15), at p. 220.

26 Akehurst, *British Year Book of International Law*, 47 (1974-1975), p. 1. Note also Cheng, *loc. cit.* above (n. 5), at pp. 537-538.

27 For this view, see Tunkin, G.I., *Theory of International Law* (trans. Butler, W.E., 1974), at pp. 123-133.

28 *Fisheries, I.C.J. Reports*, 1951, p. 116, esp. at pp. 129 and 133.

29 *North Sea Continental Shelf, loc. cit.* above (n. 4), esp. at paras. 83-99 and 101 (C) and (D).

30 For example, in relation to the two cases which are alluded to in the text at the two notes preceding this, see Waldock, *British Year Book of International Law*, 28 (1951), p. 114, and Brown, E.D., *The Legal Regime of Hydrospace* (1971), at pp. 41-71, respectively.

31 See the text accompanying the preceding note.

32 See n. 15, above.

33 Cf. Hart, *op. cit.* above (n. 2), at pp. 121-132, and Raz, nn. 15 and 22, above.

34 See the various writings of Ronald Dworkin, in particular *Law's Empire* (1986), *passim*.

35 On which, see Cheng, *loc. cit.* above (n. 5), at pp. 519-521 and 534.

36 See, for example, Brownlie, I., *Principles of Public International Law* (4th. ed.; 1990), at p. 708.

37 On these functions, see Raz, *op. cit.* above (n. 15), at pp. 169-172.

38 Cf. Raz, *ibid.*, at pp. 172-175. This is not to deny that the introduction of compulsory, binding adjudication makes a significant contribution towards enabling law better to achieve its functions. So, for example, it affords, at the very least, a means of providing the parties to a dispute with an authoritative answer to the question what it is that the law provides. On this contribution, see Raz, *loc. cit.* above (n. 3), and *op. cit.* above (n. 15), at pp. 175-176, and Hart, *loc. cit.* above (n. 2).

39 Cf. Dworkin, *op. cit.* above (n. 34), esp. at pp. 37-39 and 157-160.

40 Cf. Hart, *op. cit.* above (n. 2), at pp. 38-40, and note Dworkin, *op. cit.* above (n. 34), at pp. 189-190.

41 [1977] QB 529 at 552H-553A; [1977] 1 All ER 881 at 888*d-e*; [1977] 2 WLR 356 at 364B-C.

42 Thus, the jurisdiction which is conferred on the International Court of Justice by Article 38 (2) of its Statute to decide disputes *ex aequo et bono* contrasts with the jurisdiction which is conferred on it by Article 38 (1) to decide 'in accordance with international law'.

43 MacCormick, N., *Legal Reasoning and Legal Theory* (1978), at pp. 73 and 166.

44 For two such attempts, see Dworkin, R.M., *Taking Rights Seriously* (1978), at pp. 81-130 and 294-330, and Regan, *Michigan Law Review*, 76-II (1978), p. 1213.

45 *J.H. Rayner (Mincing Lane) Ltd.* v. *Department of Trade and Industry and others* [1989] Ch 72 at 177E; [1988] 3 All ER 257 at 301*g*; [1988] 3 WLR 1033 at 1088D.

46 For a conception of 'mistakes', see Dworkin, *op. cit.* above (n. 34), at pp. 203, 204-205, 230, 246-247.

47 For discussion of this requirement, see Dworkin, *op. cit.* above (n. 34), at pp. 65-68, 228-232 and 245-248, and MacCormick, *op. cit.* above (n. 43), at pp. 152-194.

48 See text at nn. 28-30, above.

49 A still further possibility might be to identify any specific propositions which the different bodies of practice can both - or all - be said to support. However, such an approach, which consists in looking for the 'highest common denominator', would frequently be unjustified. After all, it is often the case that certain propositions are acceptable to those advancing them only if the other propositions which they advance are also accepted. Moreover, such an approach would often amount simply to shifting the focus of the problem, since the question would remain of how to 'explain' the conflicting or inconsistent practices in respect of those issues or propositions on which agreement does not exist.

50 Hart, *op. cit.* above (n. 2), at pp. 54-56, 86-88 and 96-107. Note also Raz, *op. cit.* above (n. 3), at pp. 53-55.

51 Cf. the text at nn. 8-9, above.

52 This approach is suggested by Dworkin's analysis of customary rules: *op. cit.* above (n. 34), at pp. 65-68 and 204-205.

53 *Loc. cit.* above (n. 47).

54 After all and putting considerations of effectiveness to one side, why should a proposition which is not as just as it might be, because of the need to 'fit', be preferred to some proposition which does not 'fit', but is optimally just?

55 Certain of the explanations which are rehearsed below are proffered in the context of theories of law and legal reasoning which purport to be positivist in their approach. Nevertheless, it is believed that they are better understood as interpretations of law and legal practice which attempt to understand those phenomena by reference to the values which they secure or promote and which are, therefore, inescapably 'naturalist' in nature. See Dworkin, *op. cit.* above (n. 34), at pp. 96-98.

56 See, most famously, Fuller, L.L., *The Morality of Law* (rev. ed., 1969).

57 See Raz, *op. cit.* above (n. 15), at pp. 220-223, and Finnis, J., *Natural Law and Natural Rights* (1980), at pp. 272-273.

58 On the value of co-ordination and its role in the notion of the 'rule of law', see Finnis, *op. cit.* above (preceding note), at pp. 231-232 and 267. See also Postema, *Journal of Legal Studies*, 11 (1982), p. 165.

59 Cf. Dworkin, *op. cit.* above (n. 34), at pp. 142-143.

60 Dworkin, *ibid.*, at p. 128.

61 A further problem, which may be noted here, is that the limitation of 'fit' applies even in those areas of the law in which no-one could plausibly be said to plan his actions on the basis of what the law says.

62 See MacCormick, *op. cit.* above (n. 43), at pp. 187-188.

63 [1932] AC 562.

64 *Ex facie*, the fact that law-finding technique of the sort described is applied in the sphere of constitutional law in the same way that it is in other legal domains would seem not to be explicable by means of the justification under discussion. For present purposes, though, it is assumed that it may be. After all, it may be claimed that the judiciary should be able to engage in 'small scale' law-making in this field in the interest of 'making the constitution work', while 'large scale' law-making should be reserved to that body which has a legitimate mandate for adopting and amending constitutions. (In many countries, that body will in fact be the legislature, acting in accordance with special rules of procedure.) As in the case of other areas of law, the limitation of 'fit' may be said to create and to preserve this division of competence.

65 Thus, although the bench of certain courts in certain States of the United States is elected by popular suffrage and those who stand for election sometimes do so on what may be described as a political platform, the technique of law-finding which is employed in those courts does not differ in any significant respect from the technique which is used in legal systems in which the judges are not elected in such a way.

66 See text at nn. 32-40, above.

67 See n. 35, above.

68 For this argument, see Dworkin, *op. cit.* above (n. 34), esp. at pp. 186-216.

69 *Ibid* at pp. 93-94 and 190-192.

70 *Ibid* at pp. 167, 214 and 225-226.

71 *Ibid* at pp. 200-201, 204-205, 221 and 223 and note pp. 189-190.

72 *Ibid* pp. 204-205.

73 *Ibid* at pp. 95-96, 165-166, 213 and 216.

74 It does not follow that the law, as so identified, should always be complied with or enforced: *ibid.*, at pp. 108-113 and 218-219; and note also pp. 204-205 and 214.

75 On its own, it cannot ensure that this value is respected. That would require not only that the judge apply the limitation well, but also that the moral considerations which she employs be ones which are of the type described above at n. 71.

76 For the argument that this virtue forms one of the moral standards which we recognise, see Dworkin, *op. cit.* above (n. 34), at pp. 176-184.

77 Or, if and in so far as they would not, which derive their moral force from more fundamental precepts which, directly or indirectly, serve to justify the decisions in question.

78 Dworkin, *op. cit.* above (n. 34), at pp. 130-135 and 219-221.

79 As to which, see n. 85, below.

80 MacCormick, at some points, suggests that 'formal justice' requires that 'like cases be treated alike' and that, though this requirement may be overridden in the interests of doing justice, something of value is thereby sacrificed: *op. cit.* above (n. 43), at pp. 74-75. At other points, though, he explains the demand of 'formal justice' solely in terms of an injunction that there be no 'arbitrary differentiation between cases': *ibid.* at p. 179. As such, it does not seek to bar the doing of justice, even if injustice was done in previous cases, since there is no good reason to repeat injustice and every reason to treat the case before us differently by doing that which is just. Thus, he remarks, the requirement that 'like cases should be treated alike' holds true only if the treatment which was given to the previous case was itself just: *loc. cit.* Yet, for the reasons given below, that is to admit that the supposed value of 'formal justice' has no independent value of its own: see n. 93, below. Indeed, at still other points, he makes it clear that that 'value' is no more than a requirement of rationality in decision-making: *loc. cit.* and *ibid.*, at p. 99.

81 Cf. Dworkin, *op. cit.* above (n. 34), at pp. 204-205 and 218-219.

82 See, for example, the materials cited by MacCormick, *op. cit.* above (n. 43), at pp. 164-165.

83 Though see n. 85, below. The preceding propositions, in essence, simply reflect the truth that the adjective 'equal' in the formula 'equal concern and respect', which Dworkin employs to describe the essence of what it is that our capacity for self-government entitles us to receive from others, is utterly redundant, being inserted for rhetorical purposes only and not indicating the existence of a consideration or argument which is truly egalitarian in nature. See Raz, *Mind* (1978), p. 321.

84 Other considerations - usually epitomised in the aphorism *interest reipublicae ut finis sit litium* - generally prevail so as to make such a course of action inappropriate.

85 The existence of such vices might, at times, afford an instrumental reason for visiting less than perfect treatment upon you because such less than perfect treatment was accorded to your brother: if you being treated better than your brother were likely to excite his rage and thereby lead to the creation of a threat to the peace, say, or were apt to undermine his sense of self-respect and so impair his will to exercise his capacity for self-government in a fruitful way. Cf. Miller, *Midwest Studies in Philosophy*, 7 (1982), p. 73, and Rawls, J., *A Theory of Justice* (1974), at pp. 534-536 and 546. However, such cases are likely to be rare and are apt to occur only in the most extreme conditions.

86 For what it is worth, I, for one, find it difficult to share the intuitions which Dworkin contends that we feel in situations of the sort described: *op. cit.* above (n. 34), at pp. 178-184. Although it is but anecdotal evidence, I might add that the great majority of students whom I have taught have said that they experience the same difficulties. Perhaps any feelings of discomfort which are felt when faced with the examples which Dworkin employs in fact find their origins in the odd notion of 'fairness' which he employs to justify their creation. Certainly, though, each example which he gives can be changed in such a way as to dispel those feelings, while retaining the supposed affront to the virtue of 'integrity'. For example, the abortion example which Dworkin employs, can be altered so that half of those who request abortions are granted them, half denied them, with the decision between them being made by means of a lottery. Indeed, the public health system in the United Kingdom might be thought to operate on some such very basis.

87 *Op. cit.* above (n. 85), at p. 20.

88 Cheng, *loc. cit.* above (n. 5), at pp. 515-516.

89 See Dworkin, *op. cit.* above (n. 34), esp. at p. 166. Dworkin at times appears to hint at an explanation of the value of 'integrity' which might be thought to differ from that which has been described above: namely, that for a system's laws to exhibit the characteristic which 'integrity' is said to demand helps to create a condition of social solidarity between the members of that system, which, in turn, helps to safeguard, create or reinforce their sense of individual worth. See, for example, *ibid.*, at pp. 188, 211 and 213. However, such an argument, if it is in fact any different from that described in the text, is, like it, entirely dependent upon its application to individual human beings.

90 Similar problems exist within national legal systems in so far as the limitation of 'fit' applies also to cases involving incorporeal legal persons, such as companies.

91 Cf. Dworkin, *op. cit.* above (n. 34), at pp. 168-175.

92 Just a few of these problems are as follows. Can groups, as distinct from the individuals of which they are composed, be considered to be subjects of moral concern? If we are to think of rights in such terms,

how are we to conceive of obligations of international law? Is the content of international law such that its rules can, in any significant number, be thought of as expressing concern for other persons, whether those persons are taken singly or in groups?

93 Raz, *op. cit.* above (n. 15), at p. 204.

94 *Loc. cit.* and *ibid.*, at p. 201.

95 Certainly, Raz does not point to any specific deleterious consequences, making allusion only to the 'adverse', but unspecified, effects of 'partial reform': *ibid.*, at p. 201.

96 This is admitted by Raz: *ibid.*, at p. 205.

97 Cf. the criticism of this explanation which is made by Dworkin: *op. cit.* above (n. 34), at pp. 132-135.

98 The *S.S. Lotus*, *loc. cit.* above (n. 19). The Permanent Court of International Justice founded its approach upon the assumption that a 'closure rule' would apply in the absence of any positively created rule of customary law and proceeded to find that no rule had arisen through human action to supersede it. Nevertheless, the Court clearly felt more secure in its conclusion, having found certain instances of State conduct which assumed the very freedom which the 'closure rule' was supposed to afford: *loc. cit.* at pp. 28-29.

99 As is well known, the decision of the Court was rejected both by States in their subsequent practice and by those who drafted the 1958 Geneva Convention on the High Seas. It may also be noted that the decision of the Court in that case was determined by the casting-vote of its President.

5 LEGAL POSITIVISM - Some Lessons From Legal History

ANDREW LEWIS

'Dworkin's is, fundamentally ..., a normative theory of law, offering guidance to the judge as to his judicial duty; [Hart's and Raz's theory] is a descriptive theory, offered to historians to enable a discriminating history of legal systems to be written.'

Finnis *Natural Law and Natural Rights*.[1]

A characteristic of modern positivist theories of the Anglo-American school is a proper insistence on the importance of 'the internal point of view'.[2] Law in this light is seen not as an isolated social or moral phenomenon but as a function of practical involvement, having value primarily for those willing and able to recognise it. Excessive reliance on this criterion leads to scepticism about the reality of law: is it not merely a construction put upon the world by those who think legally? Even if this charge were sustainable, however, and from their different perspectives Finnis and Dworkin have given good reasons for thinking it not so, there would still be some interest in examining the conceptions of law formulated by those who practise it.[3] To put it as its crudest: even if all lawyers were regarded as charlatans there would be some interest in exposing the mechanisms by which they operated and sustained their trade. As there are good reasons for maintaining that there is more to the legal enterprise than cultural manipulation it follows that there is even better ground for exposing lawyers' reasons for action that mere exposure. Although the lawyer's perspective on law will only be a partial one its centrality and importance is self-evident.

This essay addresses the following question: what lessons can legal theory learn from a study of the history of the development of legal systems? Incidentally it is hoped to throw some light on the parallel question of what assistance to legal history contemporary legal theory can provide. Neither of these questions is a regular one: legal historians and legal theorists in the main occupy different intellectual territories and eschew, where they do not affect to despise, each other's endeavours. Historians study facts where philosophers study theories and each is impatient of the seeming irrelevance of the other's preoccupations. Where is the use of knowing what was once, but is no longer and will never be again, the case - even supposing, what most historians consistently doubt, that what did happen might be known with any finality? But what, equally, can be usefully learned from speculation about the theoretic underpinnings of the present legal system when it is obvious to all that, despite radical disagreements amongst the practitioners of legal theory, the actual operation of the law continues unaffected? This is not the place to attempt a refutation of these scepticisms: it is sufficient to note that since both are open to such charges the legal historian and the legal theorist would do better to join in refutation of such misplaced pragmatism than to encourage their joint enemies among the sceptics.

Legal history is a term covering a variety of practices: much can be learned of social and economic value from legal records and legal remains. But the mere utilisation of legal sources does not make a legal historian. Legal history is primarily the study of the history of the law as medical history is the study of the history of medicine and ecclesiastical history the study of the history of the church. Studies of hospitals and doctors, and church architecture and ecclesiastical vestments, might properly form part of medical, or ecclesiastical, history but might with equal or greater propriety be classed as institutional, professional, architectural and textile history. In a similar manner many legal historical studies, of the structure of the courts, of the education of the legal profession, are tangential to the main concern of legal history, which is the study of law. The question: what is law? is therefore as critical a one for the legal historian as it is for the legal theorist. That it does not always appear so is a reflection of the degree to which much legal history is about what lawyers do rather than about law: just as a modern practitioner can apparently practice without reflecting upon the theoretic bases of his actions so also did his predecessors. As a sociologist may study the lawyer and his doings without forming any wider view of the nature and justification of his activity, so may the historian study the work of his ancestors. But merely to record the doings of lawyers, or of courts, is not to study the law. The law exists, if at all, as a series of theoretical perspectives which exist within lawyers' minds and issue in advice, argument and judgment. To study the law as law one must adopt the peculiar perspective of lawyers. That is, in effect, to adopt a theory - something which many practical lawyers deny doing, even, and indeed most especially, when they are practically engaged. The professional reasons for this are plain enough in most cases: the lawyer wishes to exclude the practical consequences of his theoretical perspective from his judgement of the particular problem upon which he is engaged, just as the physician may wish to be free from the speculative aspects of a treatment whilst he is committed to its application: in each case there is a range of practical professional expertise whose effective deployment may be diminished by too much detachment. In each case, however, it will be as well to remember that there will arise hard cases in which the course to be pursued is not so easily determined, without reflection upon more basic questions going to the heart of the enterprise and the understandings which the practitioner has.

These understandings of lawyers are the stuff of legal theory and one is likely to find as wide a range of possible positions as there are identifiable legal theories. At the extremities there may even be deeply held scepticism amongst those who are, for example, devoted to legal practice for the making of money merely or those who, at the opposite end of the scale, practice for the benefit of the socially disadvantaged. Both positions appear, at least in an historical light, as parasitic, for it is difficult to see how a legal system could be sustained over time if none of its practitioners had a belief in its fundamental functions. This is, of course, no necessary refutation of the sceptical position but merely a reason to turn to others which underpin the actual practices.

Law and lawyers

Weber's is a sociological theory of law.[4] However in the course of his analysis Weber puts forward a number of distinctions and definitions of wider theoretical application. Law for him consisted of norms which were the reflection of probabilities of enforcement by officials. He proposed three ways of conceiving these legal norms. In addition to the sociological perspective which forms the main centre of his attention these are the political perspective, in which the ethical and constitutional assumptions of legal norms to be adopted are assessed against extra-legal criteria, and the dogmatic perspective within which a judge or legal scholar employs the identified norms of the system to arrive at solutions to problems within the system's own set of assumptions. Because his definition of law presupposes a staff of officials, Weber is committed to an account of the source of law which places reliance upon authority to which these officials are accountable. He famously categorised the sources of authority into three 'ideal-types', the traditional, the rational and the charismatic. Traditional authorities are whose status is modelled upon the household with religious overtones linked to ancestral religion. Charismatic authorities draw their dominance from their own outstanding and innate personal character. Rational authority rests upon the acceptance of the importance of enacted rules.

The term *honoratiores* is used by Weber (and more so by his commentators) to refer to the classes of self-regulating experts in law which arose in the early Roman and Common law systems. These are rightly seen as the catalysts for the emergence of the distinctive legal cultures of the two systems. These lawyers were responsible for the creation of two of the most important and influential legal patterns of the Western, and through the West's colonising activities most of the rest of the whole, world. Their authority can be seen in the case of Rome to be derived originally from the individual charismatic characteristics of each jurist, in the case of the Common law from the judges membership of the Royal household. What they each derive from this is an independent legal-rational authority which rapidly becomes independent of the original bases of authority.

What these lawyers thought about their law deserves to count as a central case of understanding law even if they did not articulate their conceptions as theories about law but merely left us to determine their thoughts from their actions. Though he draws much on the Roman, and to a lesser extent, the Common law, traditions Weber seems to have regarded them as exceptional in the degree to which they relied upon rational authority as evidenced by the class of *honoratiores*. The issue then becomes one of Europeo-centrism. From a perspective within one of these two dominant traditions it looks as though it is rest of legal culture which is exceptional.

Rome

If law is an autonomous institution then it is so by virtue of its acceptance as such by its practitioners. It follows that identification of the moment when a discreet caste of lawyers emerges in a particular legal culture is critical for our appreciation of its legal dimension. It would be an arid dispute to deny from a contemporary perspective the terms law and legal to practices which precede this critical historical moment, though in studying such periods and cultures it is important not to ascribe to them understandings which only become possible against a background of autonomy[5] Recent work in the two legal traditions dominant in Western legal culture, Roman law and the English Common law, has helped to determine these critical moments more precisely.

It is generally recognised that the dynamic force which led to the development of the classic Roman law of the first two centuries AD was provided, not by formal state institutions of legislation or adjudication, but by the private work of the jurists, persons of independent means who devoted their careers to the evolution and application, through advice to others, of detailed rules of law.[6] The question of how this informal legal profession created itself and, most significantly, came to distinguish itself from those who merely presented cases as orators for decision by the jury-courts of the Republic, has been most recently studied by Frier.[7] Starting from a close examination of a case (*pro Caecina*) pleaded by the famous Roman orator Cicero, Frier shows how in Cicero's own lifetime, during the last century of the Roman Republic, the nature of legal argument in court came to be modified. Cicero, though knowledgeable about law, was no jurist.[8] His strength lay in advocacy and though capable of demonstrating a technical argument in court was not an adept in the business of developing and distinguishing legal doctrine. Roman law courts were traditionally staffed by lay judges, either sitting alone or in juries of varying sizes. The more general and political the issue the more numerous the judges, the less the opportunity for technical argument and the greater the influence of powerful oratory. Cicero's great triumphs were in criminal matters with political overtones like the trial of the former governor Verres for corruption and maladministration.[9] Even in more mundane matters such as the civil case of debt brought by Roscius the actor against Fannius Cicero is happier with factual rather than legal matter.[10] When the case required it, as in the *pro Caecina*, a land dispute which provides the starting point for Frier's analysis, Cicero did not shy from legal technicalities, though he appears somewhat dismissive and embarrassed at inflicting such details upon the readers of his published speeches.

The Romans themselves attributed the foundations of Roman legal science to the three 'founders of the civil law', M. Junius Brutus, M. Manilius and P. Mucius Scaevola, who lived in the middle of the second century BC. They produced works which discussed legal matters in an analytical and systematic manner and may well have been the first to do so. Their successor, Q. Mucius Scaevola, wrote an account of the civil law in eighteen books, which may have been the first attempt at a comprehensive treatise of Roman law, though we know that it omitted many important topics, not least the law of procedure.[11] The reasons for this change in the pattern of juristic activity are not easy to determine but two factors seem relevant. In the middle of the second century BC an important piece of procedural legislation, the *lex Aebutia*, of which we know little save by inference, introduced a more flexible form of judicial process, involving reliance upon the jurisdictional magistrate's discretion.[12] This magistrate, the praetor, issued in advance of his year of office a schedule of the remedies and procedures that he proposed to follow, founded for the most part upon his own perceptions of current needs. Simultaneously, Rome discovered Greek rhetorical practices and the introduction of these on to the judicial scene produced an environment of uncertainty regarding the form and outcome of legal disputes. The jurists reacted by developing mechanisms to control the praetor's discretionary remedies and oppose the wilder flights of oratory.[13]

Although the emergence of Roman legal culture had its origins in the mid-second century, it is central to Frier's claims that it was not until the last decades of the Roman Republic that this development came to fruition. The last centuries of the Republic are characterised by a succession of political and social disputes by various groups for dominance in the Roman state: amongst these struggles for power were that between the old established senatorial class, the aristocracy and traditional political class of the Republic, and the emerging strength of the *equites*, whose prestige was derived from commerce, an activity barred to senators, was the most bitter.[14] Frier argues that it was the latter group who perceived the advantages for their class in developing a rule-based legal system which could secure their rights against the latent power of the senatorial class and who therefore, during the last century of the Republic, took up the task of particularising the position secured by the founders of the civil law in earlier generations. The plausibility of this claim is reinforced by the fact that, although the 'founders' were drawn from the ranks of the senatorial class their successors were, and remain, less prominent individuals whose main characteristic seems to have been their membership of the lower-ranking class of the *equites* and the concentration of their activity on cautelary and casuistic matters to the exclusion of the political. That the late Republican jurists' ideology was therefore developed in the course of a class social struggle in no way diminished its vitality. With the total transformation of Roman politics that accompanied the triumph of Augustus in the civil wars in which the Republic ended, the way was clear for their successors to establish the jurists' perception of law as the dominant tradition subordinate but in no way subservient to the new political regime.

It is among the merits of Frier's account that he does not suppose that once the jurists had begun to develop their own perception and methodology of law, all other perceptions and methods of handling legal issues conformed. In Cicero's own day there remained those sceptical of the jurists' claims.[15] The jurists' view of law was merely one among many throughout the Roman period. To take but one example, in the empire the function of lawgiver and judge was intrinsic to many emperors' perception of their role. They had a view of law which had little or no connexion with that of the jurists. They were not unaware of the jurists' views, since they sat in judgement with their assistance and heard their opinions cited in argument but not being themselves trained as jurists and conscious of the quasi-legislative effect of their pronouncements the emperors' must have held, when they reflected upon it at all, a much simpler view of the nature of law.[16] Nevertheless, the overwhelming importance of the Roman law tradition, both in the ancient world and beyond it, depends as much, if not more so, upon the fact that it did develop this internal juristic self-appreciation as upon the political factors which assisted its rise.[17] What distinguishes Roman law among the many legal systems of the ancient world and accounts for the survival and continuing influence of its traditions is the strength of the jurists' tradition.

Frier concludes his account of the rise of the jurists with some reflections upon the theoretical dimensions of the problem. His reliance upon contemporary socio-legal theories has earned him some stern criticism.[18] The expansion of commercial relations in the last century of the Republic went hand in hand with an expansion of the numbers of those in the *equites* class, many of them citizens newly-enfranchised in the wake of the settlement of the Social War between Rome and her Italian allies at the beginning of the century. The potential expansion in legal disputes was, Frier argues, restrained to an extent by the development of legal rules at the hands of the jurists, though he admits that on the absence of evidence this is little other than a possible hypothesis. The uniformity in understandings about law that this movement produced in turn served to enhance the reputation of the jurists, who were thus seen to control the operation of the system and to confirm their conception of the law as a dominant one within the Roman world.

Was this conception essentially a positivist one? A characteristic the Roman jurist shared with his modern Common law counterpart was a lively distrust of general theory. There is little direct evidence, therefore, of explicit legal theories amongst the jurists and we may rightly conclude that this reflects an actual absence in practice. But the absence of explicit expressions by no means argues an absence of theory and it has already been suggested that the quintessential contribution of the jurists to the Roman legal scene in the last century of the Republic and beyond is a commitment to the autonomy of law and its processes. This commitment is evidenced by the jurists' preference for intrinsic technical arguments over appeals to social or ethical utility and by their influence in progressively legalising the broad ethical standards adumbrated in the praetor's edict.[19] In all this they were adopting a very strong position on autonomy and one which, it has already been suggested, goes a long way to account for the inner strength of the Roman system which enabled it to survive and dominant competing traditions.

England

Despite persistent questions about the extent and importance of borrowings from the Anglo-Saxon period, the Norman Conquest in 1066 is generally taken to mark a *terminus post quem* for the development of the Common law. Most commonly, it is assumed that the earliest beginnings of the new system are to found in the legislative and administrative innovations of the reign of Henry II (1154-1189) particularly after the year 1166. Although individual judges and administrators can be identified from the end of the twelfth century, a distinctive legal profession, exclusively devoted to the elaboration and determination of legal issues, did not emerge until the mid-thirteenth century. Official records of judicial proceedings exist from the early 1200's and administrative records reflecting judicial business from even earlier but reports of the arguments used in court not until after the middle of the century.[20] Only with the appearance of reports of argument is it possible to identify the existence of a professional legal culture: it is of course possible that materials which have not survived would carry the emergence of a legal profession back a little further. The treatise known as Bracton, now thought to be the product of a lawyer-administrator writing no later than the 1230's, suggests that it might be possible to antedate the emergence of legal professionals by a generation or so.[21] There exist embryonic 'reports' in the form of treatises which probably belong to the period around 1260 whose instructional nature suggests that the practice of a more or less formal education in law was already being established in mid-century.[22]

The essential purpose and context for the emergence of law reporting in England was education. The reports of argument in court were a mechanism for the preservation and communication of the skills required by the early Common law pleaders to those anxious to emulate their success. They were not initially or primarily intended to assist courts in the determination of difficult issues. Typically a Year Book report records the form and structure of arguments used by pleaders to achieve success but fails to reflect the court's final determination of the case. Such a state of affairs, near incomprehensible from the perspective of the modern Common law with its commitment to the precedential value of the substance of prior decisions, reflects the dominance of procedural questions at this period. Like as not any final determination of the parties' problem would be in the hands of a jury, whose verdict was questionable only with great difficulty, or of some other less rational method of proof. What consumed the interest of the lawyers was the manner of presentation of the issue, the question which really divided the parties, to the jury, and to this end they concentrated on narrowing their pleadings. Law, the professional subject of the lawyers' and the courts' interest, consisted almost exclusively of procedural questions relating to this process.

It is an apparent paradox that one of the best accounts of the early Common law to have appeared in recent years is to be found in a book with the seemingly limiting title *The Origins of the English Legal Profession*.[23] The resolution of the paradox, it will be apparent from the foregoing, lies in the close connexion between the emergence of a legal profession and the development of an autonomous conception of law as its special field of operation. As earlier in Rome, the firm establishment of such a professional consensus by the middle of the thirteenth century did not necessarily oust competing conceptions of law such as those informing the work of the King's Council in its legislative activity towards the end of the century. The professional consensus is reflected in the practice of the pleaders recorded in the early reports and in the actual uses to which these reports were put to initiate others into the lawyers' world.[24] This professional conception of law is a distinguishing feature of the Common law.

To explain the chronology of the English development Brand points to the changes undergone by the litigation process in the century after 1166. Amongst the achievements of Henry II's reign was the establishment of national courts, both central and peripatetic, in the form of the King's courts of Exchequer and the General Eyre. These courts were staffed by an appointed judiciary charged with responsibility for decision and not merely presiding over a body of court-keepers or suitors; they sat regularly and were in session for substantial periods.[25] The control of litigation in these royal courts depended upon the issue of a royal writ to commence proceedings. Originally a matter of favour, increasing numbers of writs became writs of course (*de cursu*) during the twelfth century. A substantial body of learning grew up around the propriety of using writs for particular types of claim and this information became the first that intending lawyers had to absorb at the beginning of their professional training for generations thereafter. An appropriate writ selected and issued with the parties summoned to court on the strength of it there might be opportunities to delay for the defendant and occasion to employ mesne, that is interlocutory, process by the plaintiff. Once both were in court the plaintiff would have to make a formal claim, his count, and the defendant his defence or plea. Increasingly thereafter defendants would put in exceptions in an attempt to secure dismissal of the case by the judgement of the court rather than submitting the whole to a decision on the facts by the jury or some other mode of proof.[26] All these factors led to the appearance of a specialised body of those who could advise on and determine such particularised matters. By creating a demand for lawyers the English legal system in the century after 1166 also created the circumstances in which a new and distinctive conception of law could arise.

As in ancient Rome the crucial development in the history of the English Common law was the emergence of a specialist class of lawyers. As in Rome, albeit in a very different social setting, changes in procedure and court practice provided a catalyst. The practice of Roman and Common lawyers was importantly different: Roman jurists were not primarily forensic specialists and from an early date they seem to have concentrated on substantive rather than procedural questions. Nevertheless they shared a common conception of the specialist nature of their business.

Doubts

The lesson which legal history can teach legal theory which is argued for here is that the emergence of a profession of specialised legal practitioners is of critical importance to the rise of theoretical understandings of law. Other conceptions of law undoubtedly exist but central must be that conception held by those whose professed occupation lies in the manipulation and determination of issues which are avowedly legal in nature. Both Roman and Common law traditions have been characterised by concepts of law which emphasize its autonomous nature and it should be no surprise to find positivistic theories which support such conceptions dominant in both traditions.

Scepticism of the model of autonomy is not hard to seek. Particularly outside the law it is probably the most common position. So much of the lawyer's craft is either technical or seemingly self-serving (what Bentham called lawyers' sinister interests) that doubts about lawyers are easily transformed into doubts about law itself. The claim of legal history to a distinct character separate from social history is a claim about the importance of what lawyers have thought. Similarly, the distinctive claim of legal theory to be other than a puzzle to be taken down from the cupboard on rainy days (in Ronald Dworkin's memorable phrase), is a claim about the importance of what contemporary lawyers think.[27] Even the sceptic must concede that lawyers *think*, however mistakenly, and that those thoughts influence their actions and the outcomes of legal problems. Legal history would therefore have a point even if its field of study were to be ranked alongside astrology as an aberrant condition of the human mind.

In a recent study of the institution of the mixed jury, Constable suggests that overly positivistic assumptions by legal historians have led them to distort their account of this and, by extension, other institutions of the Common law which, if properly, non-positivistically understood, would give a different picture of law.[28] Constable's study is flawed as legal history[29] and weak on legal theory[30] but the question she raises deserves to be considered. Is it the case that legal historians have unwittingly distorted their accounts of the development of law by relying on too positivistic an understanding of law?

Let us take Constable's issue. The mixed jury, called from the sixteenth century *de medietate linguae*, existed between the middle of the fourteenth century and its abolition in 1870. Its essence was a jury chosen half of native Englishmen and half from the foreign community. Apparently first created by statute in 1353 for the benefit of alien merchants it had, by the time of its abolition, developed into an institution available to all foreigners.[31]

Constable maintains that legal historians have failed in their accounts of the mixed jury to perceive the institution for what it is: a product of a system of personal laws. 'Personal laws', where these truly exist, are systems of rules which apply to parties in court by virtue not of the jurisdiction of the court but of the personal origin of the parties. The clearest cases of personal law in modern times have been in colonial contexts where the authorities have sought to provide forums for the resolution of ethnic and religious differences. In medieval Europe a significant body of doctrine was created to deal with the difficulties posed by persons moving from one jurisdiction to another. It is arguable whether 'personal law' is a satisfactory term to comprehend this phenomenon which is, in effect, the precursor of modern conflicts of law rules.[32] Constable maintains further, and this is the theoretical point which is of interest in this context, that legal historians have been blinded to this explanation of the mixed jury by their legal positivism. Pointing to evidence for the mixed composition of inquests and proofs in the period before 1353. Constable argues that historians have been too ready to accept a model of rules which supposes that origins are to be found in authoritative law creation: the 1353 Act created the mixed jury as surely as the 1870 Act abolished it.

Constable herself is willing to accept the force of the latter remark - she does not suppose that the mixed jury continues to have any existence in English law since 1870. It is difficult to see why modelling a conception of contemporary Common law around a positive approach to statutory provision should be permissible, whereas doing so for the earlier history of the legal system is to fall into methodological error. Of course, adopting a positive approach to modern law does not exhaust the possibilities: there are many sociological and political features of the operation of a modern legal system which remain obscure on this basis. But it equally follows that the fruitfulness of anthropological or political investigations into the past does not preclude a more legalistic, positivistic, interpretation. Indeed, if one is to explain the thoughts and actions of lawyers in earlier times it is unavoidable.

Constable comes near at one point to the real explanation of the mixed jury. She acknowledges that the distinction between fact and law is maintainable for the early common law, but claims that a different sense of *fact* has to be employed, comprising actions rather than circumstances. Whilst this is not improbable, Constable fails to make the further and more telling point, following Milsom, that a different sense of *law* is in play, comprising procedural rather than substantive rules.[33] Since in the case of denizens much that would today be perceived as positive law and subject to legal argument was decided without further recourse by the jury and since such a decision would require a knowledge of practice and custom as well as circumstances, it becomes perfectly obvious and not at all puzzling that in cases involving aliens, whose practices, customs and circumstances were presumptively different, it was both just and necessary to involve fellow aliens in the jury process.

Constable is careful to acknowledge that the lawyer's positivistic theory of law is a possible conception. She claims, wrongly, that the institution of the mixed jury cannot be properly understood in such a perspective and that accordingly past historians are to be blamed for having adopted an inappropriate scheme within which to place it. It follows from acceptance of the opposite position, that the standard account of the mixed jury is a perfectly sound and comprehensible one, that the adoption by legal historians of a legal positivistic framework is wholly appropriate for certain types of enquiry. If the essence of law is what lawyers think as reflected in their practices then an appropriately *legal* understanding of the mixed jury must take this perspective as its foundation.

Conclusion

The greatest English legal historian, F.W. Maitland, was initially trained as a philosopher: in his later life, however, he paid little attention to legal theory. In his day the historical school of Maine had almost triumphed over the positivism of Austin. Maitland had little regard for Maine's projections which he regarded as poorly founded in the facts of legal history: but this did not lead him to embrace Austin. Maitland is famed for his ability to guess cautiously at matters and understandings for which in his day evidence was yet lacking. His caution in matters theoretical follows this pattern. His noted ability to get inside the minds of the lawyers whose deeds and thoughts he recorded inevitably led him to prize law's autonomy. But Maitland was far too good an historian to suppose that the law was circumscribed by the lawyer's mind and his consciousness of its interaction with, and effects upon, the social realities led him equally to doubt Austin's flat picture. He truly observed that ' the notion of law does not include of necessity the existence of a distinct profession of lawyers' but went on 'There can not well be a science of law without such a profession...'.[34] The ideas about law which such professionals have will tend to the positivistic and legal theorists who ignore such conceptions risk seriously misrepresenting thenature of law.

There are varieties of legal history and there are varieties of conceptions of law. To the historian of institutions or the lawyer sceptical about the nature of law, legal history may seem equally to compass community practices, gender biasses in litigation, frequencies and forms of court sittings and so on. These matters are of undoubted importance. But if there be a distinctive legal history - as opposed to a history of things casually labelled legal - then that history is an intellectual history and is concerned with the ways lawyers think. It follows that there is, as Hart claimed, a pre-legal state in which insufficient differentiation has occurred for it to be at all plausible to apply techniques of legal analysis. In such communities people will have a sense of customary practices and may well articulate these as rules to be followed. Again, such communities deserve to be studied, especially where, as in the case of ancient Greece or contemporary China, they achieve cultural sophistication without seemingly feeling any lack of a conception of law in a Hartian sense. But legal histories of such communities will differ markedly from those within the Western (i.e. Roman or Common law) traditions precisely because the communities involved do not easily differentiate their law from other social practices.

The bias of this essay, appropriate in a volume devoted to legal theory, has been to show what lessons legal history can teach legal theorists but before closing I should like briefly to sketch an answer to the second of the questions with which I started: what can legal historians learn from contemporary legal theory? The autonomy of the law might be thought to be under threat from those rightly concerned to integrate legal theory with legal practice. But support has emerged from an unlikely source. In his now classic exposition of Natural law thinking, Finnis demonstrates the importance of holding together simultaneously the notions that law is a product of immanent logic as well as of terrestrial judgement.[35] The study of law thus becomes not just the record of specialist intelligence, let alone esoteric and incomprehensible dogma, but rather a precious expression of man's understanding of his own humanity. The inevitable failings of the legal system, which form so many of the footnotes to legal history, are among the understandable products of a fallen humanity. More importantly, the teleological, sometimes even triumphalist, drift of classic legal history becomes at least comprehensible, though no less distorting historically, as a reflection of man's progress towards perfection. This may not place Law among the transcendental virtues but such a broad vision of the role of law accords to legal historians a rightful role in the study, not merely of lawyers, but of mankind in general.

NOTES

1 Oxford (1980) 21.

2 Most famously H.L.A. Hart, *The Concept of Law*, Oxford, 1961, pp. 111, 198; second edition, Oxford, 1994, but also Raz, *Practical Reason and Norms*, London, 1975, p. 148.

3 Finnis, *Natural Law and Natural Rights*; Dworkin, *Taking Rights Seriously*, London 1977.

4 Max Weber's main ideas about law are contained in chapter vii of his *Wirtschaft und Gesellschaft*, 4th edn, Tübingen, 1956 (ET ed. G. Roth and C. Wittich, *Economy and Society: An Outline of Interpretive Sociology*, New York, 1968 where the same chapter appears as chapter 8). An English edition of this same chapter as it appeared in the 1925 edition of the original is separately published as *Max Weber on Law in Economy and Society*, ed. M. Rheinstein, Cambridge, Mass., 1954. A useful modern account of his theories is Kronman, *Max Weber*, London, 1983, to which the present account is indebted.

5 See on ancient Greece, Todd, *The Shape of Athenian Law*, Cambridge, 1994; Foxhall, & Lewis, *Greek Law in its Political Setting: Justifications not Justice*, Oxford, 1996, Introduction.

6 Works on the sources of Roman law in general and the jurists in particular are legion. In addition to the work by Frier cited in the next note see, for a general account, Jolowicz & Nicholas, *Historical Introduction to the study Roman Law*, 3rd edn, Cambridge, 1972, pp. 86ff and, with more detail, Wieacker, *Römische Privatrechtsgeschichte*, I, Munich, 1988, pp.519ff.

7 Frier, *The Rise of the Roman Jurists*, Princeton, 1985.

8 A famous anecdote of Cicero's contemporary, the lawyer Aquilius Gallus, tells how the latter, approached by a client with a factual problem replied 'Nihil hoc ad jus: ad Ciceronem' (There's no law in this: it's one for Cicero). The apparently dismissive attitude towards his friend's legal abilities disguises

the frank admission that when it came to a question of convincing a court on the facts Cicero had no equal. Our source is Cicero himself: *Topica* 12.51.

9 Cicero, *In Verrem I & II.*

10 It has recently been argued that Cicero's argument for the defence in the *Pro Roscio comoedo* shows that the law of debt (*mutuum*) was significantly less developed at this period as compared to the later classical institution, depending more on general considerations of a sort designed to appeal to a lay juror than technical issues associated with a legal analysis of the problem, an argument which goes to support Frier's general thesis of the chronology of legal development: Birks, 'The case for Fannius', unpublished seminar paper, Institute of Classical Studies, London, 1993.

11 Pomponius, *Enchiridion*, preserved in part as D.1.2.2 (Justinian's Digest, Book I, title 2 fragment 2.)

12 Gaius, *Institutes*, 4.30. The dating of the *lex Aebutia* itself is not however without problem and, as noted, we have no direct knowledge of its contents.

13 Frier, *Rise*, 157-8.

14 The temporary resolution of the struggle at the hands of the senatorial Sulla in 82-81 BC occasioned the death of over a thousand *equites*: cf. Nicolet, *L' Ordre Equestre à l'Epoque Républicaine*, Paris, 1966-1974, i, 116ff.

15 His opponent the orator Piso for one: *Caec.* 79. Even if one supposes that Piso adopted this argument merely for the purposes of his client's case it remains that such an argument critical of jurists could be plausibly advanced at this period. See generally Nörr, *Rechtskritik in der Römischen Antike*, Munich, 1973.

16 A failure to perceive that there can be many competing conceptions of law at any one time lies at the root of the disagreement between ancient historians and legal historians over the extent of the emperor's legal role: compare, for example, Millar, *The Emperor in the Roman World*, 2nd edn, London, 1992, ch.v and p. 649 with Honoré, *Emperors and Lawyers*, 2nd edn, Oxford, 1994, Preface and ch.1.

17 See, most recently, Ibbetson and Lewis, 'The Roman law tradition' in Lewis and Ibbetson, *The Roman Law Tradition*, Cambridge, 1994, 1.

18 See, for example, the review by Birks in 7 *O.J.L.S.* (1987) 444.

19 Both points are made by Frier, *Rise*, 191-3, relying upon earlier authors.

20 Only a few scattered Year Book type reports are yet in print earlier than the 1290's but Dr Brand is about to publish the earliest reports commencing in 1268 in two forthcoming volumes of the Selden Society's publications. For the present see the discussion of these materials in Brand, 'The Beginnings of English Law Reporting', in *Law Reporting in England*, ed. Stebbings, London & Rio Grande, 1995, 1.

21 The date of Bracton's text is a long controverted matter. The traditional ascription to the eponymous author known to have been active as a judge into the 1260's has been seriously doubted in recent years: see edd. Woodbine and Thorne, *Bracton*, Cambridge, Mass., 1968-77, iii, Introduction (by Thorne) and Barton, 'The Mystery of Bracton' (1993) 14(3) *Journal of Legal History* 1. The most recent contribution to the debate, by Dr Brand, is forthcoming in the proceedings of the *Pollock & Maitland Symposium* held in Cambridge in July 1995 to be edited by John Hudson.

22 See on these treatises, Baker, 'Records, Reports and the Origin of Case-Law in England' in ed. Baker, *Judicial Records, Law Reports and the Growth of Case Law*, Berlin, 1989, 15.

23 By Brand, Oxford and Cambridge (Mass.), 1992.

24 'A substantial minority of pre-1290 reports have at some point ... a *casus* (a statement of facts relevant to the case) which is most likely to have been the work of a teacher trying to explain the case to his students': Brand, 'Beginnings', at 7. Such *casus* are a regular feature of contemporary civilian (i.e. Roman) teaching literature.

25 See for this, Brand, *Origins*, 15-17.

26 See Brand, *Origins*, 33ff. in much greater detail.

27 Dworkin, *Taking Rights Seriously*, 14.

28 Constable, *The Law of the Other: The Mixed Jury and Changing Conceptions of Citizenship, Law, and Knowledge*, Chicago, 1994.

29 Aside from the merely trivial but disturbing errors perpetrated e.g. the invention of an Australian state of Virginia whose courts cite an apparently puzzling Victoria statute, (Constable, *Law of the Other*, pp. 141-2) there is a persistent failure to read through her sources and especially to appreciate that, in using only

material that happens to have been printed and in citing early sources in English translation, she runs a great risk of distorting the history of the very institution she wishes to rescue from oblivion.

30 One quotation may suffice: 'Hart and Austin thus differ only in that Hart's officials accept their own rules as binding on themselves, while Austin's sovereign need not': Constable, *Law of the Other*, p.73.

31 The 1353 Statute of the Staple, 27 Edw.III st.2, was concerned with the establishment in England of emporia (staples) for foreign trade. The initial jurisdictional provision was for trials in cases involving foreign merchants heard in staple courts. In 1354 28 Edw. III c.13 extended the principle to courts outside the staple. The mixed jury was abolished by the Naturalization Act 1870, 33 Vict. c.14.

32 Constable fails to see that the notion of a 'personal law' is closely tied to the difficulties of assimilating different written rules. As Hooker judiciously observes: ' ... the common law is itself a customary law in the sense that it remains uncodified and uncertain. A proposition is not law until it is "found" by the judge. The relationship between English law and a local law is not usually one of conflict but of the incorporation of indigenous principles into the great body of the common law', *Legal Pluralism*, Oxford, 1975, p. 466.

33 See, for example, Milsom 'Law and Fact in Legal Development' *University of Toronto Law Journal* 17 (1967) 1 reprinted in Milsom, *Studies in the History of the Common Law*, London & Rio Grande, 1985, 171.

34 Pollock and Maitland, *The History of English Law*, second edition, Cambridge, 1898, I, p. xcvii.

35 Finnis, *Natural Law and Natural Rights*.

6 OBSERVATIONS ON METHOD IN LEGAL THEORY AND LINGUISTICS

PHILIP ROBERTS

'Legal positivism' is a term which has been used to describe a family of different theories of law. It would be difficult and probably unhelpful to attempt to provide an all-encompassing definition which purports to set out just what it is that reveals that a theorist subscribes to legal positivism. In view of the divergences between theories which attract the same label, the best that can be done is to provide some prominent family features, or point out some key distinctions between positivist theories and theories of a different stripe.

Among the five features of family resemblance for legal positivism that Hart set out,[1] the contention that there is no necessary connection between law and morality has been regarded as the tenet which at the very least positivists must hold to. As someone who has been an interpreter of Hart's work, and has written in the positivist tradition, MacCormick has characterised legal positivism

> '... minimally as insisting on the genuine distinction between description of a legal system as it is and normative evaluation of the law which is thus described.'[2]

Clearly, then, the way in which a legal theory assigns a place to the concept of normativity is crucial in revealing that theory's position in jurisprudential debate. This point is illustrated in the introduction to *Taking Rights Seriously*,[3] where Dworkin draws a useful distinction between the 'ruling theory' of law - which has a quite separate descriptive component (legal positivism) and normative component (utilitarianism) - and a 'general theory' of law in which there is interdependence between the conceptual and normative parts.

Commentary on legal theory has sometimes employed the technique of drawing upon certain concepts from the discipline of modern theoretical linguistics, which, in its relatively rapid development, has been seen as a rich source of theoretical constructs to be used for the study of rule-governed human activity. This paper explores two such theoretical devices: the concept of deep structure as used to explicate Kelsen's pure theory of law, and the further Chomskian distinction between competence and performance, originally introduced as an analogy by Rawls, but since taken up in studies of ethics and rationality.

The discussion of these concepts in the present context, allows some metatheoretical conclusions to be drawn about the role and methodology of legal theory. From these, it may be suggested that a 'deep structure' approach to law of the sort advocated by one version of legal positivism amounts to too modest a project to satisfy our intuitive demands as to the scope of legal theory. More importantly perhaps, discussion of the second analogy drawn from linguistics, the competence-performance distinction, suggests that there is room for a post-positivist theory of adjudication which allows for a degree of normativity to enter into an account of competence appropriate to judicial reasoning.

The paper is set out as follows. The next part provides an extremely brief summary of some of the highlights of the Chomskian revolution in linguistics. Following that, the attribution of a 'deep structure' approach to Kelsen is discussed. The final part places positivism and general theories of law in the context of a competence theory of adjudication.

The Chomskian revolution in linguistics

A number of writers in different fields have sought to exploit or criticise analogies with linguistic theory. The fields in question include ethics[4] and the study of everyday reasoning.[5] Although such writers allude to a linguistics analogy and provide appropriate references to the Chomskian paradigm, it is often not clear just what it is that has been so remarkable about developments in modern linguistics. In other words, imported terminology is sometimes used without the necessary explanation of the conceptual background from which it arises. Since this paper makes use of concepts from linguistics, the purpose here is to give a brief outline of the new age in linguistics which was ushered in by Chomsky's work.

In 1957 Chomsky began to publish work which was to revolutionise the discipline of theoretical linguistics.[6] In fact, it would not be going too far to say that his contributions have made the study of language a different discipline from what it was. This means that modern linguists have different concerns and aims from their predecessors.

Pre-Chomskian linguistics, which we may crudely label 'structuralist' or even 'Bloomfieldian,'[7] concerned itself with the classification of certain aspects of utterances. It was characterised by its rigorous and scientific approach to language, and was guided by the then prevalent behaviourist approach to the study of human activity. Such an emphasis on discovering linguistic structures meant, of course, that 'structuralism' was a purely descriptive discipline. In other words, structuralists were concerned to describe and classify the languages they studied, rather than formulate a school-book which taught the correct way to speak or write those languages. As will be seen, Chomskian linguistics does not produce pedagogical grammars, but it does aim to provide a genuinely explanatory theory of language rather than a merely descriptive theory. Whereas the 'structuralist' approach may be appropriate for the practical concerns of the field linguist, the abstractions of Chomskian linguistics more explicitly allow for an interdisciplinary theory of language. Katz and Bever describe the shift in theory as involving:

> '... the shift from a conception of grammar as cataloguing the data of a corpus to a conception of grammar as explicating the internalised rules underlying the speaker's ability to produce and understand sentences.'[8]

To understand Chomskian linguistics in any further detail, certain terminology needs to be introduced. Briefly, modern linguistic method now aims to formulate a grammar for a particular language, which models the linguistic competence of the native speaker of that language. Here, 'grammar' (or more fully, as we shall see, 'generative grammar') is a term of art referring to a way of systematically describing a fluent speaker's linguistic abilities. As mentioned, it should not be confused with the traditional grammars which schoolchildren (used to) learn. When linguists construct grammars from linguistic data, they produce technical specifications of language or linguistic ability, rather than a few handy rules of thumb. The acknowledgement that such grammars purport to be models of rule-governed linguistic ability - and Chomsky adheres to an innatist hypothesis regarding the 'language faculty' - makes the link with psychology and cognate disciplines.

The initial brief definition of linguistic method given above also referred to 'competence'. As should be clear from the foregoing, this term is not used in an evaluative sense in Chomsky's theory of language. It does not make sense for the purposes of his theory to say that one native speaker is more competent than another. Instead, competence is the term used to describe a speaker's unconscious knowledge of his own language. Since knowledge of a language is actually knowledge of the grammar of that language, it would be unrealistic to suppose that even the most sophisticated adult speaker could reproduce a Chomskian grammar in response to an enquiry about why he responds to sentences in a certain way. This hypothesis that native speakers have an unconscious knowledge of the grammar of their own language is often expressed by saying that grammars are 'psychologically real'.

Such competence is manifested in a speaker's ability to comprehend and utter syntactically well-formed sentences (sentences being the basic unit of study for syntactic theory). There are two important phenomena in connection with this which need to be captured by a linguistic theory. First, speakers are able to produce and process sentences which they have never come across before ('novel utterances'). Second, on many occasions sentences are produced which do not seem to be perfectly formed grammatically and yet are understood.

The first of these phenomena is evidence that, although language is a rule-governed activity, it is also a creative one. In other words, we cannot be supposed to acquire and use language simply by the habitual repetition of past utterances. In fact, the rules of Chomsky's hypothesised internalised grammar are such that people are able to produce novel sentences which are grammatical.

The competence which is claimed for native speakers of the language is therefore characterised by a grammar - composed of rules of sentence formation, interpretation, and pronunciation -which is said to *generate* all and only the well-formed sentences of that language. To refer to the grammar constructed by linguists as a 'generative grammar' borrows from the terminology of mathematics but the idea is tractable in the present context. The grammar must only generate the set of well-formed sentences of the language but as Chomsky points out, this set is infinite (hence language can truly be called a creative activity). The hypothesised psychologically real grammar is what allows a speaker to be able to produce an infinite set of novel utterances based on his finite linguistic experiences. In other words, what linguists have referred to as the 'projection problem' of language is surmountable.

Chomsky's primary concern has been to characterise syntactic (rather than semantic or phonological) competence and to this end a complex theory which has undergone a number of incarnations has grown up. In view of this complexity, only the very briefest description of the theory can be given.

Chomsky proposed that the grammar be a *transformational* grammar. This has been shown to be an economical, yet powerful generative device. The basic idea of the model provides that, syntactically, sentences have two levels of representation: a deep (or underlying) structure and a surface structure. The former is a representation of information about sentences of the language which is operated upon by rules called transformations which convert the deep structures into surface structures. In this way, 'surface' sentences which are structurally related can be generated from the same deep or underlying structure: an example of this is the conversion of active into passive sentences. Examples of structural ambiguity in surface forms - such as the sentence, 'Flying planes can be dangerous' - can also be disambiguated, accounted for by positing a level of distinct deep structures.

The second phenomenon of linguistic ability mentioned above concerned utterances which seemed to be understood and yet were imperfectly formed. This second feature focuses on the important linguistic distinction between competence and performance and raises the question of what it means to say that a grammar should characterise a native speaker's 'intuitions' about the well-formedness of sentences.

It has already been explained that the grammar constructed by the linguist is a model of a native speaker's linguistic competence. This knowledge is to be distinguished from the ways in which people actually use language in practice. The latter is described as 'performance'. Performance errors - sometimes due to fatigue or loss of concentration - mean that the corpus of utterances which the linguist takes as his data will not immediately reveal a speaker's competence. The sentences (if they are sentences) will often be imperfectly formed. Although ungrammatical (a competence concept), they may be acceptable (performance concept) to the native speaker. Nevertheless, it is the linguist's task to characterise competence. The characterisation should capture the native speaker's *intuitions* about the well-formedness and structure of sentences. In other words, it should accord with the judgements of grammaticality that a native speaker would make. It is from acceptability judgements that a speaker makes that the linguist attempts to account for the intuitions of speakers about their own language.

As a final point, Chomsky proposed that a grammar should satisfy certain criteria of adequacy. In ascending order, these are observational, descriptive and explanatory adequacy. The first just means that the grammar correctly predicts well-formed sentences of the language. Descriptive adequacy means that, as well as correct prediction, the grammar provides structural descriptions which capture speaker intuitions. In addition to this, explanatory adequacy requires that the grammar be constrained to the extent that it represents a cognitively plausible model of how speakers acquire and process their language. It is this final criterion of adequacy to which a grammar must aspire.

Although the above outline of the Chomskian model of language has of necessity been brief, it has been possible to set out two important linguistic concepts which jurists have sought to employ when theorising about law. In the remaining two parts of the paper, deep structure and the competence-performance distinction may now be respectively considered in the contexts of Kelsen's positivism and theories of adjudication.

'Deep structure' approach in Kelsen's theory of law

When students first encounter Kelsen's work they often react in one of two ways. The first is disbelief and bewilderment, followed by a vow to themselves that, although they might attend the lectures, it is most unlikely that they will attempt a question on Kelsen when it comes to the examination. After all, it is so abstract and difficult that time would be better spent working on more user-friendly aspects of the syllabus. In any case, they reason, Kelsen's work seems to lose sight of the very discipline that they chose to study.

The second reaction also involves an initial bewilderment, but it is followed by curiosity and then a sort of academic addiction. Those who undergo this process find that they have a sense that, whatever Kelsen is saying, it has the resonances of something really important. If only they could figure out just what it is that he is saying (unfortunately the commentaries do not seem to help as much as they have in other parts of the course). The addiction grows because, as the student keeps on reading and thinking, slightly more of this seemingly important theory is tantalisingly revealed.

For present purposes we can only sympathise with those who suffer from the first reaction. The reasons behind the second reaction are surely connected, not only with the relative obscurity of some of Kelsen's terminology, but also with the contention which pervades Kelsen's work that there is something 'special' or unique about law. It is not just that law is another discipline with its own set of problems and terminology, but that law, and hence any theorising about law, involves one in a different kind of mental activity, by its very nature.

Perhaps what it is that provokes interest in Kelsen's approach is its intention to remain pure itself while at the same time addressing itself to a patently impure subject matter.[9] As Raz puts it,

> 'Legal science, says Kelsen, studies the law as a normative system but without committing itself to its normativity.'[10]

Clearly, the interested student thinks, there must be something very clever going on if normativity is a central concept within Kelsen's theoretical endeavours, yet his theory remains austere. To use Raz's terminology once more, Kelsen, unlike other legal positivists, does not take the easy way out that adhering to a 'reductive semantic theory' of legal statements would afford - e.g. they are not reduced to non-normative, descriptive statements about commands - but embraces the normativity of legal statements and recognises it as the object of proper legal theorising. So one of the questions which the Kelsen student first asks is, 'How does he do that?'

In response to this question about how Kelsen is able to adhere to an austerely pure theory, an important part of the answer lies in understanding the distinctions used to make sense of 'legal statements' as theoretical subject-matter. These in turn have been explained by drawing upon the Chomskian concepts of deep (or underlying) structure and surface structure.[11]

It is essential in understanding Kelsen's theorising to keep theory (or more properly, for Kelsen, science) distinct from theoretical subject-matter. This is a straightforward enough distinction for disciplines such as the natural sciences. A geologist is hardly going to confuse the scientific propositions which issue from his scientific theory with the rocks he is studying. The situation in the case of law is different, however, and allows for the possibility of complication. Linguistic entities cannot be struck with a chisel. Kelsen's legal scientist must not confuse the statements which issue from his legal theory (or legal-scientific activity) with the subject matter of the theory (his 'corpus of data'), i.e. the norms which constitute the legal system. Kelsen sets out the task of legal science as follows:

> 'It is the task of the science of law to represent the law of a community, i.e. the material produced by the legal authority in the law-making procedure, in the form of statements to the effect that 'if such and such conditions are fulfilled, then such and such a sanction shall follow.' These statements, by means of which the science of law represents law, must not be confused with the norms created by the law-making authorities. It is

preferable not to call these statements norms, but legal rules.'[12]

The representational task set by the science of law (and upon which we will concentrate) is actually made possible by the epistemological role played by the *Grundnorm* (basic norm) in Kelsen's theory. It is the 'presupposition' of the latter which is essential to our being able to understand law as a normative system.[13]

The above crucial distinction - between *Normen* (norms) and *Rechtssätze* (rules of law) - is liable to confuse in at least two ways. First, the fact that both are linguistic in nature means that the unwary student could find himself inadvertently referring or using one when the other is intended. Although this is the case, Verengo does point out that norms could be represented in a non-linguistic way: he gives the example of red and green traffic lights.[14] For our purposes, however, this is an interesting exception which serves to demarcate norms from rules of law.

The second possible cause of confusion is that, not only are both types of entity linguistic, but for Kelsen both norms and rules of law can be subsumed under the general heading 'normative statements'. This is the case because each can be construed as an ought-statement, and indeed both may have the same syntactic representation.[15] Because of this there may be an almost overwhelming temptation to use them interchangeably.

The way out of all of this is to return to the basic distinction between theory and data and allow that, as always, the task of a theory is to refer to, describe or 'be about' its subject-matter. *Normen* and *Rechtssätze* may look syntactically identical, but whereas the former retains a thorough-going normativity by virtue of the presence of 'ought', the latter is distinguished by a different sort of 'oughtness', a descriptive or referential oughtness. It is all very well saying this in explanation, but as it is pointed out:

> 'I would agree, without much further ado, that it is not clear, *prima facie*, that a normative statement (and *Rechtssätze* are normative statements for Kelsen) might be understood as a pure description of a norm. To describe, in principle, is to enunciate a property or a set of characteristics that the object or fact described has.'[16]

One of the ways, Vernengo suggests, of understanding what Kelsen is getting at is to invoke one of the Chomskian linguistic concepts which were discussed earlier. The confusions arise, it is proposed, because we are easily fooled in present circumstances by statements which exhibit the same grammatical 'surface structure'. What is important is that although norms and rules of law may have the same syntactic surface structure, they will have different deep structures. At this underlying level, it is supposed, the two sorts of statement differ in the semantic, pragmatic and other non-syntactic information that they possess. The student of jurisprudence or the legal scientist must, it seems, avoid the possible confusion inherent in surface forms of words and work at the level of deep structure.

For this particular employment of the deep/surface structure distinction (which does not seem to make full use of the explanatory potential of Chomsky's original formulation), the point can be made in more homely, less theory-bound way. It is common practice in the ordinary use of language to utilise the same string of words to perform different functions. The same sentence can be used in such-and-such a way (e.g. to order someone to do something, or to commend someone for having done something), or it can merely be mentioned without committing the speaker to the force of the sentence (e.g. in reporting what someone has said, or in parsing a sentence when teaching an English class). Philosophers have made much of the use/mention distinction and, in written language quotation marks can be used to display or mention words which are not themselves used.[17]

While Vernengo has made one use of the deep/surface structure distinction to distinguish between the prescriptive and descriptive roles of norms and rules of law, the Chomskian separation has more commonly been used elsewhere in a slightly different way to explain the Kelsenian approach to the norms making up the legal order.[18] Here, deep structure is invoked in the context of Kelsen's claim that legal norms, addressed to officials, stipulate sanctions to be applied. The idea here is that, rather than interpret Kelsen as saying that practitioners and editors of legal texts should rewrite what they say to take account of this much lengthier full-blown representation of legal norms, the form of words stipulating sanctions is to be construed as a 'deep structure' underlying the law (presumably any representation of this deep structure will be a 'rule of law in the descriptive sense' rather than a norm itself). The task of the legal scientist, then, seems at least to involve rendering rather misleading surface structures into their underlying structures. Once again, the theorist or legal scientist is conceived of as interpreting his corpus of data at the level of deep structure.

Whichever use is made of the deep/surface structure device, it seems that the legal scientist is working at an abstract level of description below the usual way in which legal norms manifest themselves and, as such, his task is one of representation. Kelsen's concern with the underlying structure of law was mirrored by developments in logic which allowed for a growing interest in the provision of logical analyses for normative discourse.[19] It has been said that the main intention of the classical pure theory of law was to 'provide a logical analysis of law based on a logic of norm-sentences,'[20] although as Kelsen points out the use and development of logic is not an end in itself but is a means for the determination of the concept of law.[21] The interest in constructing deontic logics has persisted, especially with the growth of a computational paradigm in which to work but as some have conceded disappointingly little progress has been made in this field.[22]

By invoking an underlying abstract structure that law is claimed to have and by making his concerns representational in this way, Kelsen's approach seems strikingly modern. This, after all, is just the strategy that analytic philosophy has adopted in recent years. Philosophy, as practised in the Anglo-American tradition, began its preoccupation with language at the beginning of the century, but it was in the years after the second world war that language took on a new status within philosophical discourse as a principal study of the discipline.

In fact, although the topic of language has remained high on the analytical agenda since the war, the role that it has played has changed considerably. In the post-war period the intellectual trend was for linguistic philosophy, closely associated with work emanating from Oxford and inspired by Wittgenstein's later work on language. Writers like J.L. Austin, Gilbert Ryle and, in the field of jurisprudence H.L.A. Hart, characterised their approach to traditional philosophical problems by paying close attention to the language in which such problems had been articulated. Linguistic analysis seemed to promise a way of addressing putative problems by regarding them as linguistic puzzles. In other words, linguistic philosophy was seen as a way of doing philosophy in general, not as a branch of philosophy. In a sense, it was 'philosophy by doing linguistics'.

In more recent times, linguistic philosophy as a method has faded in popularity. One branch of analytic philosophy has, however, grown in importance as developments in logic have taken place and the potential for interdisciplinary work has been recognised. This branch is the philosophy of language, and has benefited from contributions from Quine, Davidson,

Dummett and others. In contrast with linguistic philosophy, which was itself a philosophical movement, this department of philosophy could be described as 'linguistics by doing philosophy', since it uses techniques from logic and other disciplines to study the conceptual resources of natural language.

Recent philosophy of language has been strongly influenced by the work of Donald Davidson.[23] Although arguably a system-building philosopher, Davidson has initiated a 'programme' of attempting to provide 'logical forms' for specific parts of natural language. Rendering sentences into logical forms, in this case, means trying to capture the structural semantic features of those sentences (e.g. the characteristic entailments available from such sentences) by translating them into the austere framework of first-order predicate logic with its attendant Tarskian truth theory. This is a difficult process, because standard first-order logic is of limited expressive power. To bring the logical form close to the power of 'surface structure' of the natural language sentence often means augmenting the logic with a richer ontology than the standard logic usually allows for.[24] This method is in itself, however, a useful discipline for the student of language and the analytic philosopher to adopt since it forces them to think seriously about just which concepts underlie the use of natural language (sometimes referred to as 'natural language metaphysics'). Davidson outlines the method in 'The Method of Truth in Metaphysics':[25]

> 'In sharing a language, in whatever sense this is required for communication, we share a picture of the world that must, in its large features be true. It follows that in making manifest the large features of our language, we make manifest the large features of reality. One way of pursuing metaphysics is therefore to study the general structure of our language.'[26]

In pursuing the 'Davidsonian programme', he and others have chosen problematic linguistic constructions to attempt to render into logical forms. Examples include adverbial modification,[27] and reported speech.[28] The aim of the programme seems to be to provide logical forms in an austere canonical idiom for as many fragments of the jigsaw of natural language as possible.

Not surprisingly, by operating at this abstract level of sentence analysis, Davidson has become associated with Chomsky's generative grammar: the logical forms, with their explicit, disambiguated information about structure and truth-conditional semantics, would seem to be ideal candidates for deep structures.[29] It should be noted, however, that although Davidson sometimes alludes to the Chomskian paradigm in this way, their projects are not identical. As Evnine remarks in a commentary on Davidson, although both account for actual linguistic forms in terms of abstract, underlying structures, whereas Chomsky intends to describe real, implicit speaker knowledge, Davidson is carrying out an 'explicit, theoretical reconstruction of language mastery'.[30]

With the task of the legal scientist to construct 'deep structures' from positive laws by making use of general logic of norms,[31] the Kelsenian approach so construed begins to resemble the Davidsonian programme for building up a jigsaw of underlying logical forms for a large corpus of data. Clearly, the similarities between the aims should not be overemphasised, but in general terms the approaches are comparable.[32]

If it is possible to view the enterprise demanded by the classical pure theory in this programmatic way, there is surely something unsatisfactory about the task that has been set. As has been mentioned already, it is by no means clear that progress in establishing a logic of norms has been as fruitful as was originally anticipated when work began on it. Deontic logic is simply not as dependable and domesticated as the familiar first-order predicate logic. The reliability of the latter as a canonical idiom has allowed the Davidsonian programme to advance into problem areas having set out a methodology and a rationale. The Kelsenian enterprise is one which has been preoccupied with the definition and justification of method, but which has faltered in its representational task.

In addition, and more importantly, the whole Kelsenian task begins to look less like the product of a legal theory and more like a branch of the philosophy of language, albeit a distinctive and peculiar one. More properly perhaps (in view of the role of the *Grundnorm* and the Kantianism of the classical pure theory), the danger is that it takes on the appearance of a legal analogue of the philosophy of language. The point here is that we expect more of our theoretical work about law than an assemblage of analyses. We expect more because, to go back to the earlier remarks about the uniqueness of law, there seems to be something special about the discipline which makes it more than a branch of philosophical analysis or a species of applied metaphysics. By defining and then approaching the task in a particular way, Kelsen's theory seems to have preserved but kept out of reach what many would regard the essentially legal elements such as normativity and the forces of public accountability, expectation and entitlement (such forces as may give rise, when acting on the judiciary, to a 'doctrine of political responsibility').[33]

Kelsen's account of the pure theory - his particularly austere brand of legal positivism - precludes the possibility of interdisciplinarity. This is in contrast to the modern view of representational work in different disciplines which often aims at co-operation between them. An obvious example is the emergence of cognitive science as the product of theoretical initiatives in psychology, philosophy, linguistics and computing. The strict autonomy of the Pure Theory as a version of positivism, despite its attractive and exciting characterisation of the uniqueness of law, means that its implementation can only aim at modest results. Once the excitement of understanding what the theory is has died down, the task set by it for the legal scientist can seem rather mundane.

Positivism and general theories of law in the context of a competence theory of adjudication

Of course, legal positivism as a view of law is not to be equated with the pure theory, although, as an extreme member of a family of theories, it is instructive to examine it. To return to the hypothetical but pragmatic student of jurisprudence once more, it is probable that he will have taken the view early on that, to understand any aspect of modern legal positivism, an investment of time and thought will have to made us Hart's immense contribution to jurisprudence. This will entail the student becoming familiar with the ground-breaking work in and associated with Hart's *The Concept of Law.*[34]

Any study of Hart benefits from an examination of the post-war intellectual currents which influenced his inaugural lecture as professor of jurisprudence[35] and of which there is evidence in *The Concept of Law*. The school of analytic philosophy labelled 'linguistic philosophy' has already been mentioned, along with the influential figures of the time and, indeed, the title of Hart's book provides an obvious echo to Ryle's most famous work, *The Concept of Mind*.

As well as being influenced by the linguistic method in philosophy (and hence ultimately by Wittgenstein's animadversions on language), Hart's original 1954 contribution,[36] on definitions as explanations in sentential contexts also alludes to another point referred to in our preceding discussion: words are to be explained in terms of the truth-conditional semantics of the sentences in which they occur. To this semantic component of the analysis of legal statements is to be added a pragmatic component detailing their typical uses. In this way we must work at proper explanation, rather than try to provide dictionary entries for words which are thought to be essentially 'legal'.

Raz, in the course of an essay on Kelsen,[37] gives a neat explanation of the different roles of these two components. The socio-factual aspect of the 'meaning' of legal statements is accounted for by their truth-conditional analysis whereas the normative aspect is captured by the pragmatic component:

> 'The normative [aspect] is accounted for by an explanation of the illocutionary force of the statements and by the fact that they express not only the speaker's beliefs but also his practical attitude, his willingness to be guided by certain standards.'[38]

As Raz has pointed out,[39] Hart shared with Kelsen an anti-reductivist stance: neither is prepared to eliminate law's normativity by reducing it to something factual and allegedly more primitive like the concept of a command. In other words, normativity is an irreducible element of law and legal discourse. Kelsen and Hart proposed different versions of the response to this irreducibility thesis. The former seems to have preserved the normative element of legal statements in a display cabinet for scientific scrutiny. Hart according to Raz's explanation, accounts for it in terms of a pragmatic component of legal discourse which is itself a species of normative language:

> 'The employment of the method of linguistic analysis led [Hart] to regard the use of normative language as the key to understanding the normativity of law.'[40]

Notably, then, Hart tried to explain rather than eliminatively reduce the normativity of law. However, as Raz also points out, although he concentrated at first on linguistic analysis, Hart moved from the study of language itself to substantial theory-building. This in turn paved the way for positivism to address issues in adjudication.[41]

The picture of law presented by Hart's theory is now well-known. It is one which, in its general outline, formed the target of Dworkin's attack on positivism in his influential essay, 'The Model of Rules I'.[42] Briefly, for Hart a legal system is composed of two sorts of rule: duty-imposing (or primary) and power-conferring (or secondary), which find a unity in being validated by a master secondary rule that it itself accepted from the 'internal point of view' by officials of the system.[43] For our purposes the intuitively appealing picture described by Hart represents law as a core body of settled rules surrounded by a penumbral region in which there are no settled rules. In the latter region cases - termed by Dworkin, 'hard cases' - are decided on the basis of the operation of judicial discretion. In other words, there seems, on this model of law, to be an important frontier at which rules could be said to run out. Following the resolution of a hard case, which results in a rule of law becoming settled, the frontier is extended further into what was the penumbral region. Of course there is no real question of the growth of, say, English law resulting in the total elimination of judicial discretion - uncertainty in law, like indeterminacy in language, is not like that (of course, Hart's account drew specifically on that species of linguistic uncertainty termed by Waismann 'open texture').

The point about the general feature of Hart's model referred to above, which has focused the concern of many critics of legal positivism, is that it produces an adjudicative dichotomy. Cases falling within the core are dealt with by judicial application of the law; those cases falling outside the settled region are the subject of judicial creativity. Clearly, then, at least two important concepts are bound to prompt further inquiry: the idea of a rule, and the concept of discretion.

The first of these is given a famously lucid and penetrating treatment by Hart in *The Concept of Law*. Indeed, the working out of what a rule is - albeit from a point of view which itself reveals the influence of Wittgenstein and of Oxford philosophy on Hart's theorising - is one of the single most important themes running through the book.

The second concept, judicial discretion, and the way in which this is related to application of the law is the point at which Dworkin's criticism of positivism begin its first assault. It is also the issue over which at least one extension of Hartian positivism, set out by Neil MacCormick and seemingly approved by Hart, mounts a defence.

The actual substance and evaluation of these particular debates will not concern us here. For the present purposes what is noteworthy is that at issue for a theory of law conceived of in these terms is the nature of adjudication. The traditional problem for legal positivism of what law is (which has been interpreted as demanding a descriptive or conceptual theory) begins to open out into a broader question about the nature of judicial reasoning.

Of course, questions about adjudication and the judicial role do not suddenly arise with Hart's brand of legal positivism. For example, although Kelsen distinguished the function of the judge from that of the jurist (but as it is now generally recognised the prescriptive/descriptive distinction was not always readily appreciated by those judges who were prepared to draw upon Kelsen's work, Harris offers a different interpretation of the Kelsenian enterprise.[44] This provides that judges do take part in the activity of legal science 'whose necessary objective is the systematic exposition of some corpus of legislative materials'.[45]

The point for us, however, is that Hart's theory seems to allow for the possibility, even though positivism must still regard the proper object of study as law as it is, that the nature of adjudication can be a central concern. In this context, MacCormick has proposed a number of extensions to Hart's theory, some of which at least seem to have drawn approval from Hart. MacCormick has suggested that principles - a form of non-rule standard, which in Dworkin's theory, set out individual rights and which, he argues, are left out of the positivist account of law[46] - can be accommodated within a Hartian concept of law alongside rules.[47] This extended model can be viewed within the context of a theory of legal reasoning, a summary of which is given:

> 'In summary, the theory presented in this book [*Legal Reasoning and Legal Theory*] that the judicial duty to do justice according to law is a highly complex one. It is a duty to give only such decisions as can be justified by a good justificatory argument.'[48]

In clear rule-governed cases this is fairly straightforward, with deductive argument possible, but in 'penumbral' cases the justification of decisions must look beyond rules to principles. Furthermore, there are certain tests of argumentation identified by MacCormick which are required for such a decision to be justified, namely consequentialist arguments, coherence arguments and arguments of consistency. In brief, then, MacCormick places an extended core-penumbra theory of law within the wider context of judicial argumentation or a theory of legal reasoning:

> 'A satisfactory theory of legal reasoning indeed requires, and is required by, a satisfactory theory of law.'[49]

We might say that, in the course of setting out a theory of law, MacCormick has given an account of 'judicial best practice'. Because the extended positivist theory now explicitly includes principles, which for MacCormick are vaguer than 'cut and dried' rules, judges will have a strong discretion (*contra* Dworkin) in using them to decide hard cases. Finally, even though MacCormick's account makes room for the inclusion of principles, he points out that this does not undermine the positivist thesis that the description of a legal system is to be separated from its evaluation.[50]

Signs of the nature of adjudication becoming a central issue for a theory of law may provoke words of caution from Raz, who accuses Dworkin of 'developing a theory of law out of a theory of adjudication':

> 'In fact he developed a theory of adjudication and regards it willy-nilly and without further argument as a theory of law.'[51]

As we have seen, however, it is not so much an area of concern invented by Dworkin, as a natural result in the shift of attention to adjudication resulting from Hart's positivist theory of law.

Despite Raz's misgivings, Dworkin's work represents the most important modern response to legal positivism. It would be taking an unnecessarily narrow view of his contributions to date, however, simply to regard the proposals that he has set out as merely an extended rebuttal of central positivist doctrines. This is because he is a successful example of theoretical system-builder. In turn, this means that his arguments are of interest to students of ethics, politics and philosophy as well as law. It is clear, though, that, for the purposes of what has been discussed above, Dworkin has constructed what may be termed a thorough-going normative theory of law. He contrasts this with the usual way that the 'ruling theory' (sometimes given the general label of 'positivism') of law is strictly separated into a purely descriptive (legal positivism, strictly construed) and a normative (e.g. utilitarianism) component in the introduction to *Taking Rights Seriously*:[52]

> 'The critical portions of these essays criticize both parts of the theory and also criticize the assumption that they are independent of one another … A general theory of law must be normative as well as conceptual.'[53]

The proposal that the normative and descriptive parts of a theory are interdependent rather than independent marks a definite break with the ethos of legal positivism. It is no longer going to be enough, for a genuinely unified theory of law, to recognise that law is irreducibly normative but seek to study that normativity as if it were an exhibit on display. Nor, according to Dworkin's approach, will it be enough to set out, as a theory of adjudication, value-neutral guidelines for achieving 'judicial best practice'. Here what is 'special' or unique about law is that by its very nature it demands a theory which is both descriptive and normative. In other words, by theorising about law we cannot help but engage ourselves in normative arguments about what law ought to be like. As Dworkin remarks, by providing that there be a normative component to a unified theory of law means that a wider context of moral and political philosophy will be invoked.

It has been suggested that the gulf between legal positivism and Dworkin's theory of law is so great as to make the two incomparable:

> 'So Dworkin's is, fundamentally, (though with many illuminating moments of description), a normative theory of law, offering guidance to the judge as to his judicial duty; theirs [Hart's and Raz's] is a descriptive theory, offered to historians to enable a discriminating history of legal systems to be written.'[54]

This sort of comment, however, still leaves room for the idea that a break with positivism could be made simply by producing a guide as to how judges should go about deciding hard cases. This need not engage any moral theory in support and could be presented as a theory of legal reasoning; it was what was meant earlier by 'judicial best practice'. Although normative in one sense, it would not qualify as a theory of adjudication for the sort of unified theory of law that Dworkin has in mind.

Distinctions of this sort suggest that, not only is normativity a complex concept, but that theoretical treatment of the concept falls into different types or grades. To borrow from the title of one of Quine's influential works on modality, there seem to be three grades of normative involvement to which theory can be committed (see his 'Three Grades of Modal Involvement', which considers three degrees of the acceptance of the concept of necessity in logic).[55] The first is simply the recognition that the theory's subject-matter contains an irreducibly normative element. This is what led the Kelsenian approach to demand that the legal scientist assemble a corpus of descriptive deep structures; similarly, Hart put forward his early explanation of legal statements containing pragmatic component which set out the illocutionary force of such statements. Clearly this grade of normative involvement treats normativity as an object of study without taking on a normative approach itself.

The second grade of normative involvement means that a theory is put forward which provides a certain sort of guidance to those involved in a rule-governed activity. In a sense, it describes a skill or ability but in order to do so must issue prescriptive statements as well as descriptive ones. This requirement is not immediately obvious and so further explanation is called for.

By way of analogy, we may consider the position of someone who teaches a legal skills-based course. It is currently (and rightly) seen as essential these days for that part of legal education leading to professional qualifications to cover such practice skills as interviewing, drafting, negotiation and advocacy. Each of these must be taught by a method which is quite different from the usual lecture-based courses of academic subjects. It is really not satisfactory, or even possible, simply to try to tell someone or describe to someone what, for example, negotiating is. If one does begin to try to explain things in this way, there will inevitably come a point (probably quite early on in the 'lecture') when the language ceases to be purely descriptive and starts to offer guidance or recommendations: 'if you are preparing to negotiate the terms of this sort of contract, you ought to prepare the ground by ...'

Offering 'how-to' guidance is clearly not the sole or stated aims of theories of adjudication already discussed, but the analogy is intended to show that in a purportedly descriptive project of this type, a grade of normativity is nevertheless involved. A theory of this sort of practical activity thus becomes a descriptive-normative theory.

A different sort of example of the descriptive-normative phenomenon arises in Dworkin's discussion of theories of interpretation in *Law's Empire*.[56] His preliminary discussion, which precedes the full exposition of his theory of law as integrity and allows him to conclude that law is an interpretive concept, invites us to consider various sorts of interpretation - artistic, conversational, scientific and social. He remarks that, despite the differences between them, there could be some common element unifying them all: this 'deep connection among all forms of interpretation'[57] is the so-called 'principle of charity'. This principle was set out by Quine[58] and elaborated on by Davidson[59] in his discussion of 'radical interpretation'. There, we are asked to imagine the task of a field linguist trying to interpret a remote and unknown language from scratch. It is claimed that he must employ a principle of charity to begin to understand the native speakers' responses and remarks: the assumption that this involves is that when the native speakers make assertions (assuming we know when they do make assertions), they do so largely correctly. The preferred theory of interpretation is therefore one which optimises agreement. The principle of charity is supposed to operate for much more homely cases of interpreting what is being said and so, as Quine puts it, although we are usually given to interpret English speakers' words homophonically:

> 'We will construe a neighbour's word heterophonically now and again if thereby we see our way to making his message less absurd.'[60]

Clearly, this is a useful device for Dworkin to allude to since there are clear resonances of it in his proposal that interpretation should make its object the best it can be. For the present purposes the principle of charity is also a useful concept because it is one over which theorists sometimes cannot seem to agree. The point is that it is just not clear whether, in discussing the principle, a *strategy* for interpretation is being suggested or whether (as Davidson would claim) the principle is an indispensable *precondition* for interpretation to take place at all. The former represents a normative use of the principle whereas the latter is conceptual or descriptive of the very possibility of interpretation.

In fact, even when these two roles for the principle of charity have been set out for us it does become difficult to decide just which role fits best into the theory: it is as if the two possible functions of the principle slip in and out focus. Dworkin's theory of interpretation, as instantiated in his theory of law as integrity, seems to exploit this normative-descriptive slippage between roles that the principle is capable of: giving an account of interpretation in the way Dworkin intends, as a practice, will involve both description of what interpretation is and guidance on how to be a successful interpreter.

To return to our taxonomy of normativity, the third grade of normative involvement means that a theory explicitly connects with some form of moral and political argumentation. For a theory of law, this means providing a unified theory of law the normative component of which is 'embedded in a more general political and moral philosophy'.[61] This third grade of normative involvement for a theory is now far too 'impure' for positivists to tolerate, since it means abandonment of the strict separation thesis. Yet, it could be argued that we need to advance to this stage in order to be able to argue that we are putting forward a characteristically legal theory.

Dworkin's legal theory is complemented by (or 'embedded in') a moral and political theory which is liberal and rights-based. In developing such ideas he was a member of a triumvirate of American liberal theorists who became prominent in the 1970's, the other two members of which were Rawls and Nozick. American liberalism of this sort represents a broad political spectrum, and Dworkin's views are hardly compatible with the theory presented by Nozick. There is, however, some degree of harmony and evidence of influence as between Dworkin's work and the theory of justice and accompanying account of moral reasoning set out in Rawls' *A Theory of Justice*[62] and related works.[63]

Rawls' book is a complex work with much detailed argument. The point which is of most interest here, and one which Dworkin has commented on specifically, is Rawls' description of moral reasoning.[64] 'Reflective equilibrium' is the term given to designate this model of reasoning. The equilibrium that is envisaged is the result of an interplay between, and mutual adjustment of our moral judgements and certain abstract principles that we adhere to. The method produces a process of reflective equilibrium, rather than a stable end-state. This is because any stability is liable to be upset by, for example, new cases which lead us to revise our judgements. As Rawls acknowledges, this model of reasoning need not be confined to moral theory,[65] and as will be seen the idea has been taken up by recent writers in other disciplines.

The form of coherence theory that Dworkin uses in setting out his theory of law (whether the version present in the essays of *Taking Rights Seriously* or the interpretive turn taken in *Law's Empire*) seems to owe something to the general description of reflective equilibrium set out by Rawls. Indeed, Raz seems to ascribe the burgeoning popularity of coherence theories in moral philosophy to Rawls' presentation of his methodology.[66] Dworkin's own commentary on the method concludes that there are two possible models of moral reasoning underlying the definition of reflective equilibrium: a 'natural' model and a constructive model. Guest summarises Dworkin's views on each:

> 'Generally, I think Dworkin's view is that Rawls' idea is insufficiently prescriptive and that it needs more bite than its appearance as a successful moral psychology [natural model], one that shows admirably the development of a person's moral beliefs but not clearly why any person should engage in it ... According to the [constructive model], there is a duty upon us to *make the reconciliation*, and to construct the answer.'[67]

In addition to providing reflective equilibrium as a model of moral reasoning, Rawls also introduced an analogy from linguistics. The analogy draws upon the Chomskian notion of competence (and thereby the competence-performance distinction) described earlier.

> 'A useful comparison here is with the problem of describing the sense of grammaticalness that we have for the sentences of our native language. In this case the aim is to characterise the ability to recognise well-formed sentences by formulating clearly expressed principles which make the same discriminations as the native speaker. This is a difficult undertaking which, although still unfinished, is known to require theoretical constructions that far outrun the *ad hoc* precepts of our explicit grammatical knowledge. A similar situation presumably holds in moral philosophy. There is no reason to assume that our sense of justice can be adequately characterised by familiar common sense precepts, or derived from the more obvious learning principles.'[68]

The relationship of the linguistics analogy to reflective equilibrium and its possible extensions beyond moral philosophy have provoked some comment among commentators. Although critical of the use of the analogy, Daniels gives some idea of its purported scope:

> 'Suppose we view a person as having a moral 'sensibility', a competency which should be investigated like other competencies, in particular, syntactic competency. The competency is manifested in the indeterminately large range of moral judgements people feel competent to make about a wide variety of cases, including judgements about the rightness and wrongness of acts, policies, and institutions, as well as about the moral status of agents involved in such acts.'[69]

Along with a notion of 'moral competence', the analogy draws upon other related Chomskian concepts. By characterising a moral competence, a moral version of the linguistics' 'projection problem' discussed earlier could be explained: principles can be cited to explain why people who have encountered only a finite number of moral situations could go on to make an infinite number of judgements. Daniels says that 'with some exercise of fancy'[70] the competence-performance distinction could be drawn for moral theory by analogy with linguistics. This could be said to manifest itself in cases where we find that we must revise our original moral judgements, because we discover that they are now incompatible with other judgements. Daniels describes this possibility for performance error as follows: 'We might then say that our on-line moral processor erred and failed to match our real moral competency.'[71]

Although, as noted above, critics have voiced misgivings about Rawls' use of the analogy in the context of moral philosophy, there does seem to be something appealing about it for the purposes of legal theory. This amenability is perhaps best illustrated if we recall the way that Hartian positivism allowed for a theory of adjudication to gain importance in a theory of law; adjudication, as we noted, really does occupy centre stage once we move, with Dworkin, beyond the bounds of positivist theory. When discussing matters of adjudication a distinction between competence and performance seems a plausible and intuitive one to make. It is not out of place in describing a line of cases, or a series of situations involving legal reasoning, to say of one decision or result that a judge or legal official had erred. This sort of comment need not be one which is made as the result of frustration at a decision which has not gone our way: the point is that considered attributions of legal 'performance error' are routinely made in the course of commentary and of judgements themselves. It is important to note that such attributions arise in the way that they do because common law tradition and technique seems to demand that the such a competence be assumed on the part of judges. In other words, in the same way that a performance error is not some sort of deliberate deviation made to fool a theorist, those judgements which, as Dworkin would put it, have low 'gravitational force' are to be viewed as aberrations which should not be allowed to disturb the common thread of developing law.

Indeed, the whole way in which adjudication and other legal activity is spoken of betrays such an attitude: the assumption of some sort of competence-performance distinction is an endemic feature of legal language. Although rather anecdotal, perhaps one illustration is the rather peculiar way in which judges have been said to 'misdirect themselves'. The idea here is surely that, despite possessing (as all judges must do by definition) 'judicial competence', the judge made a performance error on a particular occasion. In a rather different context this general judicial attitude was displayed by Lord Denning in explaining the way that, by draughtsmen's 'oversight', our legislation could be inconsistent with EC law.[72] In addition, certain large-scale reinterpretations and assessments of bodies of law are drawn up in a way which seems to acknowledge this methodological stance. Perhaps one example of this is the fast developing law of restitution, which seems to regard a long history of cases as manifestations of performance errors which failed to take proper account of Lord Mansfield's dictum in *Moses v. Macferlan*[73] and promulgated the misguided notion of 'quasi-contract'.

If the competence-performance distinction could be articulated in a legal-theoretic context, it would also plausibly bring with it an explanation for an adjudicative analogue of the so-called projection problem. A theory of 'judicial competence' would be designed to accommodate the fact that judges are expected to decide indeterminately many new cases based on the experience of a finite number of previous decisions and precedents. It is important to note that the sort of competence about which we are envisaging the construction of a theory is something which is *expected* of judges. This brings out a feature of judicial competence which is different from the way in which the concept is employed in linguistics (e.g. as an 'innate' faculty). We are entitled to expect from judges that they possess a certain sort of competence (such an expectation could support a 'principle of political responsibility' to which judges are subject), albeit that in certain cases performance errors are made. The attitude that we adopt towards them and, therefore, towards the process of adjudication is thus a *methodological* dualism of competence and performance. As already noted, jurists and judges do seem to talk about adjudication and the development of law as if there is such a dualism: i.e. a background theory of competence against which performance errors are to be explained.

So, unlike the data of linguistic theory, from which a model of linguistic competence is built up, law, by virtue of its traditions, techniques and the accountability of judges, seems to demand some theory of competence which has some sort of normative aspect (due to our entitled expectations noted above). By reconstruing the role of the concept of competence, as we must by virtue of employing it as an explanatory concept in legal theory, it may be possible to avoid the criticisms made of Rawls' application of the linguistics analogy to moral theory.

An early criticism of Rawls' linguistic analogy was made by Hare,[74] who claimed that such an analogy is vitiated since linguistics does not yield substantial conclusions as moral philosophy is supposed to do:

> 'It is quite alright to test a linguistic theory (a grammar) against what people actually say when they are speaking carefully: people's *linguistic* 'intuitions' are indeed authoritative for what is correct in their language ... But the only 'moral' theories that can be checked against people's actual moral judgements are anthropological theories about what, in general, people *think* one ought to do, not moral principles about what one ought to do.'[75]

This point seems a little like Dworkin's criticism of the method of reflective equilibrium viewed as moral psychology, rather than given a prescriptive interpretation. Daniels makes a similar sort of criticism.[76] He bases his evaluation on a distinction between narrow and wide versions of reflective equilibrium. The former is construed as an ordered pair consisting of a set of considered moral judgements and a set of general moral principles that economically systematises them. This form of equilibrium can characterise a task like that of the descriptive linguist's, but stops short of the sort of justificatory or prescriptive task of moral philosophy (which would be rather like prescribing one descriptively adequate grammar in preference to another). What is required, Daniels argues, is a wide sense of reflective equilibrium. This is represented by an ordered triple consisting, not only of the considered moral judgements and moral principles, but also a set of philosophical theories 'invoked or presupposed by the winning arguments for the principles' (i.e. background theories). Each of the sets would be adjusted so as to be compatible with each other. This would fulfil the prescriptive task mentioned earlier.

Wide reflective equilibrium may be the favoured model for purely moral reasoning, but in view of the uniqueness of the judicial role, evidenced by the characteristic way in which legal language reveals certain expectations of judges, there may still be a place for the sort of reconstrued methodological competence-performance distinction described earlier. Another difference between Daniels's case and present concerns is that the moral competence-performance distinction, which is criticised, is set within the context of the revisability of our *own* moral judgements; Daniels asks us to consider:

> '... cases in which we are led to revise moral judgements because they are incompatible with other judgements we hold, contrary to what we had been able to see at first.'[77]

That the moral analogue of the distinction is envisaged as one which enables self-correction of moral judgements is different from the way in which it employed in linguistics, where competence and performance error are attributed by the theorist. The latter use of the distinction is also the most appropriate one in the context of legal theory: there, an attribution of competence could be made based on the data of decided cases.

In a different context from Daniels' discussion, in an important paper on human rationality, Cohen has made explicit and persuasive use of the competence-performance distinction.[78] His thesis is that, despite psychological experiments which reveal that people make systematic errors when confronted with a variety of reasoning tasks (both probabilistic and deductive), it is the case that rationality must be ascribed to ordinary people. The way in which this thesis is supported appeals to the notions of competence, performance and the possibility of 'some malfunctioning of an information-processing mechanism':

> 'In other words, the nature of the problem constrains us to a competence-performance distinction. Our fellow humans have to be attributed a competence for reasoning validly, and this provides the backcloth against which we can study defects in their actual performance.'[79]

In pursuing the 'rationality thesis', which claims that, under the right conditions, people reason in accordance with the norms of rationality,[80] Cohen argues that any *normative* analysis of people's everyday reasoning (i.e. stating how people should reason) must rely on people's intuitions about what constitutes good reasoning. This, Cohen claims, cannot be dodged by an appeal to texts on logic or probability. However, *factual* theories which investigate the norms of everyday reasoning must also draw upon these intuitions.

> 'It follows that for every such normative theory, which determines how it is proper to act or reason, there is room to construct a factual theory that does take intuitions as its subject matter. This factual theory will describe or predict the intuitive judgements that formulate the data for the corresponding normative theory ... It will describe a

competence that normal human beings have ... This factual theory will be just as idealised as the normative theory from which it derives.'[81]

So, the idea is that, where a normative theory of the sort referred to above is developed, it is to be expected that a corresponding theory of competence (not actual performance) can be 'read off' from it. To transfer this model to a legal context, and specifically to theories of adjudication, the 'intuitions' which are referred to by Cohen and others must find their analogue in judgements or decided cases. These data are the basis and evidence which a normative theory of judicial reasoning must rely on: in order to make specific proposals about what adjudication ought to be like, there is no point in theorising in a vacuum, and so reference must be made to cases. According to a methodological legal analogue of the model proposed by Cohen, if a normative theory about how judges should make decisions has been advocated, then a descriptive theory of competence can be constructed to explain the cases. Clearly, the two components of the model are intimately linked and there is a risk of confusion, but they are distinguishable. The closeness of the descriptive-normative link has already been discussed in a rather different way in the context of the role of the principle of charity in interpretation, and it is possible that this may be accounted for by a suitably amended version of Cohen's model.

The question remains whether the normative theory of adjudication envisaged will be a theory which involves second or third grade normativity. The sort of theory of rationality envisaged by Cohen would involve second grade normativity, but there is room for the possibility of a thorough-going normative theory of adjudication which would be 'embedded in' a more general moral and political theory (in the style of Dworkin). This would of course have implications for the theory of competence to be 'read off' the normative theory. It would, however, be possible, by appropriate use of decided cases, to construct a 'general theory' of law that linked a theory of competence with a third grade normative theory.[82]

As a final point, Cohen's 'rationality thesis' has recently been criticised by Stein,[83] who compares that thesis with the possibility of an irrationality thesis (which denies that our competence matches the norms of reasoning). Unless one is of the critical or legal realist school, this question does not arise in the case of judicial reasoning: it is a methodological assumption made to understand and practise common law technique that some form of the rationality thesis holds for judges.

NOTES

1 Hart, H.L.A. *Essays in Jurisprudence and Philosophy*, (1983) O.U.P. 57-58.

2 MacCormick *Legal Reasoning and Legal Theory* (1978) O.U.P. 239-40.

3 Dworkin *Taking Rights Seriously* (1977) Duckworth.

4 Rawls *A Theory of Justice* (1971) O.U.P. and Daniels 'On Some Methods of Ethics and Linguistics' (1980) 37 *Philosophical Studies* 21.

5 Cohen 'Can Human Rationality be Experimentally Demonstrated?' (1981) 4 *Behaviourial and Brain Sciences* 317-70; Stein 'Rationality and Reflective Equilibrium' (1994) 99 *Synthese*, pp. 137-172.

6 See Chomsky *Synctactic Structures* (1957) Mouton, *Aspects of the Theory of Syntax* (1965) MIT Press, *Language and Mind* (1972) Harcourt Brace Jovanovich. For introductions to his work see: Smith and Wilson *Modern Linguistics* (1979) Penguin; Radford *Transformational Syntax* (1981) C.U.P. and *Transformational Grammar* (1988) C.U.P.

7 Bloomfield *Language* (1933) Allen & Unwin.

8 Katz & Bever (1876), 'The Fall and Rise of Empiricism' in Bever, Katz & Langendoen *An Integrated Theory of Linguistic Ability* (1876) New 12.
9 Kelsen *The Pure Theory of Law* (1967) University of California Press.
10 Raz 'The Purity of the Pure Theory' (1981) 138 *Revue Internationale de Philosophie* 451.
11 See, for example, Vernengo 'Kelsen's *Rechtssätze* as Detached Statements' in *Essays on Kelsen* (1986) Tur & Twining. Harris *Legal Philosophies* (1980) Butterworth.
12 Kelsen *General Theory of Law and State* (1946) Harvard U.P.
13 Raz *The Authority of Law* (1979) Oxford U.P. chapter 7 for exposition and criticism.
14 Vernengo *op.cit.* 99.
15 *Ibid.*
16 *Ibid.*
17 See, for example, Quine *Methods of Logic* (1952) Routledge 43.
18 Harris *op.cit.* 64-65
19 von Wright 'Deontic Logic' (1951) 60, *Mind.*
20 Weinberger 'Logic and the Pure Theory of Law' in Tur & Twining *op.cit.* 189.
21 Klectasky, Marcic & Schambeck (eds.) *Die Wiener Rechtstheoretische Schule Vol.I* (1968) Vienna 616-18, reproduced in Weinberger 'Logic and the Pure Theory of Law' in Tur & Twining *op.cit.*
22 See (1991) *Ratio Juris* vol.4 no.3, especially the introduction and von Wright's contribution.
23 See Davidson *Essays on Actions and Events* (1980) Oxford, and *Inquiries into Truth and Understanding* (1984) Oxford.
24 See 'The Logical Form of Action Sentences' (Davidson, 1980, pp. 105-122) for an example: 'adverb-dropping inferences' are accounted for by allowing quantification over events as well as objects.
25 Davidson, 1984, 199-214.
26 Davidson, 1984, 199.
27 Davidson, 105-121.
28 Davidson, 93-108.
29 See Lycan *Logical Form in Natural Language* (1984) M.I.T. for proposals along these lines.
30 Evnine *Donald Davidson* (1991) Polity Press, Cambridge 76.
31 See, for example, Kelsen, 1968, 616.
32 A further similarity to Kelsen is that Davidson's theory has been referred to by Rorty as a 'pure theory' (Rorty *Philosophy and the Mirror of Nature* (1980) Blackwell 259ff. By this it is meant that Davidson's project is pure of traditional epistemological claims about the extent of human knowledge.
33 cf. Dworkin *Taking Rights Seriously*, (1977) Duckworth 87.
34 Hart *The Concept of Law* 2nd ed. (1989) O.U.P.
35 Hart 'Definition and Theory in Jurisprudence' (1954) 70 *Law Quarterly Review* 37.
36 *Ibid.*
37 Raz 'The Purity of the Pure Theory' 138 (1981) *Revue Internationale de Philosophie* 441.
38 *Ibid*, 448.
39 *Ibid*, and Raz 'H.L.A. Hart (1907-1992)' 5 (1993) *Utilitas* 145-56.
40 *Ibid*, 147.
41 Note also Guest's comment that it does not seem sensible to separate the 'concept of law' from the idea of adjudication: Guest *Ronald Dworkin* 158n.3.
42 Dworkin *Taking Rights Seriously* (1977) Duckworth.
43 Hart *The Concept of Law*.
44 See e.g. Udoma C.J. in *Uganda v. Commissioner of Prisons, ex p. Matovu* (1966) E.A. 514. Harris offers a different interpretation of the Kelsenian enterprise: *Law and Legal Science* (1979) O.U.P.
45 *Ibid*, 2.
46 MacCormick's description of principles differs from Dworkin's, but they are still non-rule standards.
47 MacCormick *Legal Reasoning and Legal Theory* (1978) O.U.P. and *H.L.A. Hart* (1982) Edward Arnold.
48 *Ibid*, *Legal Reasoning and Legal Theory* 250.
49 *Legal Reasoning and Legal Theory* 258.
50 *Ibid*, 154 and 239.

51 Raz *Ethics in the Public Domain* (1994) O.U.P. 'The Nature of Law,' 202-203.
52 *Taking Rights Seriously*.
53 *Ibid*, 6.
54 Finnis *Natural Law and Natural Rights* (1980) O.U.P. 21.
55 Quine, W.V. 'Three Grades of Modal Involvement' in Quine *The Ways of Paradox* (1976) Harvard U.P.
56 Dworkin *Law's Empire* (1986) Fontana.
57 *Ibid*, 53.
58 Quine *Word and Object*, (1960) Cambridge, Mass. 58-59.
59 See 'Radical Interpretation' in Davidson (1984) 125-139.
60 Quine *Ontological Relativity and Other Essays* (1969) Columbia U.P. 46.
61 *Taking Rights Seriously*, viii.
62 Rawls *A Theory of Justice* (1971) O.U.P.
63 For an idea of Dworkin's own estimate of his position as a liberal see his contribution in Magee's *Men of Ideas* (1978) 240-60.
64 *Taking Rights Seriously* ch.6.
65 Rawls (1981) 20n.7.
66 Raz *Ethics in the Public Domain* 277.
67 Guest *Ronald Dworkin* 148-49.
68 *A Theory of Justice* 47.
69 Daniels 'On Some Methods of Ethics and Linguistics' 37 (1980) *Philosophical Studies* 21, 22.
70 *Ibid*, 24.
71 *Ibid*, 24.
72 *Macarthy's Ltd v. Smith* [1979] ICR 785 at 789.
73 (1760) 2 Burr 1005, 1012.
74 Hare 'Rawls' Theory of Justice' in Daniels (ed.) *Reading Rawls: Critical Studies of A Theory of Justice* (1975) Blackwell 85.
75 *Ibid*, 86.
76 Daniels, 'On Some Methods of Ethics and Linguistics' 21.
77 Daniels, 24.
78 Cohen 'Can Human Rationality be Experimentally Demonstrated?' 4 (1981) *The Behaviourial and Brain Sciences* 317-70.
79 *Ibid*, 317.
80 Stein 'Rationality and Reflective Equilibrium' 99 (1994) *Synthese* 138.
81 *Ibid*, 321.
82 Although not discussed, a connection could be made between the competence theory proposed and Dworkin's account of the mythical superjudge Hercules to whom real judges should aspire.
83 Stein, 137-72.

7 UTILITARIAN POLITICS AND LEGAL POSITIVISM: the Rejection of Contractarianism in Early Utilitarian Thought

PHILIP SCHOFIELD

In his seminal essay 'Positivism and the Separation of Law and Morals', H.L.A. Hart set out to rescue legal positivism from the critical onslaught to which it had been subjected. He approached the topic 'as part of the history of an idea', and laid stress on the legal theories of two of the 'great Utilitarians', Jeremy Bentham (1748-1832) and John Austin (1790-1859), whose insistence on the need to distinguish law as it is from law as it ought to be 'haunts their work'.[1] Bentham and Austin's purpose in making the distinction between law and morals was 'to enable men to see steadily the precise issues posed by the existence of morally bad laws, and to understand the specific character of the authority of a legal order'. Bentham was aware that the law's commands might be so evil that the question of resistance had to be faced, and it was essential that the issues should not be simplified nor obscured. By confusing law and morals, the two opposite dangers of anarchy or reaction might result: the anarchist would consider himself free to disregard any law which he thought ought not to be law; the reactionary would insist that whatever was law ought to be law.[2] According to Hart, 'the utilitarian tradition of jurisprudence' had combined the insistence on the separation of law and morals with 'two other equally famous but distinct doctrines', namely that an analytical study of legal concepts was vital to an understanding of the nature of law, and that law was essentially a command.[3] On a number of occasions throughout the essay Hart referred to the 'utilitarian distinction' between law and morals,[4] yet he did not explore the relationship between the 'utilitarian tradition of jurisprudence' and the underlying utilitarian theory itself. Hart's concern was not of course with the historical question of why legal positivism has been so closely associated with utilitarianism, but rather to begin to develop his own positivist theory of law. However, the sense in which utilitarianism entailed a commitment to legal positivism was by no means made clear.

More recently G.J Postema, in *Bentham and the Common Law Tradition*, an important reconstruction of Bentham's general theory of law, draws out the theoretical connections between Bentham's utilitarianism and his legal positivism.[5] Postema's central point is that Bentham's distinction between law as it is and law as it ought to be was part of a wider normative theory of law. Bentham's arguments rested on assumptions regarding the proper utilitarian functions of law and the features a legal system must possess to serve these functions adequately: 'His positivist theory of *laws* is one part of a more general theory of *law* which is explicitly grounded on his utilitarian social and political theory.'[6] This social and political theory assigned certain vital functions to law, in particular to create the security of expectations which was constitutive of civilized life itself. This it did by distributing rights and duties amongst the individuals in society, and by enforcing their observance, and thus allowing each individual to pursue his own conception of his well-being in so far as he respected the security of others.[7] Given the utilitarian purposes of law, 'Bentham was attracted to statutory law and the command as paradigms of his conception of law' because 'with the notion of command Bentham could capture the *artificial* character of law', as well as 'the related important idea that law is not just descriptive of social order, but its "cause" - not an expression of some deeper reality, but the *instrument* by which the social relations necessary for human life are constituted and sustained'. This meant that no existing system of law could be protected as sacred, but all law was subject to criticism and reform. The ability to distinguish between the existence, validity, and content of law on the one hand, and the justice, merit, or expediency of the law on the other was an essential condition for criticism and subsequent reform.[8] This was precisely the failing of the theory of the common law, and in particular of William Blackstone's conception of the common law which, according to Bentham, hopelessly confused the statement of facts with the making of moral judgements.[9] It was in this context that Bentham made his famous distinction between expositor and censor, between the explanation of what the law is and the observation of what the law ought to be,[10] and this distinction should not, argues Postema, be generalized beyond it. Indeed, the particular purpose of the distinction is visible when one appreciates Bentham's overall enterprise, which was to develop two of the branches of jurisprudence which he had identified, universal and censorial, the former dealing with the form laws must take, the latter with the content laws ought to have.[11] This did not equate with a distinction between the is and the ought. Both branches were in fact guided by the principle of utility: just as there was an ideal utilitarian content to law, so there was an ideal utilitarian form of law.[12] Postema argues that Bentham's attack on the common law, therefore, was not 'merely a detached philosophical assessment of a jurisprudential theory', but was 'a direct challenge to the ruling political ideology'. Bentham believed that 'the dominant jurisprudential theory was also the ruling political ideology', and 'pathologically opposed to reform'. The theory of the common law 'had to be destroyed and replaced with a radically new conception of law', namely 'statute law and its idealization, the code'.[13] In short, Bentham believed that the conception of society and of law which he offered, and of which the distinction between law as it is and law as it ought to be formed a part, better served the ends for which law was instituted. Legal positivism was one element in a wider normative enterprise.

Postema's account of the connection within Bentham's thought between utilitarianism and legal positivism is illuminating, but it would be inappropriate to assume that the utilitarian commitment to legal positivism was a result of a desire for codification and radical political reform. Postema's account perhaps suffers at this stage in losing sight of Bentham's critique of natural law as opposed to his critique of the common law. Bentham's attack on the common law was directed against the reactionary implications of confusing the distinction between law and morals; but his attack on natural law, and its claim that an immoral law was not valid law, emphasized the opposite danger of anarchy. It was the dangerous political implications of Lockean contract theory, with its talk of natural law and natural rights,[14] which encouraged the development of utilitarianism as predominantly a conservative political theory in the late eighteenth and early nineteenth centuries. This gained immense significance with the outbreak of the French Revolution, and the perceived challenge of radical ideology, encapsulated in the

Declaration of the Rights of Man and the Citizen, to the stability of the British social order.[15] Some thinkers - amongst whom Austin himself might be numbered[16] - combined utilitarianism and legal positivism with a defence of the common law and distinctly conservative politics. Bentham's own 'Anarchical Fallacies', his famous criticism of natural rights, was of course written around 1795 at a particularly threatening period of the struggle with Revolutionary France.[17] Other utilitarian thinkers who criticized the doctrine of natural rights and their political manifestation in the contract theory of government included William Paley (1743-1805), Samuel Cooper (1739-1800), and Richard Hey (1745-1835), all Anglican clergymen, and all associated with the University of Cambridge.[18] Cooper and Hey must have been familiar with Paley's influential *The Principles of Moral and Political Philosophy*,[19] but so were Austin and Bentham.[20] Austin's close reading is testified by the detailed references to it in *The Province of Jurisprudence Determined*,[21] while its appearance was in some measure responsible for Bentham's decision to publish *An Introduction to the Principles of Morals and Legislation* in 1789, almost ten years after it had been first printed.[22] Twenty years later, Bentham subjected Paley's defence of capital punishment, put forward in *Moral and Political Philosophy*, to a detailed critique.[23] Furthermore, it is possible to read Bentham's *An Analysis of the Influence of Natural Religion on the Temporal Happiness of Mankind*, which was edited by George Grote and appeared under the pseudonym of Philip Beauchamp in 1822, as a rebuttal of the system of natural religion developed by Paley, and which underpinned Paley's utilitarianism, even though neither Paley nor anyone else is mentioned by name.[24] There are other scattered references to Paley throughout Bentham's works, usually suggesting that Paley had misunderstood or misused the principle of utility.[25] According to Bentham, Paley had made the same mistake as Blackstone in defending those laws and institutions which existed merely on account of their existing.[26] Bentham took Blackstone's phrase, 'Every thing is now as it should be', made in the context of a discussion of the offence of heresy in his *Commentaries on the Laws of England*,[27] to be characteristic of Blackstone's attitude to the British political system as a whole. Paley likewise belonged to 'the every-thing-is-as-it-should-be school'.[28] As with the people at large, explained Bentham, so with Paley, 'practice is the only proper or intelligible standard of right and wrong: with them as with him and Blackstone, so long as every thing is as it is wont to be, every thing is as it should be'.[29] In a note to himself, Bentham asserted: 'Paley an Utilitarian - a false brother'.[30] Bentham's disagreement with Paley, and with the mainstream of utilitarian thought at the end of the eighteenth century, centred on two issues: firstly, Paley's ultimate appeal to the will of God as the standard of right and wrong, to which the principle of utility was, in Austin's phrase, the 'index'; secondly, Paley's political conservatism. Yet where all these thinkers agreed was in their appeal to the principle of utility as the standard of moral judgement, a rejection of natural law theories, and the associated doctrines of natural rights and the contract theory of government, on account of their anarchical tendencies, and a positivist theory of law, even if, as in the case of Paley, Cooper, and Hey, such a theory was not systematically developed. How, then, were these elements linked?

If Paley was 'the clearest ... representative of the doctrine' of theological utilitarianism,[31] as the tradition of thought which gave utilitarianism a theological basis has become known, then Austin was perhaps its most succinct. In outline, their theories were identical - the duty to promote the greatest happiness originated in the will of God, and was enforced by the fear of punishment and hope of reward in an afterlife. Paley defined obligation as being '*urged by a violent motive resulting from the command of another*'. The motive had to be sufficiently strong, since a slight sanction would not produce a feeling of obligation, and it had to issue from the command of a superior, since the mere offer of a reward would amount to an inducement or persuasion. There was no uniform sense in which the words obligation and obliged were used, 'but, wherever the motive is violent enough, and coupled with the idea of command, authority, law, or the will of a superior, there, I take it, we always reckon ourselves to be *obliged*'. This meant that there could be no obligation without the prospect of gain or loss, since there would not otherwise be a violent motive.

> As we should not be obliged to obey the laws, or the magistrate, unless rewards or punishments, pleasure or pain, some how or other depended upon our obedience; neither could we, without the same reason, be obliged to practise virtue, obey the commands of God, do what is right, or [do] any thing else.

The violent motive upon which moral obligation rested was 'the expectation of being after this life rewarded ... or punished', resulting from the command of God. Man's motive was his own eternal happiness, and the will of God his rule. Therefore, 'the foundation, upon which the whole fabric rests' was the distribution of rewards and punishments in an afterlife.[32]

Since the will of God was man's rule, in order to discover what was his duty, or what he was obliged to do, on any occasion, he had to ascertain what the will of God required. There were two methods of ascertaining the will of God: first, from the revelations contained in Scripture; and second, by studying God's 'designs and disposition from his works, or, as we usually call it, the light of nature'. The evidence drawn from both sources coincided, but as far as the light of nature was concerned, 'The method of coming at the will of God, concerning any action, ... is to enquire into the tendency of the action to promote or diminish the general happiness'. The beneficial tendencies of all the contrivances established in nature, and the fact that nothing was contrived to produce pain and misery, led to the conclusion that God 'wills and wishes the happiness of his creatures', and consequently those actions which promoted that will and wish must be agreeable to him. Hence, 'Whatever is expedient, is right.- It is the utility of any moral rule alone which constitutes the obligation of it.'[33]

Austin's explanation of moral obligation was merely a modified version of that put forward by Paley. His starting point was the idea of a command (not only the key to the science of jurisprudence, but also to the science of morals), since it contained within it the notion of obligation. A command was the expression of a wish that another person should do or forbear from some act, coupled with the power to inflict some evil on that person should he not comply with the wish. A command was distinguished from other expressions of desire, such as a request, by 'the power and the purpose of the party commanding to inflict an evil or pain in case the desire be disregarded'. Without the power to harm, the expression of a wish was not a command. The person commanded was thereby bound or obliged by the command, in other words under a duty to obey it: 'Command and duty are, therefore, correlative terms'. The evil, usually a punishment, which would probably be incurred in the event of disobedience was a sanction. Austin criticized Paley for arguing, in his analysis of obligation, that it was necessary for the motive to compliance to be violent. Whether this meant that the evil was certain, or that it was great in magnitude, was irrelevant in this context. Both these factors might increase the efficacy of the command, but they did not constitute it: instead, 'where there is the smallest chance of incurring the smallest evil, the expression of a wish amounts to a command, and, therefore, imposes a duty'. The sanction might be 'feeble ... but still there *is* a sanction, and, therefore, a duty and a command'.[34]

Moral obligation had its source in the divine laws, which were the commands of God, the sanctions enforcing them consisting of 'the evils, or pains, which we may suffer here or hereafter, by the immediate appointment of God, and as *consequences* of breaking his commandments'. The divine laws were either revealed or unrevealed; there were some duties which could only be known through Revelation, but the rest might be known 'by the light of nature or reason'. The light of nature was in effect the principle of utility: 'the laws of God, which are not revealed or promulged, must be gathered by man from the goodness of God, and from the tendencies of human actions. In other words, the benevolence of God, with the principle of general utility, is our only index or guide to his unrevealed law.' Austin summarized his argument as follows:

> God designs the happiness of all his sentient creatures. Some human actions forward that benevolent purpose, or their tendencies are beneficent or useful. Other human actions are adverse to that purpose, or their tendencies are mischievous or pernicious. The former, as promoting his purpose, God has enjoined. The latter, as opposed to his purpose, God has forbidden.[35]

The divine law was the standard by which positive law and morality were to be judged, and so it was 'an all-important object of the science of ethics ... to determine the nature of the index to the tacit commands of the Deity, or the nature of the signs or proofs through which those commands may be known'.[36] In short, moral obligation rested mediately on the principle of utility and ultimately on the will of God.

Bentham of course differed from Paley and Austin in rejecting the will of God as the basis of his theory of moral obligation, replacing it with a theory of human psychology. The opening passage of *IPML* made this clear:

> Nature has placed mankind under the governance of two sovereign masters, *pain* and *pleasure*. It is for them alone to point out what we ought to do, as well as to determine what we shall do. On the one hand the standard of right and wrong, on the other the chain of causes and effects, are fastened to their throne. They govern us in all we do, in all we say, in all we think: every effort we can make to throw off our subjection, will serve but to demonstrate and confirm it.[37]

The principle of utility had two dimensions, one psychological, the other ethical. The psychological principle explained why a man acted as he did - in order to maximize his own pleasure and minimize his own pain, to promote his own happiness - while the ethical principle set down the standard by which a man's actions were to be judged, in other words pointed out the way in which he ought to act - in order to maximize the pleasure and minimize the pain of all the persons affected by his action, to promote the greatest happiness of the greatest number. There were important occasions when there would be a conflict between the promotion of the individual's happiness and that of the greatest number, in other words an opposition of interests between the two. It was the role of the legislator to discourage those actions which diminished the greatest happiness by annexing punishments to them, and in a more limited sense to encourage those actions which increased it by annexing rewards.[38] In his mature constitutional theory, Bentham recognized that the legislator himself had his own particular or sinister interest to promote, and so means had to be found to identify his interest with that of the community in general.[39]

Having established the principle of utility as the standard by which actions were to be evaluated, Bentham, Paley, and Austin followed similar strategies in their attack on natural law theories, and on the contract theory of government. In the first place, all ethical theories not founded on utility, natural law included, were dismissed as amounting to no more than mere personal likes and dislikes. Hence Bentham reduced notions such as moral sense, common sense, law of nature, and right reason, to 'the principle of sympathy and antipathy'. They were all devices for avoiding an appeal to an external standard, and for setting up in its stead the opinion or sentiment of the person advocating them.[40] Bentham then used this analysis as the basis of his criticism of Blackstone's view of political obligation, namely that men were bound to disobey any human law which contradicted the law of nature and the law of revelation. The tendency of such a doctrine, argued Bentham, would be 'to impel a man, by the force of conscience, to rise up in arms against any law whatever that he happens not to like'. The principle of utility, measuring a law by its mischievousness or inexpediency, was the only standard by which both parties to a dispute could agree to appeal for a decision, and which could be appealed to in respect of any and every government:

> It is *then*, we may say, and not till then, allowable to, if not incumbent on, every man, as well on the score of *duty* as well as of *interest*, to enter into measures of resistance; when, according to the best calculation he is able to make, *the probable mischiefs of resistance* (speaking with respect to the community in general) *appear less to him than the probable mischiefs of submission*. This then is to him, that is to each man in particular, the *juncture for resistance*.

However there was no sign or '*common* signal alike conspicuous and perceptible to all' by which the juncture for resistance could be identified - there was only an 'internal persuasion of a balance of *utility* on the side of resistance' which would 'serve as a particular sign to each particular person'.[41]

Nevertheless, those who defended and those who opposed a law would stand a much better chance of solving their disputes by appeal to the principle of utility - men would either come to an agreement, or would see, after a discussion of the real grounds of dispute, that no agreement was to be hoped for. The discontented party would assess whether it was worth their while to resist, while the chance of reconciliation would be greater in that 'they saw that it might be not a mere affair of passion, but a difference of judgment, and that, for any thing they could know to the contrary, a sincere one, that was the ground of quarrel'. Otherwise one was reduced to mere assertion: '"*I* say, the legislature can*not* do this - *I* say, that it *can*. *I* say, that to do this, *exceeds* the bounds of its *authority* - *I* say, it does *not*."' There was no discussion of the grounds of the dispute, and the disputants 'may go on irritating and perplexing one another for everlasting, without the smallest chance of ever coming to an agreement.'[42]

It was in the context of a similar argument, in part refuting Blackstone's conception of natural law, that Austin made his famous statement concerning the distinction between law and morals:

> The existence of law is one thing; its merit or demerit is another. Whether it be or be not is one enquiry; whether it be or be not conformable to an assumed standard, is a different enquiry. A law, which actually exists, is a law, though we happen to dislike it, or though it vary from the text, by which we regulate our approbation and disapprobation.

This 'truth', though 'single and glaring', had been overlooked by Blackstone, whose view that human laws which conflicted with the divine laws were not binding, in short were not laws, was 'stark nonsense'. The most pernicious laws, and thus most opposed to the will of God, had been and were continually enforced as laws by courts. However, 'this abuse of language is not merely puerile, it is mischievous'; indeed, 'to proclaim generally that all laws which are pernicious or contrary to the will of God are void and not to be tolerated, is to preach anarchy'.

The moral sense, innate practical principles, or conscience, were 'merely convenient cloaks for ignorance or sinister interest'. If a man said that he hated the law, therefore it was not binding and ought to be disobeyed, no one would listen; but by calling his hate his conscience or moral sense, he put the argument in a more plausible form. In contrast, it might be useful to show by appropriate reasons that a law was pernicious, since this might lead to its repeal; and it might also be useful to incite resistance 'by determinate views of *utility*', for resistance was sometimes beneficial.[43]

Although obedience to established government was generally enjoined by God, for without obedience to government there would be little security and little enjoyment, the established government might be oppressive, and the principle of utility might justify resistance.

> Disobedience to an established government, let it be never so bad, is an evil: For the mischiefs inflicted by a bad government are less than the mischiefs of anarchy. So momentous, however, is the difference between a bad and a good government, that, *if it would lead to a good one, resistance* to a bad one would be useful.

The question of resistance had to be decided by assessing the mischief done by the existing government, the probability of replacing it with a better, the evil of resistance itself, and the probability of good should resistance prove successful: 'by comparing these, the elements of their moral calculation,' the members of a political community, 'must solve the question before them to the best of their knowledge and ability'. If both contending parties in a community based their calculations on the principle of utility, even though it 'would afford no certain solution', at least it provided 'an intelligible test', and made possible 'a peaceable compromise of their difference'. On the other hand, such a compromise would not be possible if the parties 'appealed to unmeaning abstractions, or to senseless fictions', such as the rights of man, the sacred rights of sovereigns, unalienable liberties, eternal and immutable justice, original contract or covenant, or the principles of an inviolable constitution. The only recourse where such phrases were bandied about was to weapons.[44]

Having established that theories of the natural law variety did not involve an appeal to an external standard, but were merely a disguise for personal preferences, the same strategy was employed to reject the contractarian theory of government, which relied on natural law or natural rights to provide the substance of the social contract or compact. Bentham's view was that the original compact was either useless or mischievous. The compact was said to be made between the king and the people, the people promising a general obedience to the king, and the king promising to govern the people in a manner that was subservient to their happiness. At one time there had indeed been some use in this fiction, in that the propositions that men were bound by compacts, and that if one party did not perform his part the other party was released from his, were accepted without question, or on the grounds of such phrases as justice, right reason, or the law of nature, 'all which are but so many ways of intimating that a man is firmly persuaded of the truth of this or that moral proposition, though he either thinks he *need not*, or finds he *can't*, tell *why*'. Men found it easier to judge when the king had broken his promise, 'than to decide directly and avowedly on the delicate question, when it was that a King acted so far in *opposition* to the happiness of his people, that it were better no longer to obey him'. But the compact solved nothing, for in order to determine whether the king had broken the compact, the people still had to determine whether he had 'acted so far in *opposition*' to their happiness 'that it were better no longer to obey him.'[45]

The only reason that men ought to keep their promises was that it was for the advantage of society that they should, and to this extent punishment should be employed to make them.

This was the same reason that kings should avoid measures which were detrimental to the happiness of their subjects, and why subjects would obey kings so long as they conducted themselves in this way - and, added Bentham, 'no longer; why they should obey in short *so long as the probable mischiefs of obedience are less than the probable mischiefs of resistance:* why, in a word, taking the whole body together, it is their *duty* to obey, just so long as it is their *interest*, and no longer'. This being the case, there was no need to say that the king promised to govern in such a way, and that the subjects promised to obey so long as he continued to do so. Indeed, there was no duty to observe a promise which would produce mischief. The validity of a promise did not depend merely on its being made, but rather upon its utility - 'The principle which furnishes us with that *reason*, which alone depends not upon any higher reason, but which is itself the sole and all-sufficient reason for every point of practice whatsoever.'[46]

Paley's dismissal of the alternative moral theories to utilitarianism as inadequate, and his condemnation of contractarianism, followed similar lines. In Paley's view, the moral sense, with its variants - innate maxims, natural conscience - did not exist, or at least if it did, it could not be distinguished from prejudices and habits. It could not, therefore, provide a satisfactory basis for moral reasoning: 'it is no safe way of arguing, to assume certain principles as so many dictates, impulses, and instincts of nature, and then draw conclusions from these, as to the rectitude or wrongness of actions, independent of the tendency of such actions, or of any other consideration whatsoever'. Such instincts would merely justify opinions and practices already established, or else provide no restraint at all against evil-doing.[47] Paley identified these same dangers, the unthinking defence of existing institutions and the exclusion of useful change on the one hand, and the setting up of individual caprice without reference to an external standard on the other, as the fundamental problems of the contract theory of government. He rejected Locke's idea of the social compact, on the grounds, first that it was false in fact, for 'if it be not a fact, [it] is *nothing*, [it] can confer no actual authority upon laws or magistrates, nor afford any foundation to rights, which are supposed to be real and existing', and second, on account of its 'leading to dangerous conclusions'. It was impossible to determine what was meant by the fundamentals of a constitution which were supposed to have been settled by a convention meeting prior to the establishment of the legislature, and which the legislature consequently had 'no right to alter, or interfere with': the result of speculating on these fundamentals was 'extremely to embarrass the deliberations of the legislature, and affords a dangerous pretence for disputing the authority of the laws'. Next, if the subject owed obedience to the government on the basis of a compact, it would follow that he ought to submit to the established form of government no matter how absurd or inconvenient it was. Finally, every violation of the compact on the part of the governor released the subject from his allegiance, and dissolved the government - this would endanger the stability of every government, and 'has in fact always supplied the disaffected with a topic of seditious declamation'.

While the idea of the social compact was 'unfounded in its principle, and dangerous in the application', the proper basis for 'the subjects' obligation' was 'THE WILL OF GOD AS COLLECTED FROM EXPEDIENCY'. It was the will of God that human happiness be promoted; civil society was conducive to that end; civil society could not exist unless the interest of the whole were binding upon each member of it; and

> that so long as the interest of the whole society requires it, that is, so long as the established government cannot be resisted or changed without public inconveniency, it is the will of God (which *will* universally determines our duty) that the established

> government be obeyed' - and no longer...
> This principle being admitted, the justice of every particular case of resistance, is reduced to a computation of the quantity of the danger and grievance on the one side, and of the probability and expence of redressing it on the other...
> But who shall judge of this? *Every man for himself.*

There was no common arbitrator in contentions between the sovereign and the subject. Like Bentham and Austin, Paley argued that each person had to decide for himself when the point of resistance had arrived, and that such a decision had to be made by reference to an external standard, the principle of utility.

Paley went on to draw a number of 'inferences' from his substitution of 'public expediency' to compact as the basis for political obligation. One of these in particular revealed that Paley's utilitarianism, and rejection of the contract theory of government, had led him to a form of legal positivism. There were, according to Paley, no immutable laws:

> No usage, law, or authority whatever, is so binding, that it need or ought to be continued, when it may be changed with advantage to the community. The family of the prince, the order of succession, the prerogative of the crown, the form and parts of the legislature, together with the respective powers, office, duration, and mutual dependency of the several parts, are all only so many *laws*, mutable like other laws, whenever expediency requires, either by the ordinary act of the legislature, or if the occasion deserve it, by the interposition of the people.

There might be good reason to think that the laws of the constitution should be treated with greater deference and respect than other laws, but this was merely a product of their greater importance.[48] The point was emphasized in Paley's discussion of the right of government to interfere in religious matters. He dismissed the claim put forward by contractarians that the concerns of religion were excluded from the social compact, and made an unequivocal statement concerning the extent of civil authority:

> The reasoning which deduces the authority of civil government from the will of God, and which collects that will from public expediency alone, binds us to the unreserved conclusion, that the jurisdiction of the magistrate is limited by no consideration but that of general utility: In plainer terms, that whatever be the subject to be regulated, it is lawful for him to interfere, whenever his interference, in its general tendency, appears to be conducive to the common interest. There is nothing in the nature of religion, as such, which exempts it from the authority of the legislator, when the safety or welfare of the community requires his interposition.[49]

The legislator was here constrained as to what he ought to do by the principle of utility, but there were no *a priori* limitations on his legal authority.

The theme re-emerged in Paley's discussion of constitutional law. Given that there were no fundamental laws, no original constitution, by which government itself was bound, all that was meant by a constitution of a country was 'so much of its law, as relates to the designation and form of the legislature; the rights and functions of the several parts of the legislative body; the construction, office, and jurisdiction of courts of justice'. Constitutional law was distinguished from other laws 'only by the particular nature, or superior importance of the subject of which it treats.- Therefore the terms *constitutional* and *unconstitutional*, mean legal and illegal.' Paley pointed out that in England the sources of constitutional law - acts of parliament, decisions of courts of law, and customs - were the same as those of other branches of law. It was important to bear this in mind,

> as some writers upon the subject absurdly confound what is constitutional, with what is expedient; pronouncing forthwith a measure to be unconstitutional, which they adjudge in any respect to be detrimental or dangerous: whilst others again, ascribe a kind of transcendent authority, or mysterious sanctity, to the constitution, as if it were founded in some higher original than that which gives force and obligation to the ordinary laws and statutes of the realm, or were inviolable on any other account than its intrinsic utility. An act of parliament, in England, can never be unconstitutional, in the strict and proper acceptation of the term; in a lower sense it may, viz. when it militates with the spirit, contradicts the analogy, or defeats the provision of other laws, made to regulate the form of government.[50]

Paley's analysis of constitutional law lacked the subtlety of Bentham's,[51] or the logical rigour of Austin's,[52] though as an account of English constitutional practice it was by no means implausible. But like Bentham and Austin, Paley endorsed the view that the acts of a sovereign power could not be described as illegal[53] - in other words that there was no source of law transcendent to that made by the legislature. Paley's position, that there were no *a priori* legal constraints on what legislators might enact as law, but that what they enacted should be judged by the standard of utility, clearly implied a separation of law and morals.

Austin's strategy in rejecting the social contract, or the original covenant as he called it, as the basis of political society followed the lines marked out by Bentham and Paley - first, such a covenant was needless and belief in it likely to prove mischievous; second, it was a fiction; and third, it had no independent value. First, the original covenant was needless in that it had no intrinsic source of authority. If an original covenant had in fact ever been made been made, it would only be legally binding if based on positive law, but such a law could not be binding on the sovereign, otherwise the sovereign would not be sovereign; it would only be religiously binding if based on the divine law; and it would only be morally binding if based on the positive morality of the community. The only case in which an original covenant might generate duties by itself was where the bulk of the subjects believed that it was in virtue of the sovereign's promise to govern to a certain end that the sovereign was bound, and not because of the intrinsic worth of the end itself. The subjects might be persuaded to rebel, not on account of the misrule itself, but on account of the sovereign's breach of promise.[54] However, Austin seemed to believe that it was more likely that the effect of a covenant would be 'positively pernicious'. The members of the community, especially those following the founders, would probably impute to the covenant a worth extrinsic to its intrinsic merits, hence: 'The opinions held in an age comparatively ignorant, concerning the subordinate ends to which the government should rule, would influence, more or less, through the medium of the covenant, the opinions held, concerning those ends, in ages comparatively knowing.'[55] A government would be prevented from legislating wisely and usefully on account of the covenant. The best securities for beneficent government were not promises or oaths, but arose 'from a wide diffusion, through the mass of the subjects, of the soundest political science which the lights of the age could afford.'[56]

Second, the theory of the original covenant was 'not only a fiction, but ... a fiction approaching to an impossibility'. The formation of political society was never preceded by, and could hardly have been preceded by, an original covenant. The very idea of a covenant involved a whole series of elements - promise, acceptance, intention, expectation - which would be virtually incomprehensible to the founders of a political society. Moreover, there was no historical evidence that any political society had been founded on an original covenant. In fact, in most cases 'the constitution of the supreme government has *grown*'. It had not been decided upon all at once, or according to some scheme or plan, but rather 'positive moral rules of successive generations of the community (and, perhaps, positive laws made by its successive sovereigns) have determined the constitution, with more or less of exactness, slowly and unsystematically'. Neither the supreme government, nor the ethical maxims held by the subjects which the sovereign was constrained to observe, were coeval with the foundation of political society, but had 'arisen insensibly since the society was formed.'[57]

Third, Austin pointed out that promises or covenants were not binding simply because they had been made. The proponents of the original covenant seemed to believe that there could be no obligation without a convention, and that once a promise had been given and accepted, the promising party was obliged through the promise, 'let its object and tendency be what they may'. However, there were conventions which were condemned by positive morality, others actively annulled by positive law, and others which conflicted with the law of God: 'Consequently, although the sovereign and subjects were parties to an original covenant, neither the sovereign nor subjects would of necessity be bound by it.'[58]

Like the more famous exponents of utilitarianism, Cooper and Hey rejected the contract theory of government. A more general account of their arguments will clearly reveal the political concerns which motivated them. Cooper, in his *First Principles of Civil and Ecclesiastical Government, Delineated*, written amidst the earliest feelings of unease with the course of the French Revolution, took issue with Lockean contract theory, though the Declaration of the Rights of Man was never far from his thoughts. Much radical argument in the 1790s drew inspiration from Locke's political theory, in particular the view that government had been created in order to protect those natural rights, predicated upon natural freedom and natural equality, which each man possessed, though could not adequately defend, in a state of nature. From this, it followed that governments were legitimate to the extent that they secured the natural rights of man.[59] As far as Cooper was concerned, a state of nature was not characterized by freedom, which he defined in terms of free will, or a power of choosing one thing in preference to another. This freedom was only valuable to the extent that man had power to act in consequence of such a choice, and this power was in fact much less in a state of nature than in a state of society, where government and social distinctions were established. Cooper argued that man was in the first instance born, and of all animals remained for the greatest length of time and to the greatest extent, subject to the authority, will, and control of his parents, and that when he had escaped from this control, he was liable to be thwarted by everyone stronger, more skilful, or more cunning than himself. Indeed even the strongest man was subject to every union of those who were individually weaker.

> And consequently his NATURAL, is for the most part less, than his POLITICAL freedom. For this is the very circumstance, which from the first exercise of reason, upon long continued experience, prompts men to unite together, and willingly to submit to any, even the *most burdensome restraints*, which the very *worst species* of *civil government*, can possibly lay upon them, as far preferable, to those evils, which they endured in that state of *anarchy*, called, a *state of nature*.

Government was not founded upon the natural freedom and natural equality of mankind, and was not therefore to be measured by its approximation to man's imagined freedom and equality in a state of nature.[60]

Just as there was no freedom of any value in a state of nature, neither were there any rights. In order for a right to exist, there had to be a clear and definite rule of action. An action could only be said to be right or wrong if there were some rule of conduct with which to compare it. In a state of nature, there was no authority to lay down such a rule - the idea of an authority contradicted the meaning of 'a state of nature'.[61] Locke had argued that the possession of life and liberty in state of nature gave rise to rights to life and liberty, and that no man had a right over the life or liberty of another, or to hurt him in any respect, unless the other had done some hurt to him. Cooper retorted that possession gave no more rise to rights to life or to liberty in men than it did in animals. In a state of nature men were motivated by their passions or appetites, in other words they acted to acquire a pleasure not before possessed, or to gratify revenge for a loss sustained.[62] In fact, far from government being founded on previously existing rights, the first rights originated in government. The possessions which in a state of nature had had a precarious existence, subject to the appetites, passions, and violence of others, were converted into property and rights by government through the institution of laws.[63]

Cooper was particularly concerned to refute the view that the people enjoyed a natural right of resistance. Men's experience of the evils of a state of nature, the evils which arose when each man acted according to his own will, had led to the establishment of government, and consequently the right of the governor to command and the duty of the governed to obey. To the governor, as their legislator, the governed had entrusted not only the power but the right of judging for them what actions each man was to perform, so as to act consistently with the general good. There was no contract, stipulation, or condition of resistance whatsoever. If the subjects attempted by force to defend themselves from submission to the governor's authority, they could not plead any right, but were justly said to rebel. The governor had a right to subdue them by superior force, for invading his right and every other man's right as a member of the society. Such resistance was an attempt to dissolve and annihilate the government itself, and to involve their fellow subjects in all the anarchy, misery, and confusion which attended a state of nature. If the legislature should enact such laws as even the great majority thought had a direct contrary tendency to the good of the society, they had no right nor legal means of opposing them, except perhaps by a petition of their opinions. Any claim to oppose the laws by force would destroy the whole compact of society, which was that the subjects agreed to submit to the will and judgement of the legislature, and not that the governor's and legislator's will should submit to theirs.[64] In other words, no matter what the content of the law, there was a duty, founded on utility, to obey.

Cooper's position was extremely conservative, placing him firmly in Bentham's 'everything-is-as-it-should-be school'. He was, however, concerned about the revolutionary and anarchical tendencies of natural rights, and used a utilitarian standpoint to claim that submission to government was a duty whatever one's opinion of the merits of a law or legal system. Underlying this concern was the view that the doctrine of natural rights amounted to the raising up of individual will as the standard of judgement. Just as those who relied on their own reason, rather than God's revelation, claimed a dispensation to accept or set aside what part of God's revelation they chose, so they would choose which of the laws of the legislature they would obey, and which they would ignore.[65] However, the governor always enjoyed the right to command, and the governed always had a duty to obey.[66] This was not to say that any tyranny or cruelty in a governor could be justified - it did not follow that universal obedience to government, whatever its constitution, was equally the duty of the governed. But once a group of people in a state, not vested by the constitution in any participation in the power of making or executing the laws, nevertheless took it upon themselves to determine which laws they would obey and which they would not, they assumed a power to which they had no right. They both annihilated the government and reverted into a state of nature. There was no universal right of resistance in the people - rather it was the right of the governor to command, and if he exercised his right or duty to make and execute the laws, and met with resistance, it was the people who arrogated the power to themselves to which they had no right who were the criminals.[67]

Cooper was prepared to modify to some extent the apparently reactionary implications of his position.[68] There were a number of ways in which government might be improved. The rights of subjects might be extended in so far as this was compatible with existing rights, and could be peaceably achieved; new laws might confer a benefit on some which had not been previously enjoyed, or remove an inconvenience previously sustained; and the executive and legislative powers might relinquish a power whose exercise was no longer required by the happiness of society. The governed might petition for alterations, provided they did so with the respect due from subjects to the supreme power. However, they must quietly submit if that power thought differently from them. Under any government, there could not be any lawful appeal from its decision, nor any rightful redress from its errors and prejudices.[69]

Cooper's concern for social stability resulted in a strong emphasis on the obligation to obey the positive law, almost whatever its content. More moderate in tone was Hey's *Happiness and Rights*, published towards the end of 1792, in response to Thomas Paine's *Rights of Man*, which had drawn out the full radical implications of Lockean contract theory. Paine had said that representative government was of such a nature that it quietly decided all matters by majority. Hey was keen to controvert the view that government, and in particular representative government, had a 'nature', as distinct from being constituted by positive stipulations. For Hey, the 'nature' of representative government could only be understood descriptively, that is the nature of representative government was that instead of a large inconvenient number of persons assembling to make laws, a small number was appointed by the large one to act in their stead, the small number being said to represent the large one. If the decision of the majority were to be regarded as binding, this was because such a procedure had been prescribed by the whole of the nation - not because it was in the 'nature of representative government'. Similarly, if the nation were silent on the number of votes to be taken as binding, leaving the decision to the representatives, then a unanimous agreement among the representatives to accept a majority as binding in future would be necessary. Again this was not the result of the 'nature of representative government', but of a positive law made unanimously by the representatives. Furthermore, any other constitutional provisions - including the establishment of a monarch with a power of veto over the acts of the assembly, and the right to convene or dissolve it - were as much in the 'nature of representative government' as any other. They all stood on the same foundation - the will of the nation, or of the representatives.[70]

Like Cooper, Hey argued that rights were in effect conferred by the laws of civil society. In a savage state, the only rights which might exist seemed to be 'negative': the savages should do no harm to each other, because they could not prove any right to do it. If in such a state a man did intentional and unprovoked harm to another, said Hey, let it be assumed that it was right that he should suffer punishment or undergo restraint to prevent a repetition of the mischief. The number of men who would do harm to others, if not deterred by the prospect of punishment, was not small. It was therefore necessary to make some provision beforehand which would convince an unprincipled man that he must suffer or be restrained if he would not restrain his own mischievous inclinations. This might prove a tenable foundation for certain laws for personal protection, which might even operate on those who had not consented to them, because they forbad them to do such things only as they before had no right to do. But beyond this, laws could not operate consistently with the principles of universal liberty and perfect equality, without the unanimous agreement of every individual in a particular region. Thus property could not be established, nor could it be maintained.

> The Rights which I can conjecture (for it is *but* Conjecture) to belong to me as a mere Man, are so uncertain, or comparatively so unimportant, while the Rights which I feel myself possessed of in civil Society are so great, so numerous, and many of them so well defined, that I am strongly inclined to consider Society chiefly as *creating* and *giving* my Rights rather than *recognizing* and *securing* what I could have claimed if I had lived in an unconnected state.[71]

This was not to say that man was to regard the existing civil laws in such a way as to abstain from attempting the repeal or improvement of them by a regular established process. However, he would not abstain from injury if he attempted alterations in laws and constitutions of states by methods which tended to unsettle civil society, without a sufficient prospect of procuring advantages likely to counterbalance an evil of so vast a magnitude. The decision was left to man's virtues. Those who wished to reform the constitution of England must show the probable future condition of the nation if the projected changes were made, the probability of making them, and the rectitude of the means intended to be employed.[72] The parallels with Bentham, Paley, and Austin here are obvious. Moreover, Hey contended that rights were subservient to happiness:

> The most satisfactory idea that I have been able to form, upon those Rights which are considered as existing antecedently to Society and human Laws, and as guiding the labours of the Legislator, is this; to include them under one general conception, a Claim to all the *Happiness* which the Legislator's sagacity can supply. Under which we must include, as perhaps the principal part, all the mediate and immediate *Means* of Happiness; the placing men in such a situation as will best inable them to effect their own Happiness. For Happiness dropt into our lap, without an exertion of our own, is not a thing which Experience teaches us to look for in this world.
>
> And, amongst the *Means* of Happiness, those *Rights* which are conferred by social union or civil Laws hold a distinguished place. If any person doubt whether the Laws of Society be the sole foundation of Property, yet there seems scarcely room to doubt that they make the *Security* of Property. And on this Security each man is inabled to construct that plan of life, which he thinks likely to produce the greatest Happiness placed within his reach; and to pursue a variety of measures, tending to his Happiness, which, without such Security, he might have attempted in vain. Yet the various civil Rights, created with a view of securing the Properties, Persons, and Lives, of men, are but *Means* of Happiness.[73]

The parallels with Bentham are again striking: first, the purpose of law was to enable men to pursue their own conceptions of happiness, not to define beforehand in what happiness consisted; second, security, especially of person and property, was of crucial importance as a means to this end. Hey went on to point out that to pursue rights so intently as to injure happiness was analogous to the folly of a miser who pursued money so as to destroy the happiness which alone gave money its value. The best laws were those which were most productive of happiness to the community at large, and it was the duty of legislators to make the happiness of the people their object. Liberty, for instance, was not connected with happiness in such a way that every additional degree of liberty was an additional degree of happiness. There was a liberty in being free from the violence of rapacious individuals, and this liberty was increased by the imposition of well-judged restraints. Such restraints contributed to happiness.[74]

What was appealing to all these thinkers was the flexibility of the utilitarian doctrine. It did not prejudge the question of whether a particular government should be obeyed or resisted. The decision had to be made by each individual himself, not as a matter of personal likes and dislikes, but according to an external standard. Even though there would inevitably be disagreement about whether resistance was desirable or not, at least men would be talking the same language, and would be clear as to the basis of their disagreement. Natural law, on the other hand, pretended to supply an external standard, but failed in fact to do so. The point was that God, or nature, did not prescribe absolute, *a priori* rules - rules remained as the guide to actions, but the rules were founded on their tendency to promote happiness.[75] If a government was not the product of an original constitution or a fundamental law, agreed to at the founding of civil society, but had rather arisen out of the inconveniences and sheer misery of the so-called state of nature, then there was no pre-existing law to which it had to conform, or pre-existing rights which it had to protect (there were only men who had an interest in pretending that there were such things).

Natural law was, of course, a combined theory of theology, morals, and law, and once it had been rejected on theological or moral grounds, a different legal theory was also needed. Interestingly, Austin attempted to show a theoretical link between the rejection of natural law and the subsequent adoption of legal positivism. According to Austin, there were three theories concerning man's knowledge of the unrevealed law of God, or 'the index to the tacit commands of the Deity', namely the pure theory of general utility, the pure theory of a moral sense, and a theory mixed of the two others. If the moral sense were the only index to the commands of God, then the moral sentiments of all men would be the same. This was obviously false: with regard to certain actions the moral sentiments of most, though not all, men had been alike, but with regard to others they had differed 'through every shade or degree, from slight diversity to direct opposition'. Still, the perception that some moral sentiments were universal, while others differed from community to community, had given rise to the mixed theory - a compound of moral sense and general utility - whereby the moral sense was seen as the index to some of God's tacit commands, and the principle of general utility to others. Hence the positive human rules which applied to all mankind were indicated by the moral sense, while those which did not apply universally were grounded on general utility. This had been reflected in the division of positive law into natural law and positive law, a division which was only intelligible on the assumption of the mixed theory of moral sense and general utility. Of course, if one were to assume the pure theory of general utility, or the pure theory of a moral sense, 'the distinction of positive law into *natural* and *positive* is senseless':[76] in the first case all law would be natural law, and in the second all law would be positive law.

Austin's argument rested on assumptions - for instance about the range of available moral theories - which had currency in the context of late eighteenth and early nineteenth century English legal and political thought. It was highly unlikely, for instance, that anyone would go outside the empirical tradition - though Locke's political theory as described in *Two Treatises of Government* was viewed with considerable suspicion, very few had serious reservations about the epistemology advanced in his *Essay concerning Human Understanding*. Once one had rejected natural law theory, and argued that all other theories of the same ilk merely amounted to an assertion of likes and dislikes, there was little left except utilitarianism, whether one retained God's will, as most did, as the foundation of moral obligation, or looked to human psychology, as Bentham did. However, Austin's argument did not show that the adoption of legal positivism was a necessary consequence of adopting the principle of utility as an ethical standard. The principle of utility was the standard against which all actions, laws, and institutions was to be judged. It was also the standard against which a conception of law was to be judged. There would be nothing incoherent in a utilitarian stating that there were certain fundamental laws, applicable to all times and places, which were derivable from the principle of utility, that government was bound by those laws, and that any law which it enacted in contradiction of those laws was to be regarded as invalid, on the grounds that this would promote the greatest amount of happiness. The utilitarian was not constrained by his utilitarianism as such to reject this 'natural law' or 'indirect' strategy, nor to reject any other strategy. He was merely constrained to accept that legal theory which he believed would be most conducive to increasing happiness. In short, the adoption of a particular conception of law remained contingent upon political objectives.

As Hart suggested, the utilitarians wished to facilitate argument about the merits or demerits of a law, without confusing the issue with questions of validity. But as Postema points out, this amounts to a normative conception of law. The utilitarians had political reasons for distinguishing law as it is from law is it ought to be - though what Postema perhaps does not sufficiently emphasize is that these reasons might be conservative, as much as radical. Utilitarianism was welcomed as a doctrine that was politically conservative, avoiding the dangerous implications of contractarian theory, and its manifestation in the rights of man. Indeed, Bentham himself was not, at least overtly, a political radical until 1809 or thereabouts,[77] and was of course responsible for one of the most memorable attacks on the French Declaration of the Rights of Man, and the political theory on which it was founded. This suggests that Postema's account of the relationship between Bentham's utilitarianism and legal positivism needs modifying to the extent that Bentham's attack on common law jurisprudence did not lead him immediately to political radicalism. Postema is possibly mistaken in emphasizing Bentham's identification as early as the 1770s and 1780s of sinister interest as the basis of common law conservatism, since, according to Bentham's own account, he only came to appreciate in full the pernicious influence of sinister interest in the first decade of the nineteenth century. Bentham's jurisprudence may have had radical political implications,[78] but his attack on natural law, and especially on the rights of man in the 1790s, was (in the circumstances of the time) conservative in tone - the danger to be guarded against was anarchy. But the utilitarian doctrine was, as I have said above, flexible in its political implications, and Bentham's later constitutional writings, for instance, were indeed radical, democratic, and republican.[79] It so happened that at the end of the eighteenth and beginning of the nineteenth centuries, it was precisely the radical and anarchical implications of natural law and the contractarian theory of government, and which the utilitarian thinkers wished, for political reasons, to avoid, that led them to adopt legal positivism. The way in which legal positivism came to be regarded as an apolitical doctrine is another story: it belongs to the way in which students of jurisprudence in the second half of the nineteenth century interpreted Austin's demarcation of the science of jurisprudence as a subject independent from the science of ethics, and in particular from that branch of the science dealing with law as it ought to be, the science of legislation.[80]

NOTES

1 H.L.A. Hart, 'Positivism and the Separation of Law and Morals' (first published in 1958), in *Essays in Jurisprudence and Philosophy*, Oxford, 1983, p. 50.

2 *Ibid*, p. 53.

3 *Ibid*, p. 57.

4 See *Ibid*, pp. 64, 68, 70, 71, 78.

5 Postema rejects the view that Bentham's legal positivism was entailed by his 'radically empiricist-nominalist ontology and epistemology'. Bentham's theory of fictions, which regarded 'only commands and sanctions and habits of aggregates of people ... as real', did not in itself distinguish between various conceptions of law or types of law (say statute and common law), since both belonged to the category of fictitious entities. The crucial distinction lay between such fictitious entities as were beneficial and such as were pernicious, and this distinction was only to be drawn by the ultimate standard of evaluation, the principle of utility. See G.J. Postema, *Bentham and the Common Law Tradition*, Oxford, 1986, pp. 296-300. It might be added that Austin's belief in God and the existence of a divine law did not preclude his commitment to legal positivism.

6 *Ibid*, pp. 302-3.

7 *Ibid*, pp. 147-90. For a further discussion of the role of security in Bentham's utilitarianism and its relationship to his legal theory see P.J. Kelly, *Utilitarianism and Distributive Justice: Jeremy Bentham and the Civil Law*, Oxford, 1990, pp. 137-68.

8 Postema, *Bentham and the Common Law Tradition*, pp. 316-17.

9 Blackstone had stated, for instance, that 'no human laws are of any validity, if contrary to [the law of nature]': see *Commentaries on the Laws of England*, 4 vols., Oxford, 1765-9, i. 41.

10 See 'A Fragment on Government' (first published in 1776) [hereafter *FG*], in *A Comment on the Commentaries and A Fragment on Government*, ed. J.H. Burns and H.L.A. Hart, London, 1977, pp. 397-8.

11 For Bentham's division of jurisprudence into censorial and expository, authoritative and unauthoritative, local and universal, and other branches besides, see *An Introduction to the Principles of Morals and Legislation* [hereafter *IPML*], ed. J.H. Burns and H.L.A. Hart, London, 1970, pp. 293-300.

12 Postema, *Bentham and the Common Law Tradition*, pp. 305-8.

13 *Ibid*, pp. 311-12.

14 The political theory of John Locke was the most common target. Locke had argued that in the formation of political society there had been an initial or original compact, whereby a group of men unanimously agreed to form themselves into society (sometimes referred to as the contract of society), and then, by the agreement of the majority, a constitution had been established and certain men had assumed political power as a trust (sometimes referred to as the contract of government): see *Second Treatise of Government*, §§ 95-9, 134, 212. The critics of contract theory did not usually pay much regard to this distinction.

15 For differing views on how close Britain came to revolution in the 1790s see I.R. Christie, 'Conservatism and stability in British society' and R. Wells, 'English society and revolutionary politics in the 1790s: the case for insurrection', in M. Philp, ed., *The French Revolution and British Popular Politics*, Cambridge, 1991, pp. 169-87 and 188-226 respectively.

16 Though he had some leanings towards radicalism in his early career, by the late 1820s Austin's politics had become decidedly conservative, and remained so: see L. and J. Hamburger, *Troubled Lives: John and Sarah Austin*, Toronto, 1985, pp. 26-52, 168-77; and W.E. Rumble, *The Thought of John Austin: Jurisprudence, Colonial Reform, and the British Constitution*, London, 1985, pp. 193-217.

17 'Anarchical Fallacies' had been first published as 'Sophismes anarchiques: Examen critique de diverses Déclarations des Droits de l'Homme et du Citoyen', in *Tactique des Assemblées législatives*, 2 vols., Paris, 1816, one of the French recensions of Bentham's works produced by his Genevan editor, Étienne Dumont, and was then re-edited for the Bowring edition of Bentham's works: see *The Works of Jeremy Bentham*, ed. J. Bowring, 11 vols., Edinburgh, 1843, ii. 489-534. For commentaries see W.L. Twining, 'The Contemporary Significance of Bentham's Anarchical Fallacies', *Archiv für Rechts- und Sozialphilosophie*, lxi (1975), 325-56; R. Harrison, *Bentham*, London, 1983, pp. 77-105; and J. Waldron, ed., *'Nonsense upon Stilts': Bentham, Burke and Marx on the Rights of Man*, London, 1987, pp. 29-45

18 Paley was a Fellow of Christ's College from 1766 to 1776; Hey was a Fellow of Magdalene College from 1782 to 1796; and Cooper was educated at Magdalene College, which awarded him the degrees of BA in 1763, MA in 1763, and DD in 1777.

19 It had been first published in 1785, had soon established itself as the text on the subject at Cambridge, and had reached a seventeenth edition in 1809.

20 For Austin's relationship with Bentham see A.D.E. Lewis, 'John Austin (1790-1859): Pupil of Bentham', *Bentham Newsletter*, ii (1979), 18-29. It is unclear which of Bentham's works, apart from *FG* and *IPML*, had been studied by Austin.

21 See for instance *The Province of Jurisprudence Determined* (first published in 1832) [hereafter *PJD*], ed. W.E. Rumble, Cambridge, 1995, pp. 71-2, 82-3, 103-4.

22 George Wilson to Bentham, 24 September 1786 and 30 November 1788, *The Correspondence of Jeremy Bentham*, vol. iii, ed. I.R. Christie, London, 1971, pp. 489-93, and vol. iv, ed. A.T. Milne, London, 1981, pp. 15-17.

23 Bentham's essay, 'Law versus arbitrary power:- or, A Hatchet for Dr. Paley's Net', written mainly in January and February 1809, is in the Bentham Papers, University College London, box cvii, fos. 199-206, with a copy at fos. 278-343, and related manuscript at fos. 183-8, 267-77.

24 Paley's *Natural Theology*, in which he argued that the works of nature demonstrated the existence of a benevolent deity, had appeared in 1802.

25 See *Deontology together with A Table of the Springs of Action and Article on Utilitarianism*, ed. A. Goldworth, Oxford, 1983, pp. 52-3, 328; and *Official Aptitude Maximized; Expense Minimized*, ed. P, Schofield, Oxford, 1993, p. 351.

26 For an overview of Bentham's lifelong engagement with Blackstone see J.H. Burns, 'Bentham and Blackstone: A Lifetime's Dialectic', *Utilitas: A Journal of Utilitarian Studies*, i (1989), 22-40. The development of Bentham's own theory of law in response to Blackstone is admirably treated in D. Lieberman, *The Province of Legislation Determined: Legal Theory in Eighteenth-Century Britain*, Cambridge, 1989, pp. 219-90.

27 Blackstone, *Commentaries on the Laws of England*, iv. 49.

28 UC cvii. 239.

29 UC cvii. 211.

30 UC cvii. 214.

31 L. Stephen, *History of English Thought in the Eighteenth Century*, new edn., 2 vols., London, 1962, ii. 105.

32 *Moral and Political Philosophy*, pp. 49-54.

33 *Ibid*, pp. 54-61.

34 *PJD*, pp. 21-3.

35 *Ibid*, pp. 38-41.

36 *Ibid*, p. 14.

37 *IPML*, p. 11.

38 This, very crudely, is the basic argument put forward in *IPML*. For a discussion of Bentham's conception of the principle of utility see Kelly, *Utilitarianism and Distributive Justice*, pp. 14-70.

39 See *First Principles preparatory to Constitutional Code*, ed. P. Schofield, Oxford, 1989, pp. 232-7, for a concise statement of Bentham's strategy in solving this problem.

40 *IPML*, pp. 25-8.

41 *FG*, pp. 482-4.

43 *PJD*, pp. 157-9.

44 *Ibid*, pp. 53-5.

45 *FG*, pp. 441-3.

47 *Moral and Political Philosophy*, pp. 8-17.

48 *Ibid*, pp. 414-27.

49 *Ibid*, pp. 570-1.

50 *Ibid*, pp. 463-4.

51 For discussions of constitutional law and the related issue of sovereignty in Bentham's legal theory see J.H. Burns, 'Bentham on Sovereignty: an Exploration', *Northern Ireland Legal Quarterly*, xxiv (1973),

399-416; H.L.A. Hart, *Essays on Bentham: Jurisprudence and Political Theory*, Oxford, 1982, pp. 220-42; and Postema, *Bentham and the Common Law Tradition*, pp. 230-62.

52 See Rumble, *Austin*, pp. 88-108.

53 Cf. Bentham, *Of Laws in General*, ed. H.L.A. Hart, London, 1970, p. 16: 'the mandate of the sovereign be it what it will, cannot be illegal: it may be cruel; it may be impolitic; it may even be unconstitutional: but it cannot be illegal. It may be unconstitutional, for instance by being repugnant to any privileges that may have been conceded to the people whom it affects: but it would be perverting language and confounding ideas to call it *illegal*: for concessions of privileges are not mandates: they are neither commands nor countermands: in short they are not *laws*': and Austin, *PJD*, p. 216: 'although an act of the sovereign which violates constitutional law, may be styled with propriety *unconstitutional*, it is not an infringement of law simply and strictly so called, and cannot be styled with propriety *illegal*'.

54 Bentham had also identified this as being the only use of the idea of a social compact.

55 Cf. Bentham's 'wisdom of our ancestors' fallacy in 'The Book of Fallacies', in *Works*, ed. Bowring, ii. 398-401. A similar point had, of course, been made by Paley.

58 *PJD*, pp. 280-1.

59 For an account of radical political thought in the 1790s see H.T. Dickinson, *Liberty and Property: Political Ideology in Eighteenth-Century Britain*, London, 1977, pp. 232-69.

60 S. Cooper, *The First Principles of Civil and Ecclesiastical Government, Delineated, (in two parts,) in Letters to Dr. Priestley, occasioned by his to Mr. Burke*, Yarmouth, 1791, pp. 37-43.

61 *Ibid*, pp. 43-51.

62 *Ibid*, pp. 55-63.

63 *Ibid*, pp. 74-5.

64 *Ibid*, pp. 83-7.

65 *Ibid*, p. 122.

66 *Ibid*, p. 116.

67 *Ibid*, pp. 126-34.

68 As a defender of the British Constitution, itself the product of the Glorious Revolution of 1688-9, Cooper was not in a position to condemn all resistance outright, though he seems to have gone as far as he could to do so. Conservative thinkers in the 1790s had to make sense of the Glorious Revolution in a way that did not justify a natural right of resistance in the people.

69 Cooper, *First Principles of Government*, pp. 156-66.

70 R. Hey, *Happiness and Rights. A Dissertation upon several subjects relative to the Rights of Man and his Happiness. Rights are Means: Happiness the End*, York, 1792, pp. 105-10.

71 *Ibid*, pp. 127-37.

72 *Ibid*, pp. 140-2.

73 *Ibid*, pp. 194-5.

74 *Ibid*, pp. 195-201.

75 Both Paley and Austin argued that conduct was to be guided by general rules. Even when it appeared that the particular consequences of breaking the rule would be beneficial, the more important general consequences would in fact make the action harmful. However, their position became incoherent when they admitted that in extreme circumstances there were exceptions, when the rule should be broken. See Paley, *Moral and Political Philosophy*, pp. 61-72, 87-9; and Austin, *PJD*, pp. 41-55.

76 *PJD*, pp. 91-2. See also pp. 114-15.

77 See J.R. Dinwiddy, 'Bentham's Transition to Political Radicalism, 1809-10', *Journal of the History of Ideas*, xxxvi (1975), 683-700.

78 This argument is pursued in D.G. Long, 'Censorial Jurisprudence and Political Radicalism: A Reconsideration of the Early Bentham', *Bentham Newsletter*, xii (1988), 4-23.

79 Bentham's later constitutional writings are perhaps best approached through the essays in *First Principles preparatory to Constitutional Code*, in which Bentham explained the general principles of government underlying the detailed administrative provisions of the Code itself. For a commentary on the monumental Constitutional Code see F. Rosen, *Jeremy Bentham and Representative Democracy: A Study of the Constitutional Code*, Oxford, 1983.

80 See B. Abel-Smith and R. Stevens, *Lawyers and the Courts: A Sociological Study of the English Legal System 1750-1965*, London, 1967, pp. 165-85; D. Sugarman, 'Legal Theory, the Common Law Mind and the Making of the Textbook Tradition', in W.L. Twining, ed., *Legal Theory and Common Law*, Oxford, 1986, pp. 26-61; and P. Schofield, 'Jeremy Bentham and Nineteenth-Century English Jurisprudence', *Journal of Legal History*, xii (1991), 58-88.

8 GENERAL AND PARTICULAR JURISPRUDENCE - Three Chapters in a Story

WILLIAM TWINING

Globalization

We are now living in a global neighbourhood, which is not yet a global village.[1] It is difficult to interpret these trends and it is easy to underestimate them; but it is also easy to exaggerate the extent and the speed of the process, to oversimplify its dynamics, to foreshorten history by treating a story that stretches over several centuries as if it is a recent development, to assume some inevitable, teleological progress in a single direction, and to ignore the countervailing processes of fragmentation and localisation.[2]

Recognition of these processes has stimulated a new academic industry, 'globalization theory'. In most disciplines in the humanities, social sciences and physical sciences the implications of globalization are firmly on the agenda.[3] The discipline of law has become distinctly more cosmopolitan in recent years, but its theoretical branch, Jurisprudence, seems to have lagged behind. In the English-speaking world traditional positivism, normative legal philosophy, critical legal studies, post-modernism, and even economic analysis of law seem to be have been going through a somewhat parochial or inward-looking phase, although there are some notable exceptions. The time may be ripe for a revival of a more general jurisprudence.

The literature on globalization has already sparked a series of debates, some familiar, some relatively new. Here it is sufficient to make three preliminary points that are directly relevant to my argument and about which there is widespread agreement. First, globalization needs to be considered on at least three levels: relations between states (international relations); non-state relations across frontiers (transnational relations); and the operation of the global system(s) as a whole (global relations).[4] Global relations at all three levels involve a multiplicity of actors, but this does not necessarily spell the end of the independent nation-state as one of the most important.[5] It does, however, put the concept of sovereignty back on the agenda, along with a number of conceptual questions about the relations between such notions as sovereign states, governments, peoples, nations, societies, communities and classes.

Secondly, and related to this, the significance of territorial boundaries has been radically changed by globalization. This presents a challenge to all 'black box theories' which treat nation-states or geographically bounded 'societies' or legal systems as discrete entities that can be studied in isolation either internally or at the international level. Rawls's theory of justice and any legal theory which treats municipal legal systems as discrete entities are vulnerable to this challenge.[6]

Finally, the process of globalization changes the agenda of issues with which any field of study is concerned: it revives and recasts old issues such as those surrounding sovereignty and war; it makes familiar problems more urgent, such as environmental control and the regulation of multi-national corporations; and it creates new ones such as those connected with developments in technology and communication, such as Internet and CNN World News. What are problems, what should be the agenda, what are priorities depends on a whole raft of ideological and other assumptions. But it is clear that if legal theory is to engage seriously with globalization and its consequences a critical re-examination of its agenda, its heritage of ideas and its conceptual tools is called for.

This essay is one of a series exploring the implications for legal theory and the discipline of law of globalization and globalization theory. It deals with one narrow topic: three distinct phases of the history of the distinction between 'general' and 'particular' jurisprudence within the tradition of English legal positivism: first, the place and significance of the distinction in the thought of Jeremy Bentham and John Austin; second, the fifty-year long debate surrounding Professor T.E.Holland's idea of a 'formal science of law' and his denial of the possibility of 'particular jurisprudence'; and, third, the recent revival of the distinction as a basis for arguing that H.L.A.Hart and Ronald Dworkin were involved in quite different enterprises, rather than disagreeing: Hart doing general jurisprudence, Dworkin confining himself to a particular, participatory theory of adjudication. The essay concludes with a brief consideration of the implications of this story for reflecting on globalization and law.

Jeremy Bentham and John Austin

> 'J.B.'s frame of mind.
> J.B. the most ambitious of the ambitious. His empire - the empire he aspires to - extending to, and comprehending the whole human race, in all places. - in all habitable places of the earth, at all future time.
> J.B. the most philanthropic of the philanthropic; philanthropy the end and instrument of his ambition.
> Limits it has no other than those of the earth.'[7]

Bentham wrote this in his Memorandum-book the day after his 83rd birthday. This was not just an old man's private musings. From *A Fragment on Government* and other early writings until the end of his life Bentham often explicitly adopted the standpoint of a (or the) 'citizen of the world'.[8] This standpoint was based on utility as a universal principle which extended to humankind in general, sometimes going further to include all sentient beings. It formed the cornerstone of his jurisprudence, which was in key respects truly global.[9]

As is well known, Bentham's project was to extend the experimental method of reasoning from the physical sciences to the moral sciences, especially legislation:

> 'What Bacon was to the physical world, Helvetius was to the moral. The moral world has had its Bacon, but its Newton is yet to come.'[10]

Underpinning Bentham's perspective was a quite elaborate series of distinctions, which have been succinctly summarised by Philip Schofield:

> '....Bentham's conception of jurisprudence had two branches: the first, expository, the second censorial, or the art of legislation. "To the province of the *Expositor* it belongs to explain to us what, as he supposes, the Law *is*: to that of the *Censor*, to observe what he thinks it *ought to be*."[11] He divided jurisprudence into authoritative, when it was the product of the legislator himself, and unauthoritative, the work of any other person. He then made a further distinction between local jurisprudence, concerned with the laws of one nation or a particular group of nations, and universal jurisprudence, concerned with laws of all nations. Though in substance no two nations had exactly the same laws, while others possibly had none in common, there were certain words corresponding to concepts, for instance power, right, obligation, liberty, which could be found in all.[12] It followed that universal expository jurisprudence had very narrow limits: it could not apply to the substance of laws, but "must confine itself to terminology". Censorial jurisprudence on the other hand, considering both substance and terminology, was much wider in scope: there were "leading points"[13] which it would be advantageous for all nations to introduce into their laws.'[14]

Here, three points deserve emphasis: first, the distinction between general (or universal) and local (or internal) jurisprudence was subordinate to the more fundamental distinction between expository and censorial jurisprudence. 'The expositor was to be the servant of the censor, who in turn would be the adviser of the legislator.'[15] Bentham distinguished the is and the ought for the sake of the ought.[16]

Secondly, the distinction between universal and local jurisprudence is not co-extensive with the distinction between the censor and the expositor. In *A Fragment on Government*, it is suggested that 'the *Expositor* ... is always the citizen of this or that particular country: the *Censor* is, or ought to be the citizen of the world.'[17] Elsewhere, Bentham modified this by including analysis of some fundamental concepts as part of universal expository jurisprudence, but as Schofield notes, this was very limited in scope.[18] However, this became the starting-point of Austin's conception of General Jurisprudence.

Thirdly, Bentham coined the term 'international jurisprudence' to apply to relations between sovereigns and contrasted it with internal jurisprudence, which he sub-divided into national, provincial, and local. The latter term applied to small districts, such as towns, parishes, and manors, which he acknowledged could have laws of their own.[19] He observed that: 'It is evident enough, that international jurisprudence may, as well as internal, be censorial as well as expository, unauthoritative as well as authoritative.'[20] Thus Bentham at least made provision for jurisprudence to operate at a number of different levels from the global to the very local, but he restricted the term 'international' to relations between sovereigns.

Bentham's distinction between universal and local was in part developed in connection with his critiques of Blackstone. However, it was more important in connection with his constructive project for a pannomion. He was a forerunner of the modern constitution-monger and legal 'expert' who offer their services to foreign governments.[21] Anyone involved in this trade has a vested interest in claiming that their expertise is of general application. Bentham was no exception. He was acutely aware that there was a tension between the claims of universality of the Censor and the need to be sensitive to local exigencies. He returned to this theme again and again.

At first sight Bentham did not appear to maintain an entirely consistent stance on the extent to which the censor needed to take account of local circumstances in proposing legislation. In some passages he appears to assume that the pannomion would have wide applicability in respect of substance as well as form. In *A Fragment on Government* he suggested 'That which is Law, is, in different countries, widely different, while that which ought to be, is in all countries to a great degree the same.'[22] Similarly, in offering his services as a codifier to James Madison, the President of the United States, he played down the amount to which his draft codes would need to be adjusted to local conditions in respect of either form or substance.[23] He even went so far as to suggest:

> '..that, upon a closer scrutiny, the points, which present a demand for local knowledge, would not, it is supposed be found to cover, in the field of law, so great an extent, nor yet to be so difficult to discriminate beforehand, as upon a transient glance, general notions might lead any person to imagine.'[24]

On the other hand, he usually maintained a sharp distinction between form (especially terminology) which should in most respects be universal,[25] and substance in which he was often rather cautious in recommending change. In considering directly the influence of time and place in matters of legislation, Bentham was prepared to give some weight to local customs and circumstances. And, as Michael Lobban has suggested, he acknowledged that even the common law was a rich source of raw materials for the censor, that his objections to it related much more to form than to substance, and that he was in respect of reform of substantive law remarkably cautious.[26]

Although there are differences of emphasis, Bentham's general position can be interpreted as being quite consistent: existing laws of different nations vary considerably in respect of both form and substance.[27] However, the principle of utility and the form of laws in the pannomion are of universal application; but caution needs to be exercised in legislating for a particular country in case expectations based on local customs and circumstances should be disappointed - for the non-disappointment principle is an important principle subordinate to utility.

Thus Bentham's project was to develop a science of legislation which was both 'censorial' and universal; the *construction* of precise conceptual tools what Mary Mack called 'a legislative dictionary' -[28], was one narrow, subordinate, but important, part of the science or art of legislation.

Austin

John Austin is the prototype of a disciple who subverts his master. Recent scholarship has convincingly shown that Bentham had a broader vision, a more subtle and flexible mind, and a much more radical programme than his tortured follower. Austin did follow his master in three important respects that are relevant to this paper: the sharp distinction between law as it is and law as it ought to be; a subordinate distinction between the study of one particular legal system and legal systems or law(s) in general; and the identification of analysis of concepts that transcend particular legal systems as a distinct field of study.

However, Austin's enterprise was quite different from Bentham's and he used these distinctions, and to some extent altered them, for his own purposes.

Bentham's objective was to develop a politically radical science of legislation. Austin's enterprise was to establish the study of positive law as an autonomous scientific discipline quite separate from censorial jurisprudence or the science of legislation. Bentham distinguished the is and the ought for the sake of the ought; Austin made the same distinction for the sake of isolating law as it is for detached study.

Both thinkers are subject to multiple interpretations. There may be several Benthams and at least two Austins.[29] However, in the present context some points are reasonably clear. The most important is that Austin confined jurisprudence to the analysis and description of positive law. The science or philosophy of legislation[30] was not part of Jurisprudence, but constituted a separate discipline. This was no mere semantic point: Austin wished his science to be apolitical; although he himself treated the philosophy of legislation to be important, his distinction paved the way for a conception and practice of the discipline of law that were avowedly uncritical.[31] Nothing could have been further from the spirit of Bentham.

Like Bentham, Austin distinguished between general and particular jurisprudence and explicitly concentrated on the former. Both treated the laws of individual sovereign states as the main subject of particular jurisprudence and state legal systems as the primary units of law; both emphasised the importance of studying basic legal concepts that transcended particular legal systems. Following Hobbes, Austin declared that his aim was 'to show, *not what is law here or there, but what is law.*'[32]

Austin devoted much more space than Bentham to the distinction between general and particular jurisprudence.[33] In an important passage he specified the scope of general jurisprudence:

> 'I mean then by "General Jurisprudence", the science concerned with the principles, notions, and distinctions which are common to systems of law: understanding by systems of law, the ampler and maturer systems which, by reason of their amplitude and maturity, are pre-eminently pregnant with instruction.
> Of the principles, notions and distinctions which are the subjects of general jurisprudence, some may be esteemed necessary. For we cannot imagine coherently a system of law (or a system of law evolved in a refined community), without conceiving them as constituent parts of it ...
>
> Of the principles, notions, and distinctions which are the subjects of General jurisprudence, others are not necessary (in the sense which I have given the expression). We may imagine coherently an expanded system of law, without conceiving them as constituent parts of it. But as they rest upon grounds of utility which extend through all communities, they in fact occur very generally in matured systems of law; and therefore may be ranked properly with the general principles which are the subjects of general jurisprudence.'[34]

Austin's list of examples of necessary notions is quite long. It includes the notions of Duty, Right, Liberty, Injury, Punishment, Redress; Law; Sovereignty, and Independent Political Society; the distinctions between written and unwritten law; rights *in rem* and rights *in personam*; obligations arising from contracts, injuries, and '*quasi ex contractu*';

and so on. It is a longer list than Bentham's and it is not entirely clear what he meant by 'necessary' in this context.[35] By including additional 'common' concepts and by focusing mainly on shared features of 'maturer' systems he may have extended the scope of his concept of General Jurisprudence a bit beyond Bentham's universal expository jurisprudence, but overall his conception of law and of its study is much narrower than Bentham's.

Austin emphasised the distinction between general and particular jurisprudence because he wished to lay a foundation for an autonomous discipline distinct from the Science of Legislation and from historical and empirical enquiries. General jurisprudence was anterior to and the necessary foundation for the systematic study of both particular jurisprudence and the science of legislation.[36] It was the theoretical part of law as a discipline.

Austin did not advocate the study of jurisprudence for its own sake. In his lecture on 'The Uses of the Study of Jurisprudence' he emphasised its pedagogical value as the basis for the 'theoretico-practical' study of English law. By providing a map of the whole and making clear the rationale of law in general and of its practice, it would contribute to more efficient vocational training for legal practice and public life. It would also be of value in understanding foreign legal systems, in daily legal practice, in adjudication, in law reform, and in the development of 'a juridical literature worthy of the English Bar.'[37] Austin's vision was of an institutionalised, autonomous discipline of law which would at once be as systematic as that of Prussia, but without the 'secluded habits' of German Professors. 'In England, theory would be moulded to practice.'[38] Significantly, he asserted: 'The only practical jurisprudence is particular.'[39]

David Sugarman and Philip Schofield have sketched the story of the rise of analytical jurisprudence (not Austin's term) and 'the expository tradition' of academic law in the late nineteenth century.[40] The outlines are familiar: Austin sterilised and narrowed Bentham's jurisprudence; the followers of Austin further narrowed down Austin, by excluding his discussions of utility and by shifting the focus to particular jurisprudence. Bentham was rendered impotent by a combination of misunderstanding, misinterpretation and neglect. It was claimed that Bentham was essentially a destructive thinker, whereas Austin was constructive and that Austin's theory of law was an improvement on Bentham's.[41] Such claims are specious. A more plausible interpretation is that the pioneering full-time academic lawyers were concerned to establish their credentials with both the practising profession and the scholarly community. Bentham's radicalism and antipathy to the common law would antagonise the former; Austin's rigorously 'scientific' approach might persuade the latter of the intellectual respectability of this new discipline. This story is broadly correct. But, in the present context, it requires to be modified in at least two respects. Austin was never accepted uncritically even within English positivism and, as we shall see in the next section, the distinction between general and particular jurisprudence was the focus for a long-running and rather sterile debate that was symptomatic of a wider unease about the development of academic law.

Poor John Austin! A public and a private failure in his lifetime, after his death he was elevated to the status of 'Father of English Jurisprudence' to be used for purposes quite different from what he had intended and to serve as a whipping-boy until he was decently buried by Herbert Hart. It was Austinian Jurisprudence that was said to stink in the nostrils of the practising barrister;[42] Austin provided the main target for attack by Henry Maine, James Bryce and other proponents of historical jurisprudence; some of his closest disciples, Clark, Holland, and Salmond, carped and criticised him; by 1945 Buckland could say: 'He was a religion; to-day he seems to be regarded rather as a disease.'[43] In recent years scholars have usually treated Austin as a lesser figure than Bentham. In 1961 Herbert Hart secured his own reputation by destroying Austin's, only for a series of well-intentioned scholars to disinter him - in one case to use him as a launching-pad for a virulent and largely irrelevant attack on Hart.[44] These 'debates' can mostly be read as a series of family squabbles with strong Oedipal overtones within English legal positivism. Since World War II the most persistent attacks on analytical jurisprudence have been from without: on the one hand, the attack on the alleged amoralism of positivism exemplified by the criticisms of Hart by Devlin, Fuller and Dworkin - a line of criticism that largely ignores the significance of Bentham's distinction between expository and censorial jurisprudence; on the other hand, the broader critique of formalism and the expository tradition, most recently exemplified by Morton Horwitz's categorisation of the English analytical tradition as being unhistorical, unempirical, uncritical, and based on an outdated hermeneutics.[45]

It was Austin's intention to develop and disseminate Bentham's ideas, not to dethrone him. He can hardly be blamed for the uses to which he was put after his death. His originality as a thinker and his influence have often been greatly exaggerated, except perhaps in his role as someone to react against.[46] A charitable interpretation suggests that he struggled valiantly, but unsuccessfully, with some intractable problems;[47] a less kind view is that he was hopelessly confused. He deserves to be reburied and allowed to rest in peace.

Holland and his Critics

From 1863, when Austin's lectures first became available, until the 1890s there is a case for saying that his doctrines 'dominated the teaching of Jurisprudence in England and the Commonwealth.'[48] Several factors explain this: Austin's positivism and his antipathy to Natural Law; the apolitical and 'scientific' nature of his analytical jurisprudence; his relative sympathy with the common law tradition compared to Bentham; and, above all, the absence of rivals.[49]

However, such claims to Austin's 'dominance' should be taken with a large pinch of salt. First, university legal education in this period was new and very small in scale. Second, it took some time for jurisprudence to become firmly established in the curriculum. In London, Austin's successors in the Chair in the subject were more notable for their rapid turnover, their lack of students and their interest in other subjects than for their productivity - the major exception being Sheldon Amos.[50] In the older universities for a long time jurisprudence was almost 'unheard of'.[51] Furthermore, Austin was the subject of persistent criticism after the publication of his lectures, and for a time the Historical School, led by Sir Henry Maine, threatened to become a serious rival.[52]

In the 1880s Jurisprudence began to be recognised as an important element in legal education, even by the Inns of Court.[53] But it was felt that there was no satisfactory student text on the subject. Thomas Erskine Holland decided to fill the gap.[54] His *The Elements of Jurisprudence* was first published in 1880. At one level it was a success; it went through 13 editions in his lifetime, and was reprinted several times after his death in 1926; it was pirated in the United States and for almost fifty years it was the most widely used textbook on jurisprudence in England - but again one should bear in mind the relatively small scale of academic law throughout that period.[55]

Holland was a quite suitable person to follow in Austin's footsteps. He was a strong positivist, a lucid writer and 'the whole bent of his mind was towards orderliness and simplification.'[56] He was impervious to criticism, precise to the point of pedantry, and well read in Roman Law and English Law as well as International Law and History. Above all he was a good expositor. As Pollock said, compared to Austin's work, 'Professor Holland's is concise without abruptness, flowing without tediousness, and distinct without wearisome repetitions.'[57]

Holland considered himself to be a pioneer. Bentham and Austin had helped to highlight the need for a formal science, but Bentham had muddied the waters by his distinctions between expository and censorial and authoritative and unauthoritative jurisprudence. Censorial Jurisprudence, Bentham's main interest, referred to the Art of Legislation rather than the Science of Law; 'authoritative' jurisprudence is nothing more than a body of law; 'unauthoritative local jurisprudence' is mere commentary; only 'unauthoritative general jurisprudence' is scientific and Bentham contributed little to this.[58] Austin made a significant contribution, presenting, in Holland's words, 'the spectacle of a powerful and conscientious mind struggling with an intractable and rarely handled material'.[59] Unfortunately, 'the defects of the work are even more widely recognized than its merits'.[60] Austin's work was fragmentary, repetitive, neglecting large tracts of his subject, while devoting too much space 'to digressions upon questions, such as the psychology of the will, codification and utilitarianism'.[61] Holland found little in modern civil law scholarship, except among pandectists, that bore directly on analytical jurisprudence as he conceived it.[62]

The way was therefore open for the first systematic work on the formal science of law. Holland followed Austin and Clark in concentrating on general analytical jurisprudence. However, he went one step further in refusing to recognise particular jurisprudence as a serious or even a proper pursuit. For him, the issue was not just one of semantics, a loose extension of the term 'jurisprudence' to the study of particular municipal legal systems. Jurisprudence is 'the formal science of positive law'[63] and science must be general. 'Particular jurisprudence' might mean either of two things: it might be a general science derived from observation of the laws of one country, in which case the particularity applies to the sources from which the science is derived, rather than to the science. Thus, one might start to build up a science of geology by observing strata in England, but the outcome would not be 'English geology', for the findings would only be scientific if the generalizations would hold good everywhere, 'insofar as the same substances and forces are everywhere present.'[64] Alternatively, particular jurisprudence may mean acquaintance with the laws of a particular people; 'but it is improper to apply the term 'science' to such merely practical and empirical knowledge'.[65]

Holland argued that a better analogy was with Grammar -'the science of those ideas of relation which, in greater or less perfection, and often in most dissimilar ways, are expressed in all the languages of mankind.'[66] There is a fundamental difference between learning a particular language and studying the scientific principles of grammar. The formal science of law is concerned with 'those few and simple ideas which underlie the infinite variety of legal rules' (in all systems).[67]

Here we are only concerned with Holland's idea of a formal science of positive law. Holland was a rigid positivist and a severe formalist and, as such, open to attack by critics of such positions. But his conception of analytical jurisprudence was also criticized from within legal positivism by Pollock, Buckland and Gray among others. Holland stood his ground and only made passing reference to his critics.

Frederick Pollock was the first critic of consequence. In a review article on 'some recent contributions to Legal Science' [68], he criticized Holland's conception of a formal science on educational grounds. The analogy with Grammar was 'felicitous, and only too felicitous', for there is little demand for books on the science of grammar. One learns grammar through learning one concrete language and not *vice versa*. The saving grace of Holland's book is that the author, while denying its possibility, in fact practises particular jurisprudence concisely and intelligibly. However, jurisprudence of this abstract kind is doomed to vacillate between two unsatisfactory alternatives: a pure theory of legal classification ('a catalogue of blank forms') or partial exposition of a particular system. An institutional work on English Law, a successor to Blackstone's *Commentaries* or analogous to the German *Pandekten* would serve the needs of students and practitioners better than a purely abstract study of legal ideas.[69]

John Chipman Gray of Harvard challenged Holland's conception of Jurisprudence, also mainly on grounds of practicality. There are three kinds of Jurisprudence: Particular; Comparative; and General. All are scientific, in the sense that they involve systematic study. Particular Jurisprudence is more than the particular law of a particular people - 'It means the scientific knowledge of the law of a particular people.' Particular Jurisprudence is of much more utility to intending practitioners than Comparative or General Jurisprudence.[70]

One particularly harsh critic, Albert Kocourek, criticized Holland for not staying loyal to his conception of an abstract science.[71] But Kocourek's own contribution to abstract jurisprudence was dismissed or ignored as being totally impractical and useless. This supports the hypothesis that Holland's *Jurisprudence* survived in spite of rather than because of his commitment to a formal science.[72]

The most interesting criticism of Holland's 'formal science' came from W.W.Buckland of Cambridge. This took the form of one of the longest-running non-debates in the history of Anglo-American jurisprudence. In 1890, Buckland published an article in *The Law Quarterly Review* on 'The Difficulties of Abstract Jurisprudence', in which he attacked Holland's conception of general jurisprudence as misconceived.[73] Whereas Holland had denied the possibility of particular jurisprudence, Buckland doubted the feasibility of general jurisprudence. Holland, who was not one to change his mind, ignored the criticism in successive editions. Fifty-five years later, Buckland renewed the attack in almost identical terms, claiming that he saw nothing to alter in what he had said.[74]

Buckland followed Pollock in doubting the utility of abstract jurisprudence, while praising Holland for improving on Austin in respect of his exposition and arrangement. But he launched a more substantial attack on his conception of the subject. Holland defined jurisprudence as 'the formal science of those relations of mankind which are generally recognised as having consequences.' This assumes that there are legal concepts that are widely shared among systems of law: to what extent that is true, even of Western systems, is an empirical question to be determined by detailed comparative study of actual bodies of law.

If jurisprudence is a formal science like grammar, it is of very limited utility. If it is an empirical science, the analogy with geology is inappropriate: one may start to build up a picture of geological strata because they are subject to physical laws which are everywhere the same; but law is dependent on its social context. The extent to which there are shared legal concepts is an empirical question requiring proof by comparative study of many systems. But where is the evidence? Holland either assumes what he set out to prove or else was relying on *a priori* axioms reminiscent of German transcendentalism; in that case, like John Austin, he may be suspected of being a closet natural lawyer.[75] In fact, Buckland as a comparatist and Roman lawyer, knows of some evidence which suggests that there are a few common notions, such as duty, but their bulk is not great and a 'science' based on these alone would be meagre at best.[76] The fundamental notions of law are not everywhere the same, for law is 'to a great degree the product of the milieu in which it has developed.'[77] Holland's analogy with grammar might be apt, but it suggests at most the limited scope and utility of such a science; on the other hand, the analogy with geology was misleading because geology is subject to universal physical laws, whereas law is culturally relative.

For Buckland, general jurisprudence is either empirical and speculative or else it is formal, in which case it is both narrow and useless. On the other hand, particular jurisprudence, as the study of the underlying notions of one system of law is both feasible and useful. The method is scientific, but the subject is empirical. Its aim, to show 'the underlying principles and broadest generalisations' of a given system as a foundation for the study of domestic law.

In several respects the differences between Holland and his critics were not very great.

First, Holland, Pollock and Buckland, and in different ways, Gray and Kocourek, were all committed legal positivists who maintained a sharp distinction between law and morals and sought to establish the study of positive law as a distinct discipline, separate from politics, ethics and sociology. Holland, Pollock and Buckland all criticised Austin for treating utilitarianism as part of Jurisprudence.[78] For example, Pollock referred to it as 'irrelevant and mostly bad moral philosophy'[79] - a far cry from Bentham. Buckland insisted that Jurisprudence was 'Austin's real subject. This was the analysis of legal concepts.'[80]

Secondly, they shared a conception of law that treated municipal legal systems as the primary subject of the study of law. Each was sympathetic to the idea of viewing Public International Law as analogous to municipal law; and they treated it as dealing almost entirely with relations between sovereign states.[81] In short, they all held similar, strong versions of a 'black box' theory of law.

Thirdly, Holland and Buckland wished to confine Jurisprudence to the analysis of concepts; Pollock was more circumspect. All placed the study of legal doctrine at the centre of legal education. The fact that all three fought hard for this admittedly narrow enterprise does not mean that they were narrow-minded as men or as scholars. Pollock is well-known for the breadth of his interests. Buckland was a Roman lawyer and linguist who was familiar with German and French legal literature. Holland wrote extensively on the history of International Law and, largely through frequent letters to *the Times*, participated in many contemporary public debates, while maintaining a rigidly positivistic stance on the interpretation and application of principles of International Law.

Fourthly, Pollock doubted whether discussions of uses of the word 'law' and the theory of sovereignty - the subject of the first two chapters of Holland's *Elements* - were properly within the scope of jurisprudence, but rather should be treated as prolegomena. Buckland agreed, but took a stronger line:

> 'Jurisprudence has no independent existence. Its formulae are meaningless except in relation to concrete legal rules. It is a part of the law. That the same jurisprudence is a part of all law is a point to be proven not assumed.'[82]

This was a crucial part of his argument that analytical jurisprudence is in first instance particular. Its primary task is analysis of the basic legal concepts of a single municipal legal system. It is an empirical question to what extent, if at all, even advanced legal systems have common concepts. This is a matter for comparative legal research. Buckland, on the basis of his knowledge of Roman Law and some contemporary civilian systems, was inclined to scepticism. He suspected that the universalism of Bentham, Austin and even Holland undermined the distinction between the is and the ought and opened the way for natural law to re-enter by the back door. Buckland it seems was a relativist in respect of both ethics and culture. However, he was as committed as any to the systematic study of legal doctrine.

What was at stake in these debates? It was not a merely or mainly a semantic question about the meaning of the term 'Jurisprudence'. The main concerns were pedagogical: the search for a suitable underpinning for the detailed study of English Law. It is striking that Buckland's article of 1890 begins with reference to the attitude of 'disgust and scarcely veiled contempt' of practical lawyers towards Jurisprudence as a subject. In the context 'abstract' is used pejoratively. The article assumes that most undergraduate law students are intending barristers. This fits the thesis, convincingly developed by David Sugarman, that the establishment of a narrow expository orthodoxy by legal scholars, who were themselves far from narrow-minded, represents a compromise aimed at establishing the study of English Law in universities as being at once scientific and of clear practical value. In the present context the primary reference group was the practising Bar. This required that Jurisprudence should be simultaneously rigorous, uncritical and in tune with the legal culture of the common law. This in turn necessitated a distinct shift of emphasis from general jurisprudence to a form of particular jurisprudence that was closely integrated with the study of substantive doctrine - the basic concepts of common law talk rather than of talk about law.

On revisiting these largely forgotten texts, one is struck by the modesty of their intellectual ambitions. Unlike Bentham, Austin and Maine, who were serious theorists, Pollock, Holland and Buckland were competent legal scholars who were suspicious of philosophy. The debate between universalists and particularists took place in the context of the preparation of elementary student texts by lawyers, for whom jurisprudence was an avocation. Over time the particularists won the day and by 1945 Buckland could write: 'Most English writers deal with Particular Jurisprudence.'[83] Bentham was ignored, Austin was bowdlerised, and Maine was marginalized. Holland was at first treated as a particularist *malgre' soi* and was in due course superseded.

Hart and Dworkin[84]

I began my study of law in Oxford in 1952, the year in which Herbert Hart was elected to the Corpus Chair of Jurisprudence in succession to A.L.Goodhart. So when I embarked on the study of jurisprudence towards the end of my second year, I found myself at the cusp of two traditions of English legal positivism. I experienced both versions.

By the early 1950s taught jurisprudence had become rather eclectic, exemplified by the main textbooks, Paton and Salmond. Some cursory attention was paid to 'schools', such as Natural Law, the Historical School, and Sociological Jurisprudence. More emphasis was placed on particular analytical jurisprudence, which fell into two parts: the sources of English Law as they were treated, for example, in C.K.Allen's *Law in the Making*, and analysis of concepts, including law, sovereignty, legal personality, ownership, possession, *ratio decidendi*, rights and duties. A typical essay topic was: 'Does English Law have a theory of possession? Does it need one?' One approached such questions by reading a mixture of cases and secondary writings. These were interpreted as 'Num-questions', that is questions expecting the answer 'No'. So in dealing with possession one compared the use of the term in cases on larceny, bailment, sale of goods, trespass to land and goods and concluded that it had a slightly different definition in each context, thereby confirming 'the pragmatism' and distrust of abstraction of English legal culture.

Such exercises were particularistic in two ways: the focus was on concepts of English law and they were studied at a relatively low level of generality. However, the approach was not entirely parochial. One might read (or read about) Savigny on possession, German theories of corporate personality, and American writers on rights. One made regular comparisons with Roman Private Law, possibly referring to Buckland and McNair.[85] Buckland's argument about the possibility and value of particular analytical jurisprudence was fully vindicated. It was clearly relevant to other subjects that we were studying; it served to break down the artificial boundaries between fields of law and to make a number of connections; and it helped one to see the common law - especially private law - as a whole, if not quite as a system.[86] For the degree I took two papers in Roman Law (having also done Roman Law for the preliminary examination, 'Mods') and one in Legal History. When I revised for my Finals, I studied the English and Roman law of contract, the history of English contract doctrine, and Hohfeld's analysis of rights simultaneously. It made a lot of sense. This kind of 'particular analytical jurisprudence' has virtually disappeared. From an educational point of view, something of real value was lost as these exercises in applied jurisprudence were replaced by more abstract enquiries.

Of course, this kind of study had distinct limitations. It was narrowly focused; it was somewhat uncritical;[87] it bore little relationship to law in action in society; and it was strikingly atheoretical, especially in respect of method. The subject, as Buckland had suggested, was part of English law; one *did* it as one did any other subject: one read secondary writings and some cases and one wrote an essay.

In his inaugural lecture on 'Definition and Theory in Jurisprudence', Hart seized on the methodological weaknesses of traditional or classical jurisprudence.[88] Questions framed in such terms as 'What is law?', 'What is a right?', 'What is a legal person?' were misposed. They invited answers in the form of definitions of single words *per genus et differentiam*; this was inappropriate for elucidating familiar abstract terms and it failed to dissolve the puzzlements underlying the questions. While theory in law was welcome, the growth of theory on the back of definition was not. In one seminal lecture Hart re-established links with philosophy and provided some powerful tools of analysis of potentially wide application. Significantly, he explicitly gave the credit to Bentham for the main tool, paraphrasis, by implication dismissing the methods of all of the intervening jurists in the analytical tradition, including Austin.

In his lectures, which culminated in *The Concept of Law* in 1961, Hart focused mainly on those concepts which particularists like Pollock and Buckland treated as prolegomena to jurisprudence - law, legal system, command, rule, sovereignty, sanction and the like. However, he drew no sharp distinction between general and particular jurisprudence and some of his best later work - on causation, intention, responsibility and rights - could reasonably be interpreted as contributions to particular jurisprudence. For much of his life, such categorisations were unimportant.

The main challengers to Hart, such as Fuller, Dworkin, and Devlin, and defenders, such as Raz and MacCormick, have generally concentrated on issues relating to his positivism and modified utilitarianism. The approach has been philosophical and the debates have normally taken place at a rather abstract level, often quite far removed from the particularities of English law.[89] There has, of course, been criticism from a variety of other perspectives. In considering the distinction between general and particular jurisprudence it is worth referring briefly to two of these. First, Brian Simpson, drawing on his deep knowledge of English legal history, has argued that Hart's concept of a legal system just does not fit the 'muddle' of the English common law.[90] This can be interpreted as turning on its head Bentham's argument that the common law is not law.[91] Simpson's argument is that a theory of law which excludes the common law must be defective. Subsequently, Charles Sampford has argued at a more general level that it is fundamentally misleading to think of law anywhere as 'systematic'.[92] His picture of law as being part of a 'social melee' at both national and international levels is very much in tune with the thrust of those aspects of globalization theory, and of legal pluralism, which challenge all 'black box' conceptions of law. At first sight Simpson's thesis looks particularistic, Sampford's general. But both represent important challenges to theories of law that treat legal systems as self-contained and 'systematic' in a strong sense. As such they are contributions to general rather than particular jurisprudence, if the distinction has any value.

A second challenge to Hart took the position that his kind of analytical jurisprudence, by focusing on lawyers' talk, divorced law from its social context and diverted attention from sociological enquiries that are essential to understanding legal phenomena. One of the first versions of this line of criticism, by Edgar Bodenheimer, was made before the publication of *The Concept of Law*.[93] It provoked an immediate response from Hart, who argued that his form of conceptual elucidation was as important for sociology as for law and that sociologists could do well to put their own house in order. For jurists clarity begins at home. It may be that the exchange with Bodenheimer was behind the famous claim in the Preface that *The Concept of Law* 'may also be regarded as an essay in descriptive sociology.' This statement has provoked hoots of derision from the sociologically inclined, but little analysis.

My own view, as one who is committed to developing broader approaches to law, has been that Hart 'won' the battle with Bodenheimer, but by not following through in making the case for the importance of conceptual elucidation in *any* approach to the understanding of law, he missed an opportunity to extend the scope of analytical jurisprudence. In short, he exposed the naiveté of traditional analytical jurisprudence in respect of *method* (Bentham excepted), but accepted uncritically its *agenda*.[94] One implication of this argument is that, if legal theory is to respond adequately to the challenges of 'globalization', it needs, *inter alia*, to develop a sophisticated conceptual apparatus for the task. That is a theme for another occasion. Here, however, it is pertinent to note that the generalists as well as the particularists in the analytical tradition are equally open to the charge of 'narrowness', insofar as they concentrated almost exclusively on legal concepts (with a few 'prolegomena'), that is on 'law talk' to the almost total exclusion of 'talk about law'.

It is sometimes suggested that Hart's *The Concept of Law* is solely concerned with 'linguistic analysis' and in this sense is semantic. Buckland, as we have seen, equated analytical jurisprudence with 'analysis of legal concepts'.[95] However, Hart's conception of a descriptive jurisprudence goes far beyond this: it includes both elucidating concepts and *using* them;[96] Concepts and models (such as the model of law as a system of rules) are tools of description; *The Concept of Law*, and general descriptive jurisprudence, go beyond conceptual clarification to describing common features of the form, structure and content of legal systems.[97]

The distinction between general and particular jurisprudence was for a long time treated as of little significance and the debates surrounding it were usually treated as trivial logomachy. However, the distinction was revived in a symposium based on a conference in Jerusalem held in honour of Hart. Commenting on some draft chapters of Dworkin's *Law's Empire*, shortly before it was published, Ruth Gavison wrote:

> 'Dworkin's analysis of law as an interpretive concept, under his own model of interpretation, makes classical legal theory impossible. In other words, Dworkin is challenging here the possibility and the value of 'general jurisprudence', the attempt to analyse societies at their most general (like the attempt to analyse human nature) and identify those features common to all social organizations which might lead to the need for similar institutions and practices. Law is one such social institution found in all societies and exhibiting a core of similar features.'[98]

Hart made a similar point in the same volume, but developed it much further in his Postscript to *The Concept of Law*, which was published posthumously in 1994. Here he defended his views largely in terms of two propositions: that Dworkin has misrepresented his position on a number of key issues and that he and Dworkin were involved in two different, not necessarily incompatible, enterprises, the one general, the other particular.

Hart claimed that he and Dworkin have very different conceptions of legal theory. Hart's is *general* 'in the sense that it is not tied to any particular legal system or legal culture';[99] and it is *descriptive* 'in that it is morally neutral and has no justificatory aims'.[100] Dworkin's jurisprudence is in large part evaluative and justificatory and 'is addressed to a particular legal culture', which is typically the theorist's own.[101] Dworkin is concerned to interpret the settled law and legal practices of a particular system and to provide the best moral justification for them.[102] Hart considers that these two enterprises are so different as not to involve any substantial joinder of issue that need constitute a disagreement.

The Concept of Law deals with the nature of law in general rather than the law of a given society. Hart's work is clearly in the tradition of general jurisprudence, occasionally concretised by particular applications to English or to Anglo-American law. But can we say that Dworkin is doing particular jurisprudence? At first sight it looks absurd to confine Dworkin's ideas in this way. For example, the idea that interpretation of a social practice involves 'showing it in its best light'[103] or the distinction between semantic and interpretative theories are not ideas that are linked to any given legal system. Are not Dworkin's ideas on democracy, equality and liberty founded on some idea of universalisability? Hercules clearly has roots in American legal tradition. He may not be a citizen of the world, but does he not provide one model for judging in any liberal democracy both in respect of his conception of his role and his method of interpretation? Does not Dworkin advance a prescriptive theory of adjudication that is general, if not universal? And, surely, Dworkin's criticisms of legal positivism are not confined to England and the United States.

One possible interpretation of the claim that Hart and Dworkin are involved in significantly different enterprises is that they are addressing different questions. Jurisprudence is a wasteland of false polemics and one way of disposing of such squabbles is to show that the best interpretation of two apparently conflicting positions is that they provide answers to different questions rather than rival answers to shared questions. Prima facie this looks attractive in the present context. In *The Concept of Law* Hart's explicit agenda was to consider three recurrent issues: (1) How does law differ from and how is it related to orders backed by threats? (2) How does legal obligation differ from and how is it related to moral obligation? (3) What are rules and to what extent is law an affair of rules?[104] Dworkin claims that *Law's Empire* is centrally concerned with the problem of sense, that is the truth conditions for correct interpretation of propositions of law. Here, one needs to distinguish between a general theory of legal interpretation or of legal reasoning and what constitutes the best interpretation of a particular rule in a given system. One might render this in the form: 'Under what conditions is it true to say that 'rule X means this' or that 'this is the correct interpretation of rule X'? This is a different question from those listed by Hart, but it is in similar form at the same level of generality as Hart-type questions, such as: 'Under what conditions is it true to say that a legal system exists?' or 'Under what conditions is it true to say that X has a right?' *All* of these questions are general in that they are not confined to or derived from a single legal system and they can be asked of many, if nor all, legal systems. Similarly, for both Dworkin and Hart, questions such as 'Is this the best interpretation of rule X?' or 'Does Y have a right to delivery of goods from the seller?' require local knowledge of a particular legal system as well as a general theory guiding the answer. Here, the distinction between general and particular jurisprudence provides no basis for distinguishing between the theories of Dworkin and Hart.

It is also doubtful whether the technique of attributing different questions to different positions will take us very far. Hart and Dworkin have different, but overlapping agendas. For example, Dworkin is interested in Hart's questions (2) and (3) and Hart acknowledges that his theory has implications for adjudication and interpretation. He also acknowledges that they do have some substantial differences of view.[105] There are some grey areas, for example where Hart claims that Dworkin has misinterpreted or caricatured his position, but insofar as Dworkin does not accept this, they are disagreeing about the best interpretation of Hart.[106] What is significant in the present context is that Dworkin's criticisms of Hart and Hart's reply are almost without exception pitched at a higher level of generality than any particular legal system. Neither is claiming that they are solely or even mainly arguing about English law or some American jurisdiction or even the common law family. So, again the distinction between general and particular jurisprudence explains almost nothing about the exchanges between Hart and Dworkin.

However, it is Dworkin who insists that: 'interpretive theories are by their nature addressed to a particular legal culture, generally the culture to which their authors belong.'[107] In the same passage he draws a distinction between 'the very detailed and concrete legal theories lawyers and judges construct for a particular jurisdiction' and the abstract conceptions of law that philosophers build, which are not so confined.[108] He argues that an abstract philosophical conception of law, still less a justificatory theory for a given system (or, semble, a family of systems belonging to one legal culture), will probably not fit 'foreign legal systems developing in and reflecting political ideologies of a sharply different character'. His main point is that one can only determine whether a given proposition of law is true for a given system by participating in that system, because this activity involves interpreting and choosing between contested meanings and that necessitates taking sides. For Dworkin there is no such thing as neutral interpretation.[109] However, in making these *caveats*, Dworkin may be being unduly cautious about the general significance of his theory.

A charitable interpretation of Dworkin's emphasis on the particularity of interpretation may include two points which we have already encountered. He may draw almost exclusively on Anglo-American materials and he may leave open the scope of the applicability of his ideas to civilian and other systems on the grounds of limited expertise, but so did Austin, Maine and Holland, all of whom claimed to be doing general jurisprudence. This seems rather like Holland's example of a geologist who has only studied English strata and who is cautious about generalising beyond his data base.[110]

Secondly, in emphasising the importance of local knowledge, Dworkin seems to be making a similar point to that made by Buckland in his critique of Holland. If general jurisprudence is confined to describing the features that are common to all or nearly all legal systems, the description will almost certainly be rather thin because in fact legal systems are quite diverse and the interest of a legal system lies typically in its detail. General jurisprudence on its own will be too abstract to be useful or interesting. In so far as Dworkin is concerned with interpretation, argumentation and justification by legal practitioners and judges, he would agree with Austin that jurisprudence to be practical has to be local and particular. But that does not mean that the core elements in his theory only apply to one system.

Moreover, only by studying all legal systems in detail can one identify which features are universal or common. Dworkin's variant on this argument is that general jurisprudence cannot deal with the problem of sense, that is the attribution of truth values to propositions of law.[111] This seems to conflate a general theory of adjudication or legal interpretation with its application in a local context. The former may be lean, but that does not mean that it is not important. *Law's Empire* advances a general theory of law, or at least of adjudication; it contains very few concrete examples of interpretation and those are mainly illustrative; some of Dworkin's other writings are more local, but these can be interpreted as applications of his general approach.[112]

A less charitable interpretation of Hart and Dworkin is suggested by Atiyah and Summers, who advocate 'jurisprudential relativism' in the interpretation of legal cultures:

> 'In our view, then, the primary subject-matter of jurisprudence is not a single universal subject matter, abstracted from the variant phenomena of law in all societies. It should, rather, consist of relevant features of the phenomena of law in one or more particular societies.'[113]

Atiyah and Summers were comparing and contrasting the legal cultures of England and the United States which are closely related by history, language, and continuing links. Interestingly they suggest that the two cultures even have different conceptions of some concepts which are usually allocated to the meta-language of general jurisprudence, such as 'law' and 'rule' and 'legal validity'. In their view, both Hart and Dworkin are best interpreted as contributing to, or as being most useful at the level of, particular jurisprudence. Dworkin's theory is both derived from American intellectual tradition and fits American culture better than English. Conversely Hart is recognizably English in respect of the derivation of his ideas and their application. For example, the ideal role for judges and legislators is dependent on context, for political institutions are fashioned by history, tradition and culture:

> 'What is the practical utility of a theory which postulates how Hercules J. ought to behave on the bench, if appointing authorities insist on nominating judges who do not even want to emulate Hercules?'[114]

This ethnographic perspective raises many intriguing questions that cannot be pursued here. Atiyah and Summers acknowledge that it may be possible to identify some features and concepts which are common to the phenomena of law in all societies, but the list is likely to be short and its explanatory value meagre. This is very like Buckland's view that law is culturally relative and that jurisprudence must in the main be particular. I have some sympathy with this position, but I do not think that this is an interpretation that makes Hart's and Dworkin's theories the best they can be. I would rather suggest that both theories largely stand or fall on an assessment of their value as contributions to general jurisprudence.

Dworkin is not a strong cultural relativist.[115] It is one thing to claim that a thick description of any society or culture or social practice must depend on local knowledge and hence be particular; it is another to claim that a society or culture or practice can only be described, interpreted or explained solely in its own terms. Most writing by historians and social anthropologists is particular and local, because they tend to study events and phenomena that are unique in important respects; but those writings are based on theories, methods and concepts that have some claim to generality - and some may be unknown locally. Conversely, it is a truism, accepted by both Hart and Dworkin, that to give an adequate account of a particular social practice or legal system typically involves taking into account the internal point of view of participants in that practice or system, including their concepts and language. One cannot give a 'thick' account of English or Tiv or Barotse law either solely in terms of some foreign or meta-language, which does not capture the ways of thought of the participants, nor solely in terms of the folk concepts of the participants themselves.[116] Hart is not committed to ignoring or discounting the internal point of view; Dworkin is not committed to treating local concepts as exclusive for purposes of justification or description. For example, in the standard example of a foreign anthropologist describing and interpreting a rain-making ceremony, the external observer needs to take into account the belief of some or all participants that it does indeed make rain, but s/he could explain and possibly justify the practice in terms of social solidarity: 'Whether or not it makes rain, it serves a useful purpose for them'.

What colour is Hercules's passport? He may be of American origin, have a slight American accent, and possibly some deep-rooted American cultural biases.[117] But clearly he is offered, and deserves attention, as a possible role model for judges in many systems - certainly the common law family, almost certainly Western civilian systems, possibly the European Union and judges of international tribunals, perhaps even the judiciary in an

Islamic state. The reason for this is obvious: the basic ideas underlying Hercules's approach are not derived from nor confined to any one legal system or culture: law as integrity; interpretation as making a system the best it can be; reasoning by the two stage process of fit and justification; justification in terms of institutionally embedded principles of political morality. All of these concepts are not system-specific. Hercules has strong claims to be a citizen at least of the West, and possibly of the World.

Let us consider some possible objections to this. First, it might be argued that these ideas are not sufficient conditions for appointing Hercules as a judge in any jurisdiction. Of course, that is correct. In order to be able to perform the role of a judge well one needs a number of other qualifications, including a good deal of local knowledge about, for example, the general prescriptions of the legal system concerning authoritative sources of law, including any rules of priority and interpretation; and about other factors subsumed under the idea of 'fit'.[118] Similarly in interpreting the law in a hard case, Hercules' duty is to resolve difficulties by reference to fundamental principles of political morality which give *this* system integrity. These will typically be contested, but in Dworkin's theory this does not mean that Hercules should merely resort to his personal opinions; rather he should seek for the 'best' solution in the system's own terms. Such justificatory principles are not purely local, but form part of a coherent theory of political morality which, one assumes, makes some claim to generality. Dworkin makes clear his commitment to a particular version of liberal democratic theory of wide application, but he recognises that Hercules may serve in a system based on a different moral theory. Presumably that moral theory is basically compatible with Hercules's own values, for he could not otherwise in good conscience have taken the judicial oath.[119] Hercules's characteristics are not sufficient conditions for judicial appointment; they are presented as desirable, ideal, perhaps even necessary, standards for good judging.

A second objection, suggested by Atiyah and Summers, is that Hercules just does not fit most actual legal systems. If he were a candidate for judicial appointment in England, he would probably not be appointed. Dworkin has two possible answers to that: first, if a system does not subscribe to his aspirational standards for judging, more's the pity. His is 'the best theory' prescribing an ideal. Secondly, Dworkin - more controversially - claims that his theory describes good practice in the Anglo-American system. In this view, Atiyah and Summers misrepresent English practice.

A third objection is that Dworkin advances a general theory of adjudication, but courts and judges are institutionalised in different ways in different societies and so have different roles, methods and so on. Even in modern Western societies third party adjudication is only one of several modes of dispute-processing and, in terms of frequency and accessibility, it is often one of the least important in practice. What precisely is the role of courts in a given society varies considerably according to time and place. This argument can be extended in two ways: first, as any comparative lawyer knows, even terms like 'court', 'judge', 'lawyer', 'case' and 'trial' are culture-specific. Second, some societies do not have any institutionalised third-party adjudication at all.[120]

This is a powerful argument that needs to be taken into account by any legal theory that claims to be even minimally sensitive to 'social realities'. It is particularly pertinent in considering globalization, given the relative unimportance of 'courts' in international, transnational and other global relations. Here I think that Dworkin may have done himself a disservice by claiming to advance a theory of adjudication. What he is really advancing is a theory of correct interpretation of legal norms. Hercules is not just a role model for actual judges; rather he is a symbol for the Upright Interpreter, who is loyal to the system - that is for anyone who is concerned to reach the correct or 'best' or 'right' interpretation of the law.[121] This includes upright officials, good citizens, and other participants who wish to make decisions based at least in part on clear understandings of what the law prescribes. One doubts whether labelling Dworkin's theory as 'a theory of adjudication' is making it the best it can be. It has a much wider reach than that.

Finally, Atiyah and Summers draw a distinction between their 'jurisprudential relativism' and moral (or ethical) relativism, which they reject. They also express scepticism about Utopian universalism in the field of law and, as we have seen, dismiss Hercules as representing an Utopian ideal with regard to the role of judges. It seems that they are more sympathetic to Hart's concern to develop a descriptive theory that fits the facts of actual legal phenomena, but they place more emphasis on cultural or local specificity than Hart does.[122] Here, there is a more fundamental difference with Dworkin; for although he makes some allowance for cultural diversity, he considers that law and its interpretation are a moral and an argumentative enterprise, founded on a moral theory that is a general theory of political morality and a theory of rationality that is similarly based on general principles of valid reasoning. Thus, at its core, Dworkin's seemingly particularistic theory is at least as general as its positivistic rivals.

Hart's Postscript and the mutual courtesies of the two friendly protagonists suggest that the differences between them can easily be exaggerated. They come from a shared philosophical tradition, but from somewhat different legal cultures. Neither has drawn much inspiration from anthropology, sociology or history. They both present a picture of law in terms of monistic unity: law as a system of rules and law as integrity treat the laws of independent nation states as units of analysis in ways that approximate to the ideal type of 'black box' theories. Even at what many consider to be the key point of differentiation between positivist and anti-positivist positions, many would argue that they may not be very different. On the one hand, some would interpret Dworkin as a 'positivist' in that Hercules must look for underlying principles that are institutionally embedded in an existing system; conversely, Hart's insistence on a sharp distinction between the is and the ought has sometimes been interpreted as a conservative attempt to legitimate legal systems - conservatism masquerading as neutrality. A more plausible reading is that for Hart, as for Bentham and Holmes, separating the 'is' and the 'ought' serves clarity of thought, which in turn is based on a moral concern: one needs a vocabulary for depicting actual legal institutions and systems in terms than can depict the true awfulness of many such exercises of power - like The *Bonfire of the Vanities* writ large. I am personally more sympathetic to this last interpretation, but in the present context the main point is that the distinction between general and particular jurisprudence does little or nothing to illuminate the similarities and differences between Hart and Dworkin.

Some Concluding Observations

This paper is one of a series of essays exploring the implications of globalization for legal theory. It suggests that sharp distinctions between general and particular jurisprudence are of limited value. Its starting-point was the suggestion that some Anglo-American jurisprudence seems to have been going through a somewhat parochial phase and continues to be dominated by theories which treat societies, nation-states and legal systems as largely self-contained units. In this context, 'parochialism' can relate to focus, or to sources, or to perspectives. Jurisprudence, can be inward-looking in respect of its agenda, ethnocentric in respect of its perspective, or limited in respect of its sources and inspiration. Globalization brings to the fore a wide range of issues at transnational, international and global levels and is rapidly changing the significance of national boundaries. As such it challenges 'black box theories', it is inimical to ethnocentric perspectives on transnational issues, but it does not minimize the importance of the local. 'The citizen of the world' may still be a rooted cosmopolitan, in Bruce Ackerman's phrase,[123] setting the study of local issues and phenomena in a broad geographical context.

This preliminary study of one aspect of the vast heritage of jurisprudence suggests that the English positivist tradition has tended to emphasise general more than particular jurisprudence; it has been quite cosmopolitan in outlook, but over time it increasingly narrowed its focus to a relatively narrow range of concepts and issues relating mainly, but not exclusively, to English or Anglo-American legal doctrine. Of the individuals studied, Bentham was the one who was most consistently committed to the viewpoint of 'the citizen of the world' and, although he did not develop his ideas very far in this respect, he was more sensitive than most of his successors to the limitations of 'black box' theories of national or municipal legal systems.[124]

It is worth commenting briefly on each of these points. First, English legal positivism since Bentham has usually placed more emphasis on general than on particular jurisprudence. Bentham, Austin, Maine, Holland, and Hart all fit this category, as do many others. Holland's English critics, such as Pollock and Buckland, were not being parochial or ethnocentric in respect of perspective. They were mainly concerned that an over-abstract approach to the teaching of Jurisprudence would be less useful than the systematic study of the basic concepts and principles of English Law and would reinforce the resistance of the practising profession to the academic study of law and especially to legal theory. I have argued that the differences between Hart and Dworkin cannot be usefully explained in terms of a distinction between general and particular jurisprudence and that Dworkin's central ideas, both explicitly and implicitly have general, if not universal, significance.

Secondly, the English tradition of academic law has generally been quite cosmopolitan. Historically, the study of Roman Law, Canon Law, Public International Law, and to a lesser extent, Comparative Law have been an important part of our intellectual tradition. The British Empire, the Commonwealth, the European Union, and the strong networks within the extended family of common law jurisdictions have usually kept in check any tendencies to confine legal studies to English domestic law. Even the advocates of particular jurisprudence such as Buckland and Pollock were hardly Little Englanders. They were familiar with Roman Law and contemporary European legal thought. Like them, generalists such as Austin and Maine, drew most of their examples from Roman and English Law. The recent decline in the study of Romanist systems, the confining of 'core subjects' to domestic law, and the general parochialism of modern professional examinations, will almost certainly prove to have been a relatively short historical phase. The European Union, the internationalization of much legal practice, and the broader processes of globalization will ensure that.

Thirdly, analytical positivism was, however, narrow in a different sense. The sharp distinction between the is and the ought and between law and other disciplines supported a tendency to confine the study of law to the exposition and analysis of legal doctrine. The expository tradition tended to become ahistorical, decontextualised and uncritical.[125]

Despite a series of challenges it remains the dominant force in our academic legal culture.[126] This is clearly illustrated in the work of our most influential modern jurist, Herbert Hart: his method was of potentially very wide application, his commitment was to general jurisprudence, but his focus and agenda for jurisprudence were quite narrow. Conceptual clarification ard formal description are as important for broader approaches to law as for legal dogmatics, but Hart neither applied his great analytical skills to the basic concepts needed for such approaches nor did he encourage others to do so. Similarly, Ronald Dworkin's agenda for Legal Philosophy is really quite narrow. Insofar as his main interest is adjudication, he confines his focus to questions of law in hard cases, ignoring almost entirely the whole range of problems of interpretation and justification involved in other important decisions in legal contexts.[127]

Another limitation of the tradition has been to treat societies and municipal legal systems as self-contained units and to pay scant attention to transnational and global relations and to legal pluralism. Even in respect of traditional Public International Law, theorists as different as Hart, Rawls and Dworkin, who share the tendency to treat 'legal systems' as isolated and self-contained phenomena, and as a result they tend be at their least convincing at the international and transnational levels. How far their central ideas can be rescued from such criticism requires further exploration.

Finally, the distinction between general and particular jurisprudence has a function, but it has been and is likely to be of limited value in setting an agenda for the discipline of law and for jurisprudence as its theoretical part. I, for one, benefited as a student from exposure to particular analytical jurisprudence and regret its passing. But 'general' and 'particular' are relative matters and the distinction cannot bear much weight. In considering the implications of globalization for legal theory, it will be necessary to be concerned with a wide range of questions at different levels of generality. 'Thick description' of local particulars set in broad geographical contexts will be as important as ever in the development of a healthy discipline of law in a more integrated world.[128]

NOTES

1 For example, *Our Global Neighbourhood*, The Report of the Commission on Global Governance (Ingvar Carlsson and Shridath Ramphal, Co-Chairmen) (1995).

2 See generally, Fred Halliday, *Rethinking International Relations* (1994).

3 A fairly typical summary reads as follows: '...in social science there are as many conceptualizations of globalization as there are disciplines. In economics globalization refers to economic internationalization and the spread of capitalist market relations... In international relations, the focus is on the increasing density of interstate relations and the development of global politics. In sociology, the concern is with increasing world-wide social densities and the emergence of "world society". In cultural studies, the focus is on global communications and world-wide standardization, as in CocaColonization and McDonaldization, and on the post-colonial culture. In history, the concern is with conceptualizing "global history"...' Jan Nederveen Pieterse 'Globalization as Hybridization' in M.Featherstone, S.Lash and R.Robertson, *Global Modernities* (1995). Equally typically, there is no mention of law.

4 Halliday at p.1.

5 'A wide range of actors may be involved in any one area of governance. To cite just one example, those with a role in bringing order to international trade in sugar and sweeteners include transnational firms, national and international authorities in charge of competition policy, a global group (The International Sugar Council) with specific responsibility for trade, and a host of smaller

private associations, including plantation workers, beet farmers, and dieticians. An international organization may easily develop an interest in a local issue, as when the World Bank finances an agricultural project in a country. A local voluntary association may just as easily become a participant in an international regime.' *Our Global Neighbourhood, op. cit.* n.3.

6 This theme will be developed in a later paper. For a general critique of Rawls along these lines see Thomas W.Pogge, *Realising Rawls* (1989). Pogge states: 'In the modern world there are no self-contained national societies; a closed background system exists only at the global level. The question, therefore, is whether Rawls's conception, if it applies at all, applies to open national societies (as Rawls seems to prefer) or to the closed social system of humanity at large (as I maintain in Part Three).' (*Ibid.* at 7-8). See further, Halliday, *op. cit.*, 78-81.

7 *Works*, vol. xi, 72.

8 *A Fragment on Government* ed. Burns and Hart (CW, 1977) at 397-98; cf. *Introduction to the Principles of Morals and Legislation* (*IPML*) ed. Burns and Hart (CW, 1970) 8.22 294-95.

9 See further, William Twining, 'Reading Bentham', *Proceedings of the British Academy* (1989) LXXV, 97, at 129 ff. It is pertinent to note that Bentham claimed to be doing *universal* jurisprudence, Austin '*general*', Buckland and Gray favoured '*particular*' and '*comparative*', and Bentham allowed for '*local*' (i.e. sub-national). see further, below n..

10 *Jeremy Bentham's Economic Writings*, ed. W.Stark, (1952-54) vol.1, 100-101.

11 *Fragment, op. cit.* at 397.

12 In *IPML* at 295 Bentham ends this list of examples with the significant words 'and many others'. Earlier, in the same work, he talked of 'the short list of terms, the exposition of which contains all that can be said with propriety to belong to the head of *universal jurisprudence*.'. He listed as examples 'obligation, right, power, possession, title, exemption, immunity, franchise, privilege, nullity, validity, and the like.', *ibid.* at 6; cf. *Works*, iii 217.

13 'Points' here refers to the substance of laws. *IPML* at 293-95.

14 Philip Schofield, 'Jeremy Bentham and Nineteenth-Century English Jurisprudence', 12 *Jo. Legal History*, (1991) 58, at 59.

15 *Ibid*, at 61. Bentham was quite explicit about his lack of interest in simple exposition: 'The business of simple exposition is a harvest in which there seemed no likelihood of there being any want of labourers: and into which therefore I had little ambition to thrust my sickle.' *Fragment*, Preface, at 404. The context of this statement is a passage in which he justifies his attack on Blackstone in the character of Expositor, because 'the imbecility' of his treatment of the censorial infected his exposition of English Law.

16 Oren Ben Dor has pointed out to me that the is/ought distinction for Bentham operates at different levels; here I am concerned with the distinction between law as it is and law as it ought to be.

17 *Fragment* p.398.

18 'To be susceptible of an universal application, all that a book of an expository kind can have to treat of, is the import of words: to be, strictly speaking universal, it must confine itself to terminology.' IPML, p.295.

19 *IPML*, at 296-97 He suggested that 'particular' might be substituted for local, but in the present context I shall confine the term particular jurisprudence to what he called 'internal' in this passage, but which he referred to at different times as 'local' and 'national'. He criticised Blackstone's use of 'municipal' to apply to national law and the term 'law of nations' to apply to international jurisprudence rather than internal (laws of nations). The terminology is unimportant; but Bentham's willingness to recognize a multiplicity of levels is significant.

20 *Ibid*.

21 For example, J.Bentham, *Constitutional Writings for Greece and Tripoli,* ed. P.Schofield (CW, 1990) and below n. . See further, W. Twining, 'Some Aspects of Reception' (1957) *Sudan Law Jo. and Reports* 229, and 'Constitutions, Constitutionalism and Constitution-mongering', in Irwin P. Stotzky, *Transition to Democracy in Latin America: The Role of the Judiciary* (1993), ch. 25. A less sceptical view, closer to Bentham's position on the transferability of laws, is developed by Alan Watson in *Legal Transplants* (1974).

22 *Fragment*, 397-98; cf. *IPML* at p.295.

23 Letter to Madison, 30 October 1811, 8 *Correspondence* 182-215 ed. S.Conway (CW, 1988). A version of this long letter was published as part of *Papers Relative to Codification and Public Instruction* (1817) and was partly reprinted in the Bowring edition, *Works*, vol. iv, 453-67. It can be read as an example of sustained special pleading, but is consistent with his general position. The central argument is that only in a few areas would the preparatory work he had already done (on penal law, civil law, judicial establishment, procedure, evidence, and constitutional law) require extensive amendment to fit local conditions. For example:

> 'Thus in the case of Penal Law. Of the *genera* of Offences, as distinguished or distinguishable by their generic names - Murder, Defamation, Theft, Robbery and so forth - definitions for the most part are the same all the world over. But for particular species, occasion may be afforded, by particular local circumstances: and so in regard to causes of aggravation, extenuation, justification, or exemption, with demand for corresponding varieties in respect of *satisfaction* or punishment. And so in regard to *contracts*.' (*Ibid.* p.203).

24 *Ibid.* at 202. This general statement needs to be read in context: Bentham was making the case for employing an Englishman as legislative adviser to a political leader whose legal system was historically and culturally closely related to English Law, but who had to be wary of local nationalist sentiment. Bentham was careful to show his familiarity with American legal developments and to pronounce them to represent 'prodigious improvements' on English Law (at 211). Local knowledge could be supplied by locals, who in any event would have the final say.

25 For example, *Of Laws in General* ed. H.L.A.Hart (CW, 1970) (*OLIG*) at 233-34, discussed by Hart in his *Essays on Bentham* (1982) ch.5 especially 125.

26 See M.Lobban, *The Common Law and English Jurisprudence 1760-1850* (1991), 179-84 which contains a useful discussion based on a variety of published works and unpublished manuscripts from different periods.

27 For example, *IPML*, 295. The distinction between form and substance in the thought of Bentham and other writers discussed below deserves further exploration. Professor Robert Summers is currently working on a major project on 'the formal character of law', which, *inter alia*, reminds us that the description of the form and structure of legal systems and of laws is not solely a matter of elucidation of concepts. For preliminary reports see Summers, 'The Formal Character of Law', 51 *Camb.L.J.* 242 (1992) and 'The Formal Character of Law III' 25 *Rechtstheorie* 125 (1994).

28 Mary Mack, *Jeremy Bentham: An Odyssey of Ideas 1748-1792* (1962); cf. Douglas Long, 'Censorial Jurisprudence and Political Radicalism: A Reconsideration of the Early Bentham', 12 *The Bentham Newsletter* 4 (1988), arguing that 'Bentham was a radical *about* political terms.'

29 Lobban, *op. cit.* 256. On the general theme of 'Benthamic ambiguity' see William Twining, 'Hot Air in the Redwoods', 86 *Michigan L.Rev.* (1988) 1523, at 1536-39 and 'Why Bentham?' 8 *The Bentham Newsletter* 34 (1984).

30 In several places Austin used the terms 'science' and 'philosophy' interchangeably, e.g. J.Austin, 'The Uses of the Study of Jurisprudence' (1863, ed. Hart, 1954) 365 (hereafter *Uses*).

31 Austin included Legislation among the subjects that should be studied as a preparation for legal practice or politics, *Uses* at 387-88. He stressed the need for law to be based on ethics, but his interpretation of utility was more conservative than Bentham's (see Philip Schofield, this volume).

32 *Lectures on Jurisprudence* (LJ) 32 (Austin's italics). Rumble has pointed out that Austin slightly misquoted Hobbes. W. Rumble, Introduction to Austin, *The Province of Jurisprudence Determined* (1995).

33 At least in print. Bentham's early manuscripts, on which Douglas Long has done pioneering work, contain some further discussions of the distinction.

34 *Uses*, 367-69. This passage is almost identical to a passage in Lecture XI of *LJ*, which contains a longer analysis of the distinction between general and particular jurisprudence. This is one of the passages which has led to controversy about the interpretation of Austin. Did his reference to utility here and his lengthy treatment of it in his lectures undermine his positivism? Indeed, some later critics suggested that he was a closet natural lawyer. And was Austin's conception of General Jurisprudence 'formal' (as Moles and Lobban suggest) or 'empirical', as is argued by W.L. Morison, *John Austin* (1982)? My own view is that there are passages in which Austin's references

to utility did threaten to undermine his strict positivism; it seems to me to be clear that he considered concepts to be *tools for empirical description*, that these were to some extent constructed from real life examples, but that his general jurisprudence did not claim to be empirical in the sense that it could be falsified by evidence, and so in that sense it was analytical or formal. See further, Lobban at 223-27. On Hart's claim to be describing 'the form, structure and content' of legal systems, see Raz, *op. cit.*

35 If it means 'logically necessary', Austin's list should have been confined to a few meta-concepts, such as sovereign, command, sanction and a very small number of legal concepts, of which duty or obligation and legal persons may be almost the only ones. In theory, one could envisage a legal system which prescribed only absolute duties, backed by sanctions that did not include punishments. If, as seems more plausible, by 'necessary' Austin meant important or basic or salient, then the distinction between necessary and common is vague and not very significant.

36 For example, *Uses*, 372

37 *Uses*, 390.

38 *Ibid*, 372.

39 *Ibid*.

40 Sugarman, 'Legal Theory, the Common Law Mind, and the Making of the Textbook Tradition', in W.Twining (ed.), *Legal Theory and Common Law* (1986), 26; Schofield, *op. cit*.

41 J.S.Mill, 'Austin on Jurisprudence', cxviii *The Edinburgh Review* (1863), 439-41, discussed by Schofield, *op. cit*. 70-71.

42 The phrase is attributed to Dicey; cf. Buckland below at n.43.

43 W.W.Buckland, *Some Reflections on Jurisprudence* (1945) 2.

44 Robert Moles, *Definition and Rule in Legal Theory: A Reassessment of H.L.A.Hart and the Positivist Tradition* (1987). Moles makes some interesting points, but his criticism of Hart rests on the secondary, and by no means uncontroversial, claim that Hart misread Austin; in his own interpretation of Austin he eccentrically pays almost no attention to his relationship to Bentham.

45 Morton J.Horwitz, 'Why is Anglo-American Jurisprudence Unhistorical?', H.L.A.Hart Memorial Lecture, May 1995 (forthcoming).

46 Apart from Bentham, the influence of Hobbes on later English positivists, such as Pollock, is often underestimated.

47 Holland see below at n.59.

48 H.L.A.Hart, 'John Austin' in A.W.B. Simpson, *Biographical Dictionary of the Common Law* (1984) 23.

49 The first generation of university law teachers believed that the production of students' works was a high priority in the struggle to establish law as an academic discipline. Works by Foster, Amos and Markby did not meet the felt need for an accessible text on jurisprudence; nor did the full version of Austin's lectures, but students' works based on them, such as those by Campbell (1874) and Clark (1883) were produced to fill the gap. See further Schofield, *op. cit*. at 72-73.

50 *Ibid*, 69.

51 *Ibid*.

52 It is significant that most of the leading pioneers of English university law teaching in this period, Bryce, Maitland, Dicey, to a lesser extent Pollock, and later Vinogradoff, distanced themselves from analytical jurisprudence. The main exception was Holland. However, nearly all went out of their way to stress the potential compatibility of these distinct enterprises.

53 Pollock *Essays on Jurisprudence and Ethics* (1882) 1.

54 Sir T.E. Holland (1835-1926) was Chichele Professor of International Law at Oxford from 1874-1910. The page citations used here are from the 10th edition (1906). Holland had earlier published *Essays on the Forms of Law* (1870). This was concerned with legislation and codification in England and could, ironically, be interpreted as a contribution to particular jurisprudence.

55 Holland's *Jurisprudence* was seen as the main vehicle of Austinian analytical jurisprudence. It was more systematic and more readable than Austin. By and large, it was treated with respect in Holland's lifetime, but it did not stand the test of time. In later writings in the tradition it was almost never cited with approval and it was used as a target for criticism by Kocourek, Stone, Dias and others. It has been almost completely ignored by writers as diverse as Friedmann, Hart and

Dworkin. Today, it seems seriously flawed in respect of both conception and execution - an elementary textbook on a subject not suited to textbook treatment. cf. W.Twining, 'Is Your Textbook Really Necessary?' XI *J.S.P.T.L. (N.S.)* 81 (1970).

56 J.L.Brierley, Obituary, 42 *L.Q.R.* 475 (1926).

57 F.Pollock, *op. cit.* (1882) at 9.

58 This is a misjudgement based on ignorance of some of Bentham's less well-known published writings as well as his unpublished work.

59 *Ibid*, Preface, vii.

60 *Ibid.*

61 *Ibid.*

62 Holland suggests that this is because 'that continental jurists find in Roman law a ready-made terminology and a typical method, upon which they are little inclined to innovate.' (Preface, at viii).

63 *Ibid*, 13.

64 *Ibid*, 10-11; cf. Maine's use of the analogy with geology in *Ancient Law* (1861) ch.1.

65 *Ibid*, at 11.

66 *Ibid*, at 7. On the link between Bentham's Universal Jurisprudence and his idea of a Universal Grammar see D.Long *op. cit.* at 16-18.

67 Holland sought to explain his idea of a 'formal science' by an example. If a scholar accumulated knowledge of every European system of law and found each to be entirely unlike the rest, there would be no basis for constructing a science; there would just be a heterogeneous body of information. 'Suppose however, *as is the case*, that the laws of every country contain a common element; that they have been constructed in order to effect similar objects, and involve the assumption of similar moral phenomena as everywhere existing; then such a person might proceed to frame out of his accumulated materials a scheme of the purposes, methods, and ideas common to every system of law. Such a scheme would be a formal science of law; presenting many analogies to Grammar...' (*Ibid*, 7, italics added). This passage is vulnerable to criticism on several grounds: first, what he describes is an empirical rather than a formal science; secondly, he lacked the evidence to support his assertion that the laws of every country contain a common element; he merely asserted what his science set out to prove; third, he includes purposes, assumed moral phenomena and methods as well as ideas. But elsewhere his formal science is presented as dealing only with analysis of concepts. This is the gravamen of Buckland's criticism. Compare the recent debate about whether Austin's jurisprudence was formal or empirical, above n.34 and below n.87.

68 F.Pollock, *op. cit.* (1882).

69 Pollock, in his *First Book of Jurisprudence* (1896) Preface, explicitly distanced himself from the analytical school.

70 J.C. Gray, *The Nature and Sources of Law* (1909) ch.7.

71 A.Kocourek, *Jural Relations* (1st ed., 1928).

72 F.H.Lawson wrote of Holland's *Elements of Jurisprudence* that it resembled Markby's *Elements of Law* 'in containing quite a good deal of what is not so much jurisprudence as law' and quoted Lord Birkenhead as saying that it was 'one of a number of books which appeared in Oxford in the eighties which made sense of English law.' *The Oxford Law School, 1850-1965* (1968) at 75.

73 W.W.Buckland, 'Difficulties of Abstract Jurisprudence', 24 *L.Q.R.* 436 (1890).

74 W.W.Buckland, *Some Reflections on Jurisprudence* (Cambridge, 1949), ch.VI, at 68. This work is fairly typical of Buckland's style: succinct, perceptive, astringent, and strongly positivist.

75 For example, *Reflections* 68.

76 *Ibid*, 70.

77 *Reflections* 69.

78 For example, Holland at vii; Buckland, *Reflections*, 2 and 42-43.

79 Pollock, *Introduction to the History of the Science of Politics* (1890) 67.

80 *Reflections* 2.

81 For example, Holland, ch. xvii; Pollock (1896); Buckland, *Reflections*, ch.2. Holland referred to International law as 'law by courtesy' (*ibid*, 127) and its study as 'the vanishing point of jurisprudence' (380).

82 (1890) at 438; cf. *Reflections* at 3: 'Law and sovereignty are not legal conceptions; they are presuppositions...' This is reminiscent of Thayer's treatment of 'relevance' as being a presupposition of the law of evidence, rather than part of it. (J.B.Thayer, *A Preliminary Treatise on Evidence at Common Law* (1898) 264-65). For both Buckland and Thayer the distinction between presuppositions and legal rules was logically, but not pedagogically, important. Buckland acknowledged that his *Some Reflections on Jurisprudence* was a misnomer as much of it dealt with what he considered to be prolegomena to Jurisprudence (Preface).

83 *Reflections* at 71.

84 Except where it is indicated otherwise, this section focuses on two texts: Hart's *The Concept of Law* (2nd ed. 1994), including his posthumous Postscript, and Ronald Dworkin's *Law's Empire* (1986) (hereafter, *LE*).

85 W.W. Buckland and A.D.McNair, *Roman Law and Common Law* (1936).

86 The standard justification for studying Roman law was that it enabled one to study a legal system as a whole. In fact, one focused almost entirely on the rules and concepts of Roman Private Law.

87 Horwitz, *op. cit.* characterises English Analytical Jurisprudence as ahistorical; unempirical; apolitical; and uncritical. This is only partially correct in respect of the version I encountered as an undergraduate at Oxford: everything one studied was suffused with history, albeit of a rather narrow kind - the tracing of the development of doctrines of English private law largely through the cases. The predominating approach was doctrinal-empirical rather than social-empirical. We were not discouraged from criticism (*de lege ferenda*) but we were not equipped to do this in an intellectual way. The predominant approach was apolitical, except that some of us drew inspiration from the writings of Wolfgang Friedmann.

88 H.L.A.Hart *Definition and Theory in Jurisprudence* (1953).

89 The problem of building bridges between abstract theorising and the study of specialised fields of law is explored in W.Twining (ed), *Legal Theory and Common law* (1986), the central theme of which is that, for purposes of legal education and legal scholarship, 'Jurisprudence should not be a subject apart'.

90 A.W.B.Simpson, 'The Common Law and Legal Theory' in Simpson (ed), *Oxford Essays in Jurisprudence*, 2nd series (1973); reprinted in *Legal Theory and Common Law*, *op. cit.*

91 For example, *OLIG*, ch. xvi.

92 Charles Sampford, *The Disorder of Law* (1989).

93 Edgar Bodenheimer, 'Modern Analytical Jurisprudence and the Limits of its Usefulness', (1955-56) 104 *Univ. of Pennsylvania L.R.* 1680; H.L.A.Hart, 'Analytical Jurisprudence at Mid-Twentieth Century: A Reply to Professor Bodenheimer,' 105 (1957) *ibid* at 953.

94 '... Hart has not in a systematic way attempted to proceed beyond the confines of Bentham's expository and censorial jurisprudence into the kind of broader perspective that is encompassed by phrases such as 'sociology of law'. He has not, for example, devoted sustained attention to analysis of key terms in the vocabulary of sociological theories about law such as society, group, class, function, process, dispute, social problem, institution or decision. He has clarified concepts, such as rule, habit, and sanction, which are important in social theory as well as analytical jurisprudence; but he has, on the whole, been content to reformulate and refine issues posed by a fairly narrow tradition of academic law, rather than to raise in a sustained way the kinds of questions which a broader social perspective is likely to treat as central or significant.' William Twining, 'Academic Law and Legal Philosophy: The Significance of Herbert Hart' 95 *L.Q.R.* 557, (1979) at 578-79.

95 Above, at n.80.

96 For example, Postscript at 240: 'As a means of carrying out this descriptive enterprise my book makes repeated use of a number of concepts...'.

97 See the passage quoted below at n.100.

98 Ruth Gavison, Comment in Gavison (ed.) *op. cit.* 28. Later Gavison continues: '...I shall risk being called a "semantic scholar" and say that for these comparative lessons to be drawn we need some universal conceptual scheme, in terms of such basic legal functions such as dispute resolution, which may help us both to understand the similarities and highlight the differences between societies.' (*Ibid*, 29).

99 *The Concept of Law*, Postscript 239.

100 *Ibid*, 240. In his response to Dworkin in the Jerusalem symposium, Hart states: '...there is a standing need for a form of legal theory or jurisprudence that is descriptive or general in scope, the perspective of which is not that of a judge deciding 'what the law is', that is, what the law requires in particular cases...but is that of an external observer of a form of social institution with a normative aspect, which in its recurrence in different societies and periods exhibits many common features of form, structure and content.' 'Legal Theory and the Problem of Sense', in Ruth Gavison (ed.) *Issues in Contemporary Legal Philosophy: The Influence of H.L.A.Hart* (1987) at 36. Hart goes on to state that descriptive analytical jurisprudence is preliminary to the articulation of a justificatory theory of a community's legal practices...' (*Ibid*, 37). I am grateful to Robert Summers for reminding me of this important passage. The main point of difference between Hart and Dworkin here is that Dworkin does not accept that description can be neutral nor that it is preliminary to interpretation (e.g. *LE* 13-14). It is not clear why Hart excludes the interpretation that Dworkin may be offering a general prescriptive theory of adjudication (including legal reasoning) or that his justificatory theory need not be limited to a particular community rather than, as with Rawls's theory of justice, any constitutional democracy. On the claim that descriptive general jurisprudence can describe the content of legal systems, compare Buckland's cautionary admonitions (above) and the 'jurisprudential relativism' of Atiyah and Summers (below).

101 *Ibid*, citing *LE* 102.

102 *Ibid*, 41.

103 *LE* 90.

104 *CL* 13; cf. Postscript, 240.

105 For example, Postscript, 248, 261, 264-67.

106 For example, 244-48.; at the time of writing Dworkin has not yet replied in print to Hart's Postscript.

107 *LE* 102.

108 *Ibid*, 102-3.

109 Dworkin agrees with Hart that one can report a debate about the meaning of a legal rule or the content of the rule of recognition from the outside, but as soon as one purports to say what any law means one is involved in interpretation and hence is participating and, in any actual or potential contest, taking sides.

110 This is analogous to Raz writing about Rawls: 'The writer's theory must, to be successful, apply to his society at the time of writing, but there is no general answer as to which societies and what other times it applies to. The applicability of the theory to different societies must be examined on a case-by-case basis.' Joseph Raz, *Ethics in the Public Domain* (1994) 63n.

111 Dworkin concedes that there are other questions for general legal theory - historical, sociological etc. which may produce illuminating propositions *about* law - but maintains that such enquiries have to build on interpretive theories about the meaning of propositions *of* law. *LE* 13-14.

112 For example, 'How to Read the Civil Rights Act', *New York Review of Books*, 20 Dec. 1979, 37.

113 P.S.Atiyah and R.S.Summers, *Form and Substance in Anglo-American Law* (1987) 418.

114 *Ibid*, 420, cf. 264-66.

115 Gavison comes close to accusing Dworkin of this: she asserts that Dworkin's theory challenges the possibility and the value of 'general jurisprudence' (above) She argues that one implication of Dworkin's subversion of the distinction between law and a theory of law 'is that a theory of law is no more than the general assumptions about law in a given community, i.e. theories of law are time- and community- dependent. (*Ibid*, 26-27). My own view is that Dworkin need not be so confined: he may be right in maintaining that to give a precise meaning to a particular provision of the US Constitution or some aspect of English doctrine is participatory, but what is interesting about Dworkin is his general perspective and approach which has wide potential application, whether right or wrong.

116 See the debate in legal anthropology between Gluckman and Bohannan about the relative importance of 'folk concepts' and meta-language for giving an account of customary law, Max Gluckman, *The Judicial Process among the Barotse of Northern Rhodesia* (1957); Paul Bohannan, *Justice and Judgment among the Tiv of Nigeria* (1957). This reflected a wider debate about 'emics'

and 'etics' in social anthropology, on which see Ward Goodenough, *Description and Comparison in Social Anthropology* (1970). It is now widely accepted that both 'folk concepts' and meta-languages are necessary tools, but that meta-languages are themselves culturally relative social constructs.

117 Atiyah and Summers, at 264-66.

118 The amount of 'local knowledge' required of some judges may not be very great. For example, the British Colonial Legal Service, whose members could be posted and transferred relatively freely from jurisdiction to jurisdiction, was an example of how a legal culture can operate relatively detached from local social contexts. Whether, many judges in that tradition emulated Hercules is another question.

119 My personal view is that Dworkin's theory is at its most persuasive when applied to the judicial oath (and all that it symbolises), for this represents an undertaking to be loyal to the system and to try to make it 'the best it can be'. For a more sceptical view of his idea of 'interpretation' in other contexts, see W.Twining and David Miers, *How To Do Things with Rules* (3rd ed. 1991), 383-85.

120 For example, P.Gulliver, *Social Control in an African Society* (1963) (an account of the Arusha of Northern Tanzania).

121 On other kinds of interpreters, see Twining and Miers, *op. cit. passim*, especially 69-74, 184-92.

122 Atiyah and Summers, as well as Hart, are interested in 'ideal interpretive method', but as a distinct enterprise.

123 Bruce Ackerman, 'Rooted Cosmopolitanism', 104 *Ethics* (1994) 516.

124 'Reading Bentham', *op. cit.* at 134-36.

125 Twining, 'Academic Law and Legal Philosophy', *op. cit.* cf. Horwitz, *op. cit.* n.45.

126 See Twining, *Blackstone's Tower* (1994) ch.6.

127 This theme is developed in my paper, 'A Nobel Prize for Law?' in Geoffrey Wilson (ed), *The Frontiers of Legal Scholarship* (forthcoming, 1996).

128 I am grateful to Oren Ben Dor, Stephen Guest, Philip Schofield and Robert Summers for helpful comments and suggestions.

INDEX